Citizen Gallery

Praise For

CITIZEN GALLERY: The Gandhys of Chemould and the Birth of Modern Art in Bombay

'Pinto writes with warmth and admirationabout K&K and with no little sadness at the loss of the generous, liberal, secular world constructed and inhabited by people like Kekoo and Khorshed [creating] a fascinating and at times hilarious tale.'

—Ruchir Joshi in *India Today*

'...a must-have for art lovers, students, historians, and a joy to read. An elegant publication indeed.'

—Mahendra Damle in *The Tribune*

'*Citizen Gallery* is a delectable read of conversations that must be heard, of art that must be seen, of photographs that must be envisioned, of letters that must be re-discovered, and of stories that must be retold...an urgent read in a world of hardening differences that refuses to engage in conversations.'

—Debashree Dattaray in *The Telegraph*

CITIZEN GALLERY

The Gandhys of Chemould and the Birth of Modern Art in Bombay

Jerry Pinto

SPEAKING TIGER

SPEAKING TIGER BOOKS LLP
125A, Ground Floor, Shahpur Jat,
Near Asiad Village, New Delhi - 110 049

First published by Speaking Tiger Books 2022

Photographs: All images except where specified courtesy
Chemould Archives, Mumbai

ISBN: 978-93-90477-05-0
eISBN: 978-93-90477-13-5

10 9 8 7 6 5 4 3 2

Book design by Maithili Doshi Aphale
Typeset in Crimson Text by Jojy Philip
Printed at Chaman Enterprises, New Delhi

This one is for Mehlli Gobhai (1931–2018),
as much a friend as a sentimental education.

Contents

PREFACE

Monsieur Friendly and Madame Noble

What a pleasure it is to reflect on dear and amazing Kekoo and equally dear and amazing Khorshed...I first met them, I believe, in 1957 in Mumbai and continued to meet them there and much later also in Panchgani. At times we travelled together by train to Poona (as it was then called) and by road to Panchgani.

They were famous for their gallery and for their framing shop, Chemould Frames, but in the circles in which I moved, Kekoo was often spoken of as perhaps the first Indian to have visited Caux, the Moral Re-Armament (MRA) Centre in Switzerland, established at the end of World War II. With that link, Kekoo became the pioneer and promoter of visits by a whole series of Indians to Caux, which in many cases resulted in profound personal changes.

Kekoo and Khorshed are therefore among the founders in India of MRA, better known now as Initiatives of Change. There were indeed a few Indians and Brits living in India in the late 1930s and early 1940s who (before the roles of Kekoo and Khorshed) practised and shared with others the idea of listening for God's guidance and accepting self-change before asking others to change.

Yet following Kekoo's pioneering visit to Caux, experiences there of other Indians gave a notable fillip to MRA's work in India.

A major memory for me is of a visit that Kekoo and I and the famous Colwell Brothers—Steve, Paul and Ralph, very young at the time—made to Vinoba Bhave in a village in the Maharashtra hinterland in the late 1950s when he was collecting land for the landless. I think much of the initiative for this visit came from Kekoo.

After the Colwell Brothers sang the MRA song, 'There is Enough in the World for Everyone's Need but not for Everyone's Greed'—singing it in both English and Marathi, Vinoba used the lines as the text for his speech.

I had the privilege also of meeting Kekoo's father and still remember his most friendly face and smile. Since I think of Kekoo as 'Monsieur Friendly', I have a feeling that his oft-recognized warmth was inherited from his father.

There was something of a born salesman in Kekoo. I know next to nothing about Kekoo's life in the art world, but I saw again and again that no matter what individual or group he was amidst, Kekoo would be befriending and winning them over in the most natural way.

In some ways, he was 'Mr Bombay' too, for he joined or helped every initiative for improving the metro's civic life and at times its political life also. I think he absolutely loved Bombay—and Mumbai as it is now known—and of course his own corner of it in Bandra.

And if Kekoo was 'Monsieur Friendly', Khorshed was 'Madame Noble'—selfless, caring, principled.

I would be remiss in not including Kekoo's cousin Dara Gandhy here. Unfortunately no longer with us, from the very start Dara has been a stalwart personality in the fight for values in Mumbai and in the work of MRA, as much a founding figure for MRA in India as Kekoo or anyone else.

When I think of the Gandhys, for some reason, my thoughts fly also towards the great figure of Dadabhai Naoroji, whose unceasing battles for a just and free India must have been among the Gandhys' chief inspirations. There must be a foundation for this belief of mine, for not many years ago Kekoo presented a wonderful Dadabhai portrait to Asia Plateau, the MRA Centre in Panchgani.

How greatly India needs the wisdom, courage and persistence that Dadabhai personified! And how we have forgotten him!

India and Mumbai can do also with a few more like Kekoo and Khorshed. Not easily found. Tradition, charm, art, love of country, love of people, a background of privilege and a lifetime of thought for others: what a combination! I was lucky to be among their friends.

—Rajmohan Gandhi

Mumbai

INTRODUCTION

The Gandhys of Bandra

> 'Kekoo, Khorshed and Shireen are an extraordinary family. So if you were to write a history of the professional lives of the Gandhy family, you would be, in a sense, writing the history of modern art in Bombay.'[1]
> —**Tasneem Zakaria Mehta,** Honorary Director and Managing Trustee, Dr Bhau Daji Lad Museum

Here is just one of the many stories I heard about a certain Kekoo Gandhy (1920-2012), the male half of a pair of Gandhys whose Gallery Chemould helped sustain and promote the Progressive Artists Group. This was a band of artistic brothers that included such names as Maqbool Fida Husain, Hari Ambadas Gade, Abdul Aziz Raiba and Krishnaji Howlaji Ara; the Gandhys kept them going before they became famous, often providing these artists with much-needed monetary support.

The story goes that Kekoo was sitting in the verandah of his bungalow and sipping a cup of tea. The street outside looked like it always did, but this was the restless eye of a man who loved his city to the point that he would do practically anything for it. To him, it seemed that the street might be improved.

'The promenade needs repair,' he said aloud, and then added, 'We should repair it.'

This was a mistake for his family was within earshot.

'Don't be silly, Kekoo. Repairing streets is the municipality's job. Why do we pay taxes otherwise?' his wife, Khorshed, asked.

'It's a walkway I use too,' said her husband. 'I also have the duty to repair it.'

'It will cost lakhs,' said his daughter, Shireen. 'Don't be silly. You should write a letter to the municipal commissioner and get it attended to.'

'That will take forever,' said Kekoo. 'By which time people may fall over and get hurt.'

'In Switzerland, those people would sue the government,' said Bernard Imhasly, son-in-law, journalist and retired diplomat.

The matter seemed to drop and conversation became general. But at lunch, Kekoo was somehow reminded of the state of the promenade.

'How much do you think it would cost?' he asked his wife.

'Far too much money,' she said impatiently. 'And I don't even think you will be allowed to repair it.'

'Why not?' Kekoo was a dab hand at repairing things. He even restored paintings on his own. If someone brought in an old work, he would put it down on his desk on the first floor of Kekee Manzil and get to work. His grandchildren, Atyaan and Areesh Jungalwala, Shireen's children, would double up as Santa's elves, fetching and carrying for him as he worked. Sometimes Kekoo used oil paints. Sometimes he used wet bread. In one possibly apocryphal story, he was found using nail polish.

'Arré, do you think anyone can just repair anything? That is government property. You are a private individual. You cannot just....'

'I am a citizen of this country. I have the right....'

Behroze Gandhy, third child and filmmaker, came from her room on the first floor for lunch. Her mother told her what Kekoo had planned.

'And where do you think you'll get the money?' she asked.

'I thought we could sell that one,' said Kekoo, pointing to an MF Husain painting that had graced the drawing room for nearly thirty years. This is the family, you should remember, that was instrumental in giving Husain his first one-man show. Kekoo often talked about it as one of his favourite works. No one is sure, at this remove, whether he was joking or he was serious about the whole thing. But his casual remark caused an explosion.

'You will not sell that painting,' said Khorshed severely.

'It doesn't belong to you, Papa. It belongs to the whole family.'

'I got Husain to....'

'It's part of our legacy....'

'We grew up looking at that work. It's part of our aesthetic world.'

Over the next few meals the idea was debated but since the painting stayed in place and the street remained in a state of disrepair, it became of less and less interest. And then one day, two things happened simultaneously. Workers appeared and began to repair the street and the painting disappeared from the wall.

The family was furious.

'You stole it,' Khorshed said.

'A man cannot steal from himself,' Kekoo said calmly. 'But I did not take the painting.'

'Then how come they're repairing the street?'

'It's the municipality men; they do work from time to time, you know. And with nothing really to help them. They have to build a fire themselves to melt the tar. I had a chat with them this morning. The *muqaddam* is a nice man called....'

'You're paying for this Papa, we know you,' said Shireen. 'And you've sold that Husain. Who did you give it to? Pundole?'

'Are you mad? Why would I let Pundole take the commission?'

'I wouldn't put anything past you,' said Shireen.

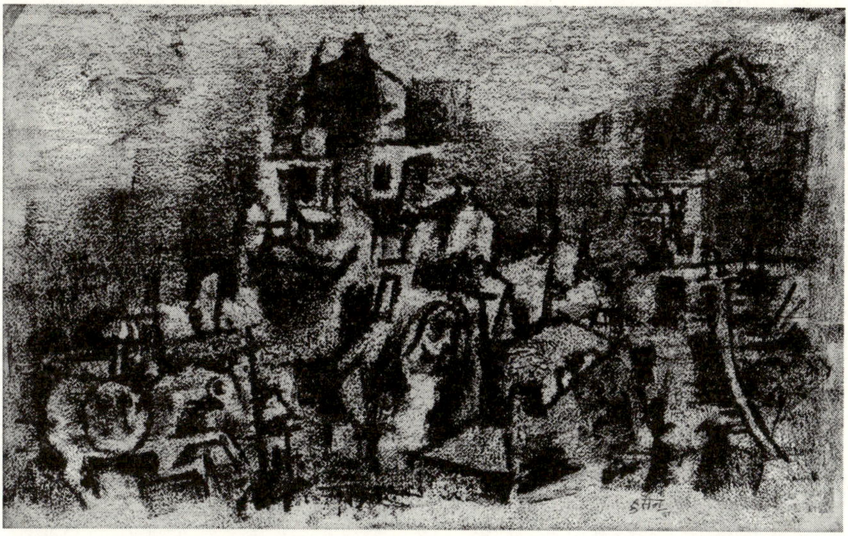

The Husain that went missing

Rashna, the eldest of the daughters, author and psychologist said, 'Every man has a patriarch male inside him; you less than most, it must be admitted, but in this case I think you have let him have his way. You could have considered the feelings of others.'

'That would be the day. His is a case of *gherno ghelo ne baaharno dayo,*' said Khorshed, deploying a fine Parsi-Gujarati phrase which means that the person in question behaves well outside but inside the house, he plays the fool.

Adil Gandhy descended from his second-floor fastness and asked what the kerfuffle was about. The lighter-coloured patch on the wall was pointed out to him. He eyed it for a moment.

'Where did it go?'

'Papa sold it.'

'To pay for road repairs.'

'Revaa de ni,' he said, 'Let it go,' and then, ignoring the angry outcries, hurried off to Chemould Frames, the still-flourishing business on Princess

Street[2], as it is still known to the Anglophone faithful. Adil's policy in family matters was often: Least said, soonest mended.

'I'll find out,' said Khorshed and she took up the phone and began to make a series of quiet but stern calls. She rang up all the galleries and auction houses and warned them that they had no right to sell a family Husain, just because Kekoo showed up with it under his arm. Again and again, she was reassured that Kekoo had not come in bearing any such painting but Khorshed was sure he had warned them not to talk and that they were quietly doing a deal over an early intimate work by the master, all cool colours and confidently sketched lines.

A few days later, the house was being painted and the sideboard above which the Husain had been hanging for all those years was shifted. And there it was: the missing Husain. Its chain had snapped and it had slipped quietly behind the furniture.

'We knew you wouldn't have done anything like that,' said Shireen.

Kekoo merely smiled.

This then is the only family that could lose an MF Husain, if only for a few days.

•

It is also the story of a Parsi couple who wrote their city on to the map of the art world with their drive, determination and large-heartedness. It is the story of a peculiar combination of visionary zeal and intense pragmatism. It takes in the world, lassoing in Iran and Switzerland, Australia and the US. It takes in Hindu spirituality, ashrams at Ganeshpuri, yoga of the BKS Iyengar variety, Midnight Mass on Christmas day and a number of Muslim friends. (And if you know your Bombay Parsis, you will know that this is rare.) It offers a vision of another kind of India, an outward-looking, eager-eyed, open-armed India.

Hence this book.

It began as a celebration of the life of Kekoo Gandhy, a Kekoonama. But in the process of researching it, I realised that this was equally a Khorshednama. She made him possible and together they made Gallery Chemould into a birthing room for Indian modernism. In 2008, Kekoo was given the Padma Shri. He promptly lost it.

I got part of the story in an email from Rashna Gandhy to me: 'As far as I remember, the whole family had attended the citation ceremony at the Rashtrapati Bhavan. We were then all heading off in different directions, Behroze and I had taken Mummy for a holiday to Kashmir and Papa had to travel back from Delhi to Bombay on his own.' The story is taken up in a letter by Khorshed Gandhy:

> This morning we phoned Kekoo to find out how he had fared on his journey back to B'bay and he told us the nightmare he had gone through! Apparently the plane developed some snag and it had to turn back. There was absolute chaos at the airport and in the midst of it all the honour scroll which he was carrying in his hand, because it would not fit in the bag, got lost! After several announcements it was retrieved and then Kekoo did not know the plane he was supposed to get into. He was in total panic, he said, and finally he landed at Santacruz sometime at 11 o'clock. Poor Dara, who was supposed to fetch him, must have had an equally harrowing time! This morning when I talked to Kekoo I said 'You had better not to go to Calcutta' (which he was to go with Adil) and he said 'Forget Calcutta—I have yet to recover from my Delhi trip'!!

No wonder his daughter Rashna told me, 'When we heard through the news that Papa had been awarded the Padma Shri, we told Mummy that she deserved to get the Padma Vibhushan for having put up with Papa and carried out all his ideas through their married life!'

•

Welcome to Kekoo's world.

And if you find that there are several versions of an event, it is only in keeping with the way memory plays a role in the world of art. Not for nothing is Mnemosyne the chief of the muses. And as JM Coetzee puts it in *The Master of Petersburg*, 'But who except the recording angel would care to write the full, dull truth?'

—Jerry Pinto
Mumbai, 2022

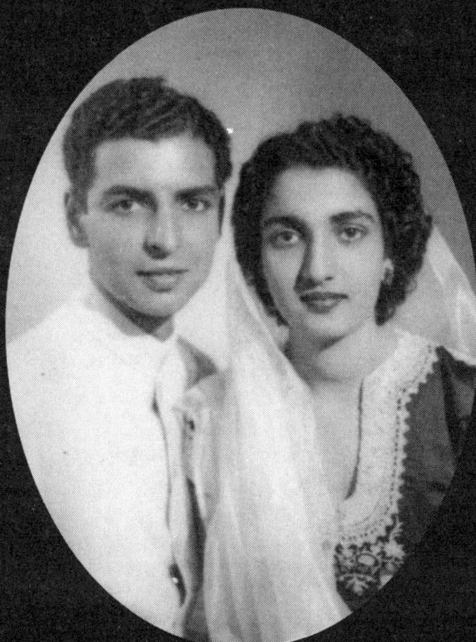

Kekoo and Khorshed Gandhy

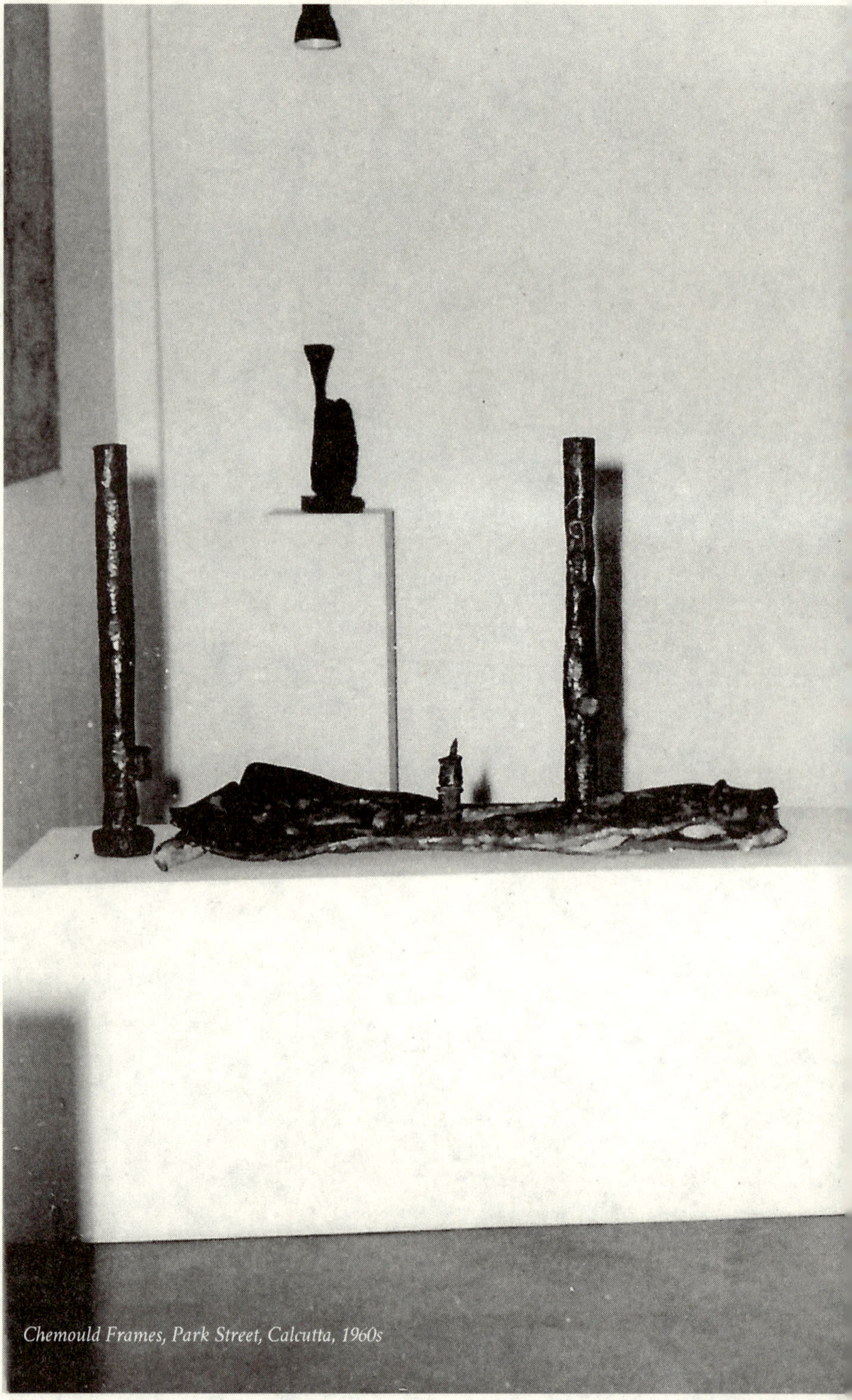

Chemould Frames, Park Street, Calcutta, 1960s

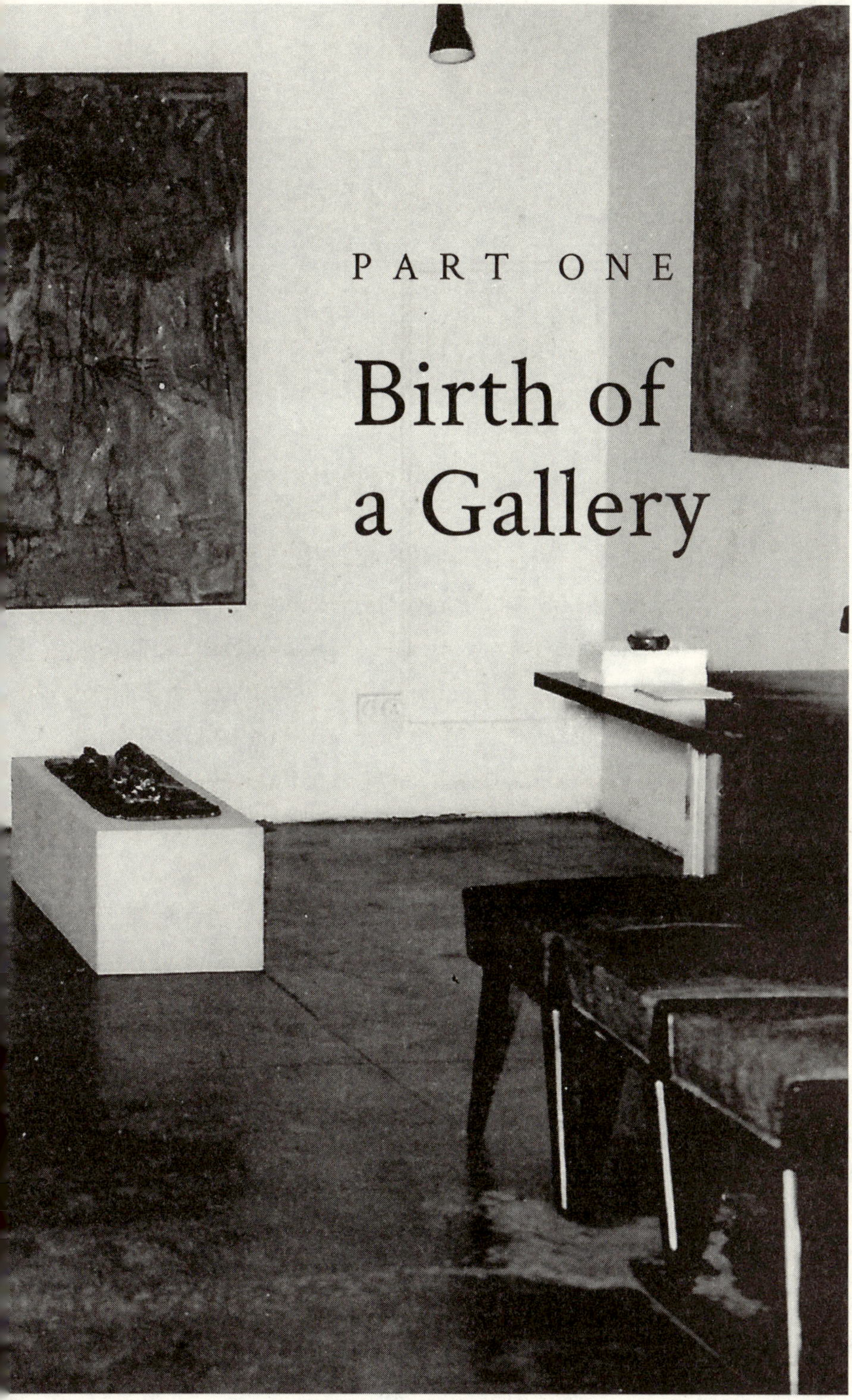

PART ONE

Birth of a Gallery

•01•

The Art of the City, the City of Art

'There were good reasons for Bombay becoming the Mecca for Indian artists. All the large corporations of the country had their head offices in the city. Some enterprises like the Tatas and Air India bought paintings to adorn their offices. Bombay also had magazines like *Marg*, financed by the house of Tatas, entirely devoted to art; and the *Illustrated Weekly of India* belonging to the Times of India group of publications, which devoted a lot of space to artists and sculptors. *The Weekly* and its Hindi counterpart *Dharmyug* had an all-India readership.'
—A Brush with Life: An Autobiography by **Satish Gujral** and **Khushwant Singh**

Dara Gandhy maintains that Chemould was 'the first frame-moulding factory in the whole of Asia'. The factory then added a frame shop designed by an Italian internee of World War II, C Conti, as Kekoo Gandhy told the poet Adil Jussawalla. Later, it sprouted an art gallery in another building in the same city, and two branches in two other cities. But did it really catalyse the modern art movement? Did it really help birth the Progressives? Is the subtitle of this book a little overblown? The overstatement of an archivist who has known the family for years?

Perhaps you should read on and decide for yourself.

To consider that it would be necessary to consider the city of its birth and its relationship to art. The story of Bombay is the story of its monies. Or at least, this is how it has been told. This is the city of Mammon, devoted to the creation of wealth; other cities did culture, notably Calcutta and Madras. Delhi did power and people smiled a little when anyone mentioned Bangalore because it was where good people went to retire. (This was when it was a garden city; today, the image one remembers is a lake covered with chemical froth so acidic that it sears the paint off cars.)

We grew up with this story and it is as false as any other generalisation. However, if you say something often enough, it is likely to be taken up and made into a cliché and in a social-media driven world, every cliché is taken to be a fact.

For if you look carefully at this city, supposedly anti-intellectual, supposedly bottom-line driven, you have to wonder how it managed to support a film industry in an entirely alien language at a time when it was not even a medium that had proved itself; how it then managed to create and support the classics of art cinema, the little jewels of middle-of-the-road cinema and the glorious excesses of Bollywood; how it gave birth to the Progressive Artists Group; how it supported the Progressive Writers Association who were decidedly pink; how it was home to poets like Narayan Surve, Namdeo Dhasal, Vinda Karandikar and Pu Shi Rege while making space for Nissim Ezekiel, Dom Moraes, Arun Kolatkar, Gieve Patel, Adil Jussawalla and Eunice de Souza and for Popati Hiranandani and Arjun Shad; how it managed to have more theatre than any other city in the country in at least four languages: Marathi, Hindi, Gujarati and English; and how it came to spawn a homegrown gharana of Hindustani art music, the Bhendi Bazaar gharana. One should be very careful when one is told something about a city; it is usually a defence mechanism or an attempt at camouflage.

But in the 1940s, this was no city for painters. There was no 'art scene' in Bombay. One argument for this is that India was a poor nation, a colonised nation and it could no more be expected to have an art scene than it could be expected to understand concepts like democracy and the vote. (You can see where this is going.) In 1950, however India went to vote and the poor, hungry, illiterate masses proved that the symbolic power of the vote was something they had understood quite well and were willing to wield quite thoughtfully. Meanwhile, they were making art all over the country.

I am not making an argument for Indian exceptionalism. There is no human society which does not undertake art nor is it an activity for one's leisure time. Art is a human necessity, built into our DNA. Or else why would we dream? Writing in *The Spectator,* Joseph Addison says that when you dream you are, all at once, the theatre, the actors, the play, the author and the audience. And dreaming, by all accounts, seems necessary to good mental health; which means art is important to our mental health, so important that the subconscious will do it for you if your conscious mind won't.

The history of art bears witness to the tenacity of the art-making instinct in human beings. When life was 'nasty, brutish and short', women and men stopped their work, work that meant the difference between the survival of the clan and its extinction, in order to create a record of themselves. They stopped to collect the berries and roots and stones that would give them colour, they stopped to paint on the walls of caves and left an astonishing record of their lives for us. And this at a time when to develop a toothache or to sprain a foot meant you would go hungry and perhaps starve to death. Even in our time, tribal art has been created in times of surplus and in times of scarcity. However, in these cases, I suspect that the artist was not a separate category of person; s/he is part of the world, an actor like any other with the same responsibilities as everyone else. In order to make the separate category of artist viable, you need people who will believe in the art, or as is often the case now, believe in the artist. (If you think you do not fall into this category, try this test. Insert your name where X is. Would you rather have it said of you: 'X has a magnificent painting on her wall' or 'X has a Sabavala on her wall'?) Thus the problem is when the artwork becomes a commodity and the commodity becomes a fetish object and begins to command huge prices. It is enough for it to happen somewhere in the world for artists to want it to happen everywhere in the world. And while the prices of art continued to climb for a select handful of Western male white artists, there weren't many buyers in Bombay in the 1940s.

So when you try to locate Chemould in the larger history of modern art in India, you're looking at the political, the economic and the aesthetic. To complicate matters, there isn't that much material. Some attempts have been made in the recent past but they have been hampered by an institutionalized amnesia. Organisations rarely keep records and when they have, these are easily pillaged. Consider the Bombay Art Society.

In *Vartman Chitrasutra,* Suhas Bahulkar quotes Professor Baburao Sadwelkar who had in the Centenary Year proposed to make a study of the Bombay Art Society's contributions to Indian art. He had 'a broad outline in mind' and wanted 'to research and get coherent records' but found to 'my dismay there was no documentary record available in the Society, nor could I find any other catalogue. Important photographs of the past, and their negatives, which I had seen some years back in the Society's collection had vanished. It would seem unbelievable to anyone, that an art society that had existed for a hundred years would not possess any records. It was alas a hard fact. All my enthusiasm to write the society's history was shattered.'[3]

Another clue to our lack of records may be found in JN Mohanty's

Between Two Worlds: East and West: An Autobiography. The freedom fighter and activist Gopabandhu Chaudhuri visits him in his rooms.

'Once when I was living in the Hardinge Hostel of Calcutta University, he came to the city and stopped by to see me. I was in college so he waited for me in my room (which was opened for him by the floor servant who knew of his relationship to me). He waited for some time and finding me late in returning, left, leaving the following note on my desk: "Sorry I missed you. Found on your desk a pile of old letters including some written by me. A philosopher should not save, that makes you cling to the past instead of being free for the future. Cultivate non-attachment."'

Non-attachment? Or erasure?

The next lines of Mohanty's memoir are plangent: 'I destroyed the letters. If some of them were here, I would have now reconstructed my story much better.'

It is against this background, that this chapter has to be read. A final caveat: this is written in necessarily broad strokes. It is not meant to be a history of art in the city but a backdrop for the main business.

•

The Bombay Art Society and the Sir Jamsetjee Jeejeebhoy School of Art can be said to be the two most important art institutions of the city before the first galleries came along. Neither can be said to have played a stellar role in the development of the Progressives or the Bombay School, two of the movements that had the greatest impact on the art life of the nation. In fact, both institutions seemed to have been prototypically, stereotypically averse to change and although many of the members of the Bombay Art Society were people who supported these very movements outside, they seemed incapable of providing a space within the institution for the new ways of painting that were being tried out.

And all this began in 1851 with that peculiarly Victorian idea, the Great

Exhibition. It was perhaps a part of the larger European idea that things could only get better from now on, since Science was going to conquer Nature (and perhaps even Man's Nature), and that if the Common Man could be made to see these wonders, his gaze would be elevated above the mundane and he would begin to see glorious vistas of possibility. In order to do this, he would need to be offered some measure of beauty and that was where the arts and crafts came in.

Those Indians who did get to England to see The Great Exhibition of 1851 were impressed by the vastness of the human enterprise and how much the 'poor, bare, forked animal' was getting done in various parts of the world. Amongst them was Sir Jamsetjee Jeejeebhoy, a great Bombay merchant and philanthropist. (In her entertaining *City of Gold: The Biography of Bombay*, Gillian Tindall says that there were 'murmurs' that Sir JJ's father's name was Bottlewalla because he was a dealer in empty bottles. It is tempting to suggest that this is the blood in Kekoo Gandhy's veins for his mother was a Bottlewalla, as we shall see.)

Sir Jamsetjee came back with a dream. He wrote a letter to the Directors of the East India Company in May 1853, offering a donation of a hundred thousand rupees to start an Art Instruction School. For its part, the company had to provide the land and bring masters out from England.

This seemed to have found favour with the directors. Perhaps they thought this might lead to the creation of an artistic (or artisanal), 'class of persons, Indian in blood and colour, but English in taste....' Such art workers could serve the Company's larger interests which were strictly commercial. Instead of just sending out raw material and unfinished products, perhaps they thought they might be able to sell the world some finished goods as well. Of this instinct was born the terms Bombay pottery and Bombay woodwork. (There are magnificent samples of both to be seen in the Dr Bhau Daji Lad Mumbai City Museum in the grounds of the Rani Baug.)

Oddly, the Sir Jamsetjee Jeejeebhoy School of Art began with drawing classes at the Elphinstone Institution commencing in March 1857. A Mr Peyton was hired to instruct such 'natives' as wanted to be instructed in drawing, although this was probably more likely to be copying from models. Then a Mr Terry took over. The school expanded and the Elphinstone Institution was probably over-run.

Sir Jamsetjee stepped in and offered his own home on Abdul Rahman Street. Three ateliers were established: decorative painting, sculpture and artistic metalwork (wrought iron work). The ateliers were headed by three English masters: Mr Higgins, John Griffiths and Lockwood Kipling (the father of Rudyard Kipling who would give us that memorable phrase, 'The White Man's Burden' and would call us 'half devil and half child'). But 1857 was a watershed year in many ways. This was the year that was marked by the First War of Independence, which also ended the hegemony of the East India Company. Bloody battles erupted across North India and when it was all over, the Crown took over and the economic encounter turned into a colonial enterprise, with all the attendant doublespeak and hypocrisy of the time. The move heralded a series of changes. To begin with the British could no longer hide behind the profit motive as a Board of Directors could. This was the Crown, this was part of the British Empire and some attempt had to be made to whitewash the encounter. It was necessary to create a myth that would cover the reality of this economic and cultural exploitation. Rudyard Kipling, born in Bombay, in love with India all his life, willingly obliged with the *Recessional*, a poem sonorous with false humility. In order to make this myth palpable, the cities of the empire began to throw up buildings that were intended to demonstrate that the White Man was willing to shoulder his burden *ad infinitum*. Three universities were established with suitably magnificent buildings: Bombay, Calcutta and Madras, all in 1857. The magnificence of the architecture of the period was a political statement; the buildings were intended to demonstrate to the natives that the Raj was there to stay.

These buildings needed decoration and the rise of what was once known as the Indo-Saracenic, or Bombay Gothic, in today's jargon, was part of that enterprise. When you go to look at what was called Victoria Terminus and is now Chhatrapati Shivaji Maharaj Terminus, you can see what these two moments combined to create. There is a genius to the whole of it that defies description. There are the standard heraldic animals of the European imagination, the lion and the tiger. There are the goddesses in fluttery finery that hold up torches and suchlike. But there are also peacocks in full strut, and jackals and foxes and monkeys all gesturing backwards to the *Panchatantra* and the *Jataka*.

Look at the Rajabai Clock Tower, funded by another merchant prince, Premchand Roychand, and named after his mother. Roychand (1831-1906) was twice kingly; he was known as the Cotton King and the Bullion King. He was also the founder of the Bombay Stock Exchange.

The outline of the clock tower looks like it was built for a European landscape but now look at the statuary, the men from different communities standing guard on the tower, each in a different community outfit. The architecture was hybrid, drawing from East and West; the detailing and ornament was local but the scale of the enterprise was colonial. It should come as no surprise then that students of the JJ were commissioned to paint the dome of the Secretariat in 1929, under the guidance of Gladstone Solomon.

And therein lies the rub. This is the native artisan in the service of the Raj. This is the genius of India made subservient to the products and processes of the West. It is wonderfully ornamental. It works not on the individual level but as a whole, because it is so out of proportion to the world around it.

This is not to say that the school itself was wrong or flawed. You judge a school by its pupils, although in that time, it seems to have been more common to judge a school by what it rejected. Many of the artists whose works are now declared national treasures got their start at the Sir JJ School of Art. Some interesting work did get done.

For good or bad, in the early period, the principal was always an Englishman. And in the way of these things, each new principal moved the school in a new direction. Sir John Griffiths joined the JJ in 1868, became the principal in 1880 and worked there till 1884. He saved Ajanta for us. Even as we speak, hundreds of tourists are walking around those caves, breathing and oxidizing the fragile paint on the walls of those caves. You don't need an appointment, you don't have to wait, you just have to show up. The guides tell you that it is not a good idea to shine torches on the paintings as they will degenerate. Then in order to pick out how the light reflects from the pearls around a maiden's neck, they will shine torches at the same walls. Meanwhile, selfie flashes abound. There are hundreds of young Indians who have gone up to the caves and left evidence that Rahul loves Preeti.

Griffiths was one of those men who saw the magic of those caves. Today, that would seem self-evident but not at his time. Europeans did not see this as art. The Portuguese used Elephanta as a shooting gallery, probably appalled at the many-armed gods and goddesses they saw. The British wanted to dismantle the Taj Mahal and auction it; they started with a jharokha from the Red Fort and when that didn't get any takers, they abandoned the plan and let the Taj Mahal languish.

Griffiths was different. He undertook the monumental work of executing facsimile copies of the frescoes in the Ajanta Caves. With a team of art school students and teachers, Griffiths worked in the caves from 1872 to 1884 and completed the work. He even hoped that the students would be drawn to paint in that manner. He wrote, 'One of the most curious and interesting of my experiences was the initiation of Hindu, Parsi and Goanese [sic] students into the mysteries of an art still congenial to the Oriental temperament and hand—I am persuaded that no European, no matter how skillful, could have so completely caught the spirit of the originals.' Writing in December 1998, Professor Baburao Sadwelkar says somewhat sadly, 'However, none of the artists of that period were drawn to the aesthetics of Ajanta but aspired to master the Western techniques of illusionistic realism.'

Precisely. Many might have been able to see what could be done but might have lacked the bravery to do it. To reclaim and reuse a past requires a sense of ownership. You must have a place on which to stand and a paintbrush long enough to be able to shift the art world to include you and your sense of what art is. In the colonized world where the buyer was white or part of a comprador class, it would be difficult to imagine a painter who could magick this sense of entitlement into being.

I like to think there were. I like to think we will one day discover someone who went down to Ajanta and painstakingly made his copies but came back and incubated what he saw and recreated his own world in painting.

The only problem with this dream is that this is Bombay and we recycle everything. There are no attics in which forgotten paintings may be lurking. They have been turned into living spaces and the contents sold to the raddiwala. The reason we have so little of our silent cinema left to us is because the film was looted for its silver content and then turned into bangles. This may be non-attachment as the philosopher preached or an excess of it.

And finally, when your school is a colonial enterprise, when your history and your aesthetic are supposed to service the White Man and your skill must be turned into bulwarks against the identity that you are trying to birth, how can you position yourself in order to reclaim a past for another man's tomorrow?

•

Captain WE Gladstone Solomon, the principal and later the director of the Sir JJ School of Art writes in his book *The Bombay Revival of Indian Art* (1924): 'It may here be mentioned that it was in the time of Mr Griffiths that India's senior art society came into existence in 1888. The Bombay Art Society was founded with the object of helping artists and particularly of encouraging the students of the School of Art. During its novitiate the Society was chiefly a vehicle for the works of European Amateurs from all over India. The successful carrying off of a prize for the black and white in 1892 by an Indian student, Mr MV Dhurandhar, encouraged his fellow students of the School of Art to try their luck; and it was Mr Griffiths' aim to show the best production of his students every year as an incitement to artists to go to Nature for their inspiration. The impetus that was thus given was so effective that several sister organisations came into being; and during the present time of revival new Art Societies are springing up all over the South West. Of the one hundred and ninety two artists who exhibited in the Annual Exhibition of the Bombay Art Society in December 1923, one hundred and thirty-six were ladies. The European Exhibits were only twenty in all.'

The Gazetteer of Bombay City and Island Vol. III, 1910 explains the origin of the Bombay Art Society:

'The Bombay Art Society was founded in 1888 with the object of encouraging art, particularly among amateurs, and of educating the native public to an appreciation of its merits. Since that date, eighteen exhibitions have been held, of which three were held in the Secretariat, two in the Town Hall, and the remainder in the School of Art building. About 10,000 pictures have been exhibited and more than Rs 20,000 has been distributed in prizes. The society has also held an annual conversazione during the last few years, at which private collections of porcelain and pottery, collections of watercolour sketches, and examples of embossed leather work have been exhibited. The society depends for its funds upon the subscriptions of members and has from time to time also received grants from Government. The publication of a Journal is under consideration.'

The said journal did come out as *A Brief Historical Sketch of the Bombay Art Society, with special reference to the period—1906–1910.* Professor OV Müller, who was then secretary of the Society, explained in the introduction that the Society had been founded 'for the purpose of encouraging art, especially amongst amateurs, and of educating the native public to a true appreciation of its merits. A very large number of the Englishmen and women, who come out to this country, have learnt to draw and paint. This art, if neglected, is apt to be forgotten. By affording opportunities of exhibiting work done, submitting it to criticism, winning medals, prizes and certificates, and at times disposing of surplus productions, the Society endeavours not only to keep alive but to develop this artistic sense. The various Arts Schools of the country are putting forth an ever increasing number of students, and these would-be artists also find in the Society's Exhibitions one of their chief supports.'

There is a condescension to this that is immediately apparent now but in an age which struggled to convince itself that colonialism was a just force for a better world order, you can see how 'educating the native public' might seem like a worthy cause.

All this needs to be read against the growth of the history of the city, perhaps a subject too vast for such a miniature portrait. I have never believed that a society of surplus is needed in order to create art. But perhaps you need a surplus to create and stimulate the growth of an *art market.*

Bombay had been a boom-and-bust city for a while. Great fortunes were made when the American Civil War broke out in 1861 and the supply of cotton to the mills of Manchester and Birmingham, failed. Indian cotton filled the gap and the money came rolling in, the mills came up on land leased for nothing from the government, and it is said that farmers who did not know what to do with the money they made lined the wheels of their bullock carts with silver. Then the war ended and when news came to Premchand Roychand, he is said to have sighed and said that he would have to begin all over and again.

When a leisured class with surplus money seeks to turn itself into an aristocracy, it mimics the powerful classes around it. The Mughals had ateliers of painters; and later so had the Rajputs and the royalty of the hills. The Nawabs had themselves painted in miniatures and so it was natural that the then-nouveau riche should be looking for something to hang in the living room.

But if we enlarge our vision for a moment, you can see an inflection point happening in the salons and galleries of the world. The aesthetic and the political are inextricably linked. The Industrial Revolution darkened the wings of moths and the skies of the cities. (The term 'acid rain' was invented in 1852 by a Scotsman, Robert Angus Smith, a chemist with an interest in air pollution.) War was a constant threat, the poor in the city worked sixteen-hour days, miners died in the shafts to bring out coal and iron, the rural poor gleaned the fields and ate potatoes. Art did not always respond directly to these realities but even when there are no poor people visible in Turner's landscapes, you can see he is making a political choice to keep them out of his eternal skies and seas and ships. The ballerinas in Degas' work are young, they are poor and they are going to be exploited. And although there was some attempt to hold it all together with Impressionism while incorporating what science had been telling us about optics, to keep looking at the mountains and the trees while breaking them down into component dabs of paint, it was all going to collapse under the weight of an unavoidable social consciousness. Art moved from the mainstream to the Salon des Refusés, but when you have been refused, you might also not be bought.

In India, the Independence Movement began to create the kind of foothold an Indian artist might need to begin the process of moving the world with the lever of a paintbrush. It should be no surprise that the Progressives burst out of Bombay around the 1940s. In one version of the foundation myth of the Progressives[4], it was a rejection that began the process. In Ila Pal's biography of MF Husain she quotes Husain as saying,

> 'No doubt the Bombay Art Society was active...it had a steadily growing band of collectors too, but it was taking too long to realign itself with the changed aspirations, which became obvious when they rejected Souza's and Ara's work.' This delivered the final blow. Ara, Souza and Raza got together and formed the Progresssive Artists Group where each of them could nominate a new member.
>
> So Ara chose Gade, Raza selected Bakre and it was Souza, who had liked Husain's paintings at the Bombay Art Society show, who invited Husain to join....'

It was an odd assortment with widely differing social backgrounds and experiences.

They were called The Progressives. It is a word that has ever since indicated a Leftist orientation, a sympathy for the marginalized perhaps because whether they were progressive artists or progressive writers, they found themselves on the margins of art production. The Progressives were trying to break away from the Bombay Art Society's clutches and constraints; Hari Ambadas Gade described it to SI Clerk of *The Daily* as a 'bad realistic Victorian style'.

India became independent in 1947 and in 1948, the Bombay Art Society celebrated its diamond jubilee. And there is a familiar name on the committee that was set up to celebrate it with an exhibition of old and new masters, covering those six decades. There was Dr Mulk Raj Anand, Professor W Langhammer, PS Chinmulgund (Secretary to the Government of Bombay), Emmanuel Schlesinger, Rudolf von Leyden, Dr DG Vyas, KK Hebbar, *Kekoo Gandhy*, VD Bhagat, Ram Chatterjee and others. That Kekoo Gandhy was already on this committee speaks volumes for he was still then only the man who made the frames.

But things were changing rapidly. The old institutions seemed hopelessly out of date. Consider what FN Souza said of the time when he began painting: 'I had begun to notice that the JJ School of Art turned out an awful number of bad artists, year after year. And the Bombay Art Society showed awful crap in its Annual Exhibitions which comprised the amateur efforts of some memsahibs in India who were pampered by British imperialism. Hence their pretty-pretty paintings together with the work of several artists coming out of the art school, exhibited once a year in the Art Society had no directions, no goal, no inspiration, no energy—regardless of the style or method they chose to work in. It then occurred to me to form a group to give ourselves an incentive. Ganging up in a collective ego is stronger than single ego. It is easier for a mob to carry out a lynching; and in this case, we found it necessary to lynch the kind of art inculcated by the JJ School of Art and exhibited in the Bombay Art Society.'[5]

This is Souzaese, the language of machismo and overstatement, but there was a real and proximate cause for the break. Two nations had been born that year in August 1947 and Ara had watched an Independence Day procession and inspired, had painted a magnum opus, 18 feet in width, 3 feet in height. He presented it proudly for inclusion at the annual exhibition of the Bombay Art Society and was turned down. It was too big, they said, though Rudolf von Leyden (of whom we shall hear more later) had said that in it, 'Ara the artist, Ara the poet and Ara the citizen have merged and cooperated.'[6]

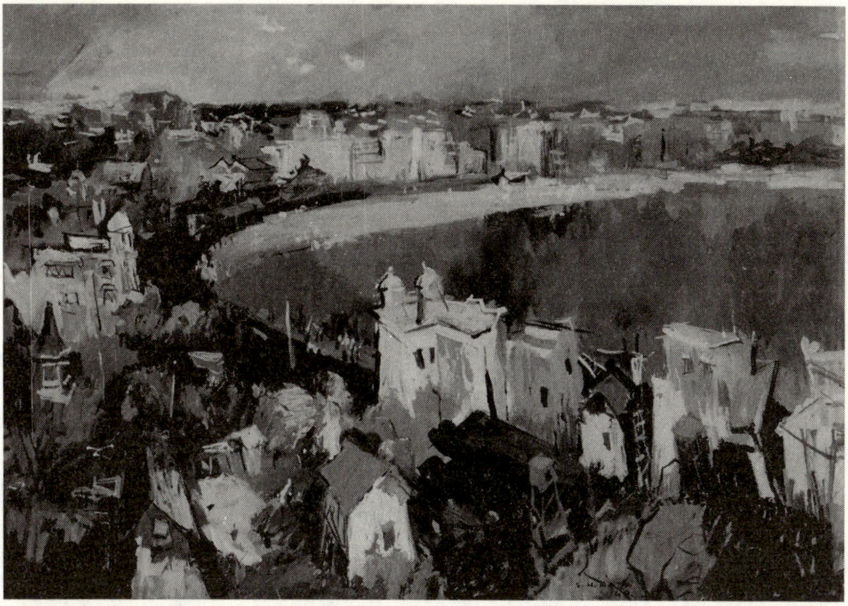

Bombay from Malabar Hill: *This unusually large gouache on board painted by Raza during his early years as an artist, won the Gold Medal at the Bombay Art Society's Diamond Jubilee exhibition in December 1948. Image Courtesy & Collection: Kiran Nadar Museum of Art*

The break perhaps was inevitable; it seems to be the dialectic of most art movements. There is an institution or maybe two. Perhaps they are symbiotically linked. They dominate the skyline and by means of educational strategies or rewards such as prizes and a spot in an exhibition, they establish the boundaries and perimeters of art. This is art, they say when they give an Indian a prize: the Native is now capable of making it. But when he begins to find his own line, his own palette, his own way of seeing, there is a distinct coldness in the air.

This is where an art gallery comes in. It might not always help. It might not always be able to sell the paintings but if there are a number of galleries in a city, it is possible for the artist to get to show what s/he is doing and the public gets a chance to see the work. They may not like it, they may not even understand it, but galleries that are open to the public are likely to constitute an education in themselves.[7]

After all, there wasn't much help coming from the Establishment. Husain told Ila Pal:

'In contrast, the attitude of our keepers of antiquity, like Dr Moti Chandra, Rai Krishnadas and Dr KM Munshi was appalling. While foreigners like E Schlesinger, Rudy von Leyden and Walter Langhammer, who had come to India as refugees and were just finding a foothold, sold their possessions to help us, these "stalwarts" treated us like pariahs. Moti Chandra went to the extent of saying that the right place for our paintings was the WC[8]—"to be put up with, not flaunted! "'

It was the same Moti Chandra who later turned down Schlesinger's offer of his fine collection of modern Indian paintings for the Prince of Wales Museum, Bombay.'[9] This attitude was alive and well for a long time. In 1985, it was still possible for G Venkatachalam to write, 'I have to confess that I have no sympathy with much of what passes for Modern Art; in fact I do not pretend to understand it at all. Much of it seems to me perverted intelligence and a delightful delusion where it is not wilful deception. I do not like this deforming of figures and torturing of forms and mutilation of limbs in the name of rhythmic design and plastic unity.' You might think that Mr Venkatachalam is venting his ire in the columns of some right-wing magazine. Or equally, in India at least, it might be a statement in a polemical Marxist magazine. But it is actually to be found in a KK Hebbar monograph, a Nalanda publication. (Hebbar is of course excused on the grounds that he is an ancient at heart. Old is always good.)

The Progressives coalesced around a negative response. Perhaps this was the reason why cracks began to appear soon enough though the group grew quickly in size and in recognition. Kekoo Gandhy gave Ila Pal his version of what went wrong: 'Because Souza was the big blabberer, he cornered more attention. Hebbar and some others felt bitter about the whole thing. So did Bendre. As a result, they formed the Bombay Group which had many other artists including Shiavax Chavda. Actually it was at Chavda's exhibition at the Princess Room in the Taj Hotel that Lady Rama Rau fired the first salvo at the Neo-Bengal School and the Royal Academy of London.'

This was a time of great intellectual excitement. Members of the Progressive Artists met with members of the Progressive Writers Association at Mulk Raj Anand's house. The Left wanted the Progressives to inject more social realism into their work but the artists, by and large, resisted, unless driven by their own internal impulses.

The problem wasn't ideological; it was commercial. Nobody was buying. Perhaps one of the reasons was that almost everyone had imbibed the Gandhian ideal of austerity in personal life and the Marxist attitude that buying art was a bourgeois practice. Art as an investment, with the classic dream sequence in which you buy for a pittance and sell for a fortune, was an idea whose time had yet to come. In the 1950s, a painting was something you bought because of the pleasure it gave you. You might think this was about as pure a motive as possible but in that long-forgotten age, even that pleasure was suspect. In her memoir, *All These Years,* Raj Thapar says: 'At Raza's very first exhibition, I bought a painting for fifty rupees and had to fight back a guilt of extraordinary size for that indulgence.'

The guilt comes out of the fact that Thapar bought the work because she took pleasure in it. She did not see it as an investment, she was certainly not thinking of its resale value. That a painting might eventually prove to be hugely profitable was unimaginable in the 1950s. Rashna Gandhy told me that Salman Haidar of the Indian Foreign Service thanked her because Kekoo had arm-twisted him into buying an MF Husain while Haider was working in the Indian High Commission in London, as Kekoo did not want to carry unsold paintings back to India!

The stage therefore is set. We need a young man with money, imagination, enthusiasm and the ability to see art as a form of personal social commitment.

Enter stage right: Kekoo Gandhy.

•02•

An Accident and a Non-Business

Like so much else that happens in the subcontinent, it seems as if Kekoo Gandhy's encounter with modern Indian art happened by accident. Like so much else that happens in the subcontinent, there are many versions of the same serendipitous encounter.

One of the two protagonists of our story, Kekoo Gandhy, had benefited from a good education in India and qualified to study economics at Pembroke College, Cambridge. He even completed a year there and was popular enough to be elected president of Majlis, the association of Indian students. When we meet him, he is back in Bombay, the city of his birth, on holiday. World War II has broken out, making return inadvisable. He does not know it now but he will never go back to Cambridge and he will never regret it.

The other protagonist is Roger Van Damme. He is Belgian and a maker of picture frames. The War has left him stranded in India.

In one version, Kekoo Gandhy and his cousin and self-confessed side-kick, Dara Gandhy, are driving on Juhu Beach and meet Roger Van Damme, a Belgian; his car has stalled. They help him dig it out of the sand and that gets a friendship going which will eventually lead to the Gandhys starting a framing business. This, in turn, will lead to them becoming the first family of modern art in India. This is Dara Gandhy's version of the story, told to me when he was eighty-five years old and we were sitting in Kekee Manzil, the house in which he too was born, seven years after Kekoo.

Adil Gandhy does not think that is quite what happened. Kekoo Gandhy's first-born, a man of near sublime cheerfulness, tells it well in an email:

'As I heard and know it, Dad [Kekoo Gandhy] was driving a nice big Austin with huge steel bumpers and there was an accident. It was the Van Damme car that suffered the damage but he was a gentleman and willing to overlook what must have been a fender-bender. They were soon chatting like old friends. It was then that Roger Van Damme introduced himself, saying that he was a Belgian businessman who had been travelling in India when the war broke out and Germany occupied Belgium. He had perforce to remain and that might explain his not-so-nice car too. His company was a trading firm called Sepulchre Brothers; he was interested in setting up a side business in framing for paintings and photographs and suchlike since he had the know-how and the machinery which was lying idle in Brussels.'

•

Loulou Van Damme, daughter of Roger and still a close friend of the family, tells it differently:

'This is my version of how the Chemould association started. My father had arrived in Bombay and his car suffered a puncture. He got out and was changing the tyre in the heat and dust of a Bombay road when a huge car drew up beside him and a man emerged, dapper in a suit and a tie and a hat, carrying a huge cigar.

"May I be of any assistance?" he asked.

This was Minocher Gandhy or Papa Gandhy, Kekoo's father.

And over a change of tyre, the two men became friends. They discovered a common circle, they discovered they worked in the same area and of that punctured tyre, Chemould was born.'

•

What is interesting is that all three versions of the same story centre around the symbol of the motor car. In two versions, the make is specified: an Austin. Dara Gandhy remembers six young students of the Cathedral School going to school in it every day until petrol rationing was imposed and they began to take the train instead. This can be read as something of a reversal in terms of status and in terms of the trajectory of development. In the first half of the twentieth century it was the train that was to represent the arrival and spread of modernity; in the second half, it would be the car that would define modernity, mobility and all the attendant ills of a civilisation still struggling to be born.

In all of the three versions, there's a moment that could have turned out differently. Kekoo and Dara could have driven past the stalled car; Roger Van Damme could have kicked up a fuss and called the police; or Minocher could have got on with his work and his cigar. (If it seems odd that Minocher, a good Parsi, was smoking, perhaps it should be remembered that he was a tobacco merchant as well and that this is a story told by a non-Parsi.)

Kekoo Gandhy would often speak about how Roger Van Damme had noticed the multitude of goddesses, gods and their various avatars in India. He would say that Van Damme insisted India was a great place for a framing business because everyone had an image, an icon, a lithograph or often a photograph of an ancestor in their homes, in front of which they offered daily worship.

'Roger would say, "The gods are crying out for a good frame," and I agreed,' Kekoo would say often. It was never clear whether this was a joke or something that Van Damme had actually said but that would have been about all it took for the young Kekoo to throw himself into the idea.

Dara Gandhy remembers his friend and cousin as a man of impulse. 'Kekoo would listen to something and if he was really paying attention, if he got excited, you could see the wheels turning in his head. Then it did not

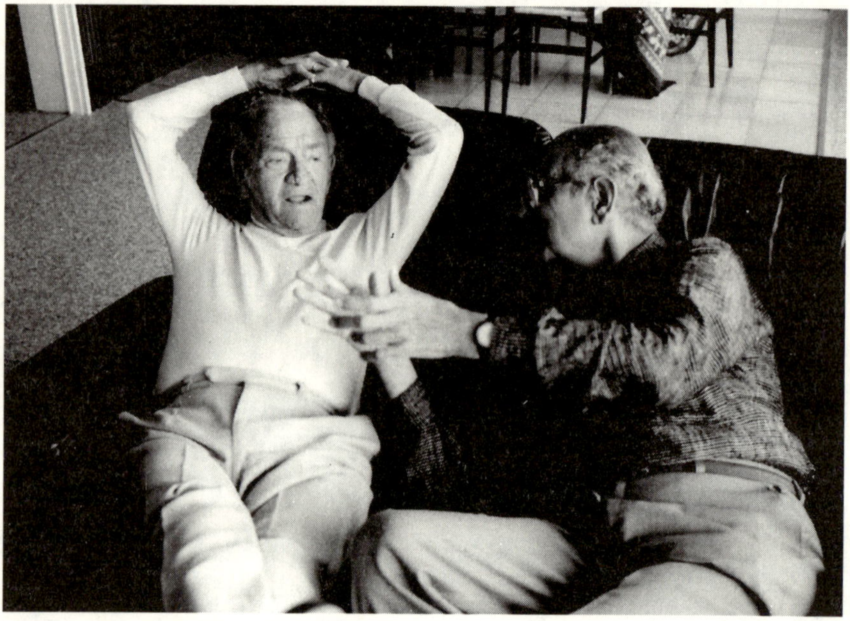

Serendipitous encounter: Roger Van Damme and Kekoo Gandhy, 1991

matter whether it seemed possible or whether we knew anything about it. We would be doing it.'

The use of the pronoun 'we' in Dara's voice has a wonderful mixture of exasperation and affection. It is an acknowledgement that if Kekoo was going to be doing it, Dara would also be doing it. 'We did not know anything about chemicals or moulds or frames or art, but it did not seem to matter. What mattered was the idea and how to get it done. And I don't know whether it was luck or optimism or energy or just that Kekoo would not give up on anything, but things eventually got done,' says Dara.

Kekoo may not have had the training for setting up a factory or running an art gallery but then young men of his class did not really train for anything. He was born to privilege. He went to Dorabji and Hirabai Vacha Primary School (which was on the grounds of what is now Mehboob Studios) and then to the Cathedral and John Connon School. He did the Grand Tour of

Europe for a year before he was admitted to Cambridge. Men of that class and time had great expectations and they knew they would take their place in a carefully orchestrated system of privileges that had been devised so as to withstand the shocks of history, the tempests of time and shifts of political allegiance. The system had held in the world of satraps and kingdoms; it had withstood the test of the colonial world and its bureaucratised criminality; it would also prove malleable enough for independent India.

The framing business was an opportunity and it was time to call in the patriarch, Minocher Gandhy.

Adil Gandhy takes up the narrative: 'Mota Papa [Minocher Gandhy] had an idea; the Gandhys owned around five to six acres of land, which was actually an orchard with wonderful mango, chickoo and coconut trees with a beautiful stone bungalow in front. The entire estate was called Shapur Baug [after its original owner, Shapoorji Bharu] and it was lying vacant. Minocher Gandhy initiated the idea of starting a joint venture with the Van Dammes. The Belgians would bring in the know-how and the machinery; the Gandhys would contribute the vacant land and they could make picture frames. That was how they came to be partners in The Chemical Moulding Manufacturing Company Private Limited.

'The frames were basically made of wood but the ornaments/designs which were laid on top were made out of a chemical composite. After the design had been decided, a steel roller was covered with this chemical composite in reverse and this was used to cover the wood. It is from this "chemical moulding" that the company got its name.'

'Chemical Moulding' explains how Chemould got its name and should lay to rest any doubts about how the name is pronounced.

Shapur Baug was not just the factory. It has, in retrospect, taken on the air of an enchanted garden, the promise of an almost Blytonian childhood. Adil Gandhy remembers the tum-tum that drew up at the station and

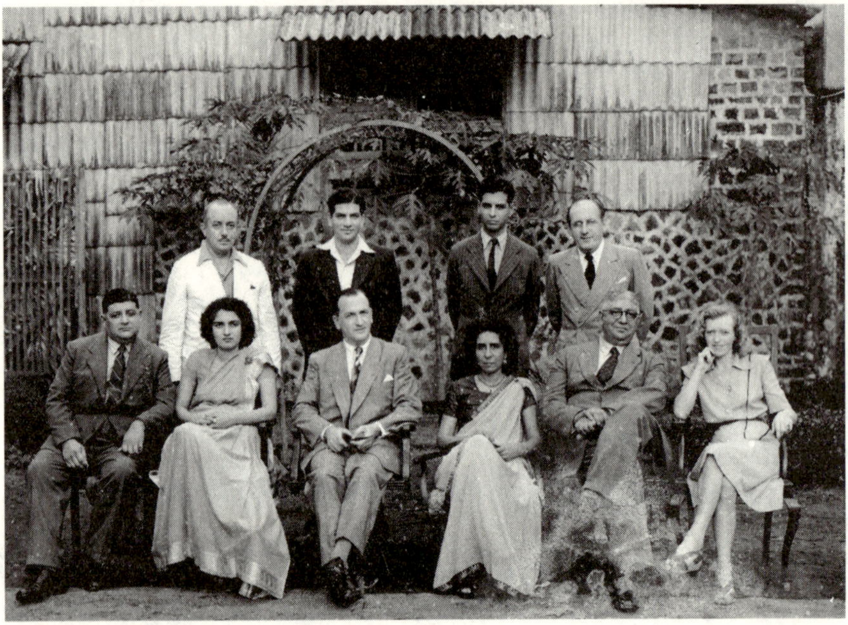

Enchanted garden: *The Gandhys and Van Dammes at Shapur Baug. Standing (l to r): Belgian manager of Gevaert, Max Verbiest, Russi Gandhy, Kekoo Gandhy; sitting (l to r): Tehmuras Gandhy, Khorshed Gandhy, Roger Van Damme, Roshan Gandhy, Minocher Gandhy, and Mrs Simon Van Damme.*

Mohammed, the old driver, who took them to the baug on weekends. Loulou Van Damme remembers: 'Whenever I hear a wood saw going, and it is not a sound I hear much now, I am immediately transported back to Shapur Baug. It was a lovely house, a dream home, Kekoo's home and we lived there too. My mother created a wonderful garden with a fountain in which we played as children. There was horse riding and picnics to Powai Lake where we went fishing.'

Thus like many things the Gandhys did, this would not only be about business. It would be about the relationships that went with the making of money. The Gandhy and the Van Damme families grew quite close because 'Van Damme also loved the house [at Shapur Baug] which was lying vacant at the time and decided he would rent it from the Gandhys. So he lived there for his entire stay in India until he left in 1959. He used to come for two to three hours in the morning to train the workers on the manufacturing of wooden mouldings and then drive into town to attend to his trading business,' recounts Adil.

The familial relationship was replicated in the two companies—Sepulchre Brothers and Chemould—which were owned in partnership. 'The Gandhys had 60 per cent of Chemould; and the Belgians had 40 per cent; as for the Sepulchre Brothers, it was 60 per cent owned by the Belgians and 40 per cent by the Gandhys. In 1963, Van Damme decided to retire and Chemould became 100 per cent Gandhy-owned and run; in return Sepulchre's ownership went back to them,' says Dara Gandhy.

So far, so good. The frame business was of a decent size and made a decent profit. Art was for other people: the Bohemians, the dilettantes. The Van Dammes had also been involved in art restoration but that had been in earlier generations when an old painting could be imagined to have a great deal of monetary value.

Then came the frame shop, an idea that must have struck the patriarch as a bit small, if not downright odd. This was after all a wealthy family which had interests in tobacco. But it was also a family that was no stranger to risk. As art historian Karin Zitzewitz writes in *The Perfect Frame,* a book that was published on the occasion of Gallery Chemould completing forty years:

> Minocher Gandhy was active in the tobacco trade, taking after his father, whose entry into this business is the subject of a family fable. Manecksha Gandhy, Kekoo's grandfather, had moved in his youth to Bombay from Bharuch, Gujarat. After some time struggling to find a good job, he became the office manager for a British dealer. One of his duties as office manager was to act as a proxy for the firm at the tobacco auctions. He returned from one such auction—at which he

had duly bought his firm's order—to discover that the dealer for whom he had worked was nowhere to be found. Having signed for his company's order of tobacco, Gandhy himself was liable for the bill.

Panicking, Manecksha Gandhy went to the District Collector and explained his situation. The Collector, taking pity on the young man, himself gave the loan that allowed Gandhy to fulfill his obligation to the market and enter the business himself. A businessman of no small talent, he was able to pay back the loan and make a friend in the Collector. The moral of this story—that risk should be viewed as an opportunity and, when properly taken advantage of, can catapult one into favourable circumstances—has clearly been absorbed by Kekoo Gandhy. It animates many of his own tales.

There was enough money for the patriarch, Minocher Gandhy, to build Kekee Manzil, a fine three-storey stone building, on a small rise on the coast of Bandra when his wife Roshan delivered his heir, Kekoo, on 2 February 1920.

The area is saturated in the history of the family. The mansion next door was called Villa Vienna and it was home to Kekoo's mother, Roshan Bottlewalla. The house had been built by her father Maneksha Bottlewalla, who made a huge amount of money, travelled abroad, fell in love with Europe's grandeur and came home to build himself a house with columns and gables.

'But as often happens,' Shireen Gandhy, the youngest of the four Gandhy siblings and the one who runs Chemould now, says, 'Maneksha lost a lot of money and came to the point where the Gandhy family had to bail him out. That was when the Gandhys bought over Maneksha's Matheran property (which was already mortgaged) and Shapur Baug to tide him over some tough times.'

After Maneksha Bottlewalla died, two of his sisters continued to live in Villa Vienna. One of them passed on naturally; the other was found dead, a mystery still unsolved. The property passed through a succession of owners until it ended in the hands of Shah Rukh Khan who renamed it Mannat.

And hereby hangs a delightful Kekaesque tale. When the house was sold, Kekoo immediately saw an opportunity to sell Shah Rukh Khan some art and spent many days scuttling next door to hang paintings on the superstar's walls.

'That too during Holi,' moaned Shireen, remembering. 'Who takes a painting outdoors during Holi?'

'Anyway, all this was of no use,' Khorshed Gandhy snorted. 'He never bought a single painting but he had the benefit of them hanging in his house for some time.'

But on Holi, Kekoo was invited to a party thrown by Shah Rukh. He came home delighted at how gently the actor had lowered him into the swimming pool.

•

Money often seems stable from the outside. You look at Kekee Manzil and you see an edifice that is going to be there for another few hundred years. Were you to do a time-lapse film, the buildings around would rise and fall but the three-storey building would continue unchanged, a fulcrum around which the area turns. But anyone who has money will tell you how unstable money is, how a patriarch may spend sleepless nights thinking about the old saying, 'From shirtsleeves to shirtsleeves in three generations.' If the shopfront on Princess Street had been an off-shoot of the business, Mota Papa might have understood and even applauded this move. Control the supply chain and you can make profit all along the line or amortise some

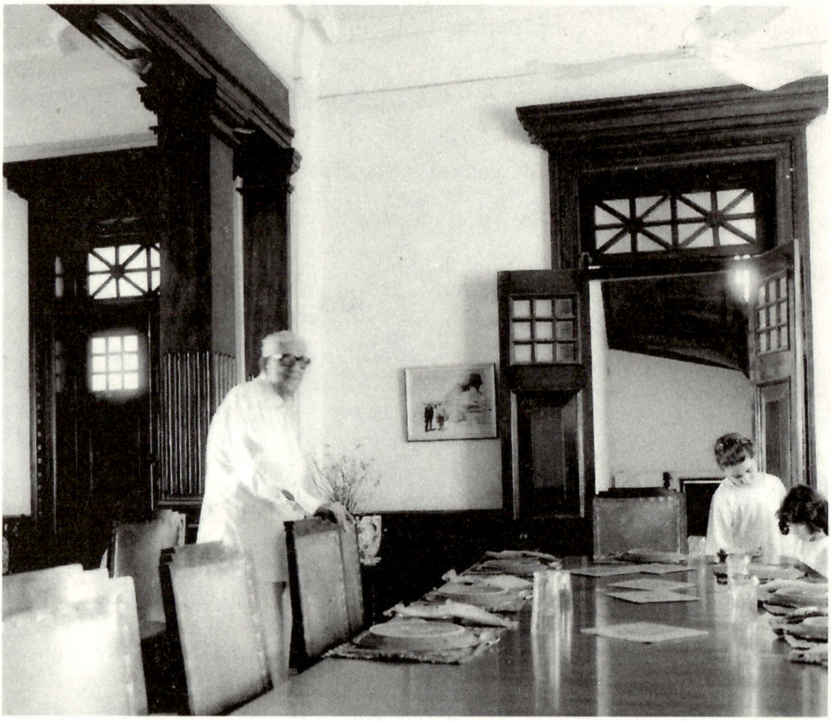

The patriarch of Kekee Manzil: Minocher Gandhy. Photos: Above and on facing page: Cynthia Stroud-Watson

losses. But when his son began to spend an increasing amount of time at the shop, hobnobbing with down-and-out artists, he must have wondered what was going on.

'My father-in-law always said: What is this art about? This is a non-business,' said Khorshed Gandhy. 'I wonder what he would have said today.'

For even if the original idea was a chemical moulding frames factory—which the family ran for many years—it was the art that was contained in them that soon began to fascinate Kekoo Gandhy.

'Really, I didn't know much about art or artists, ' Kekoo said again and again. He said it so often that you know he did not really believe it nor did he expect his auditors and interlocutors to take this as anything but the standard modest proclamation of ignorance.

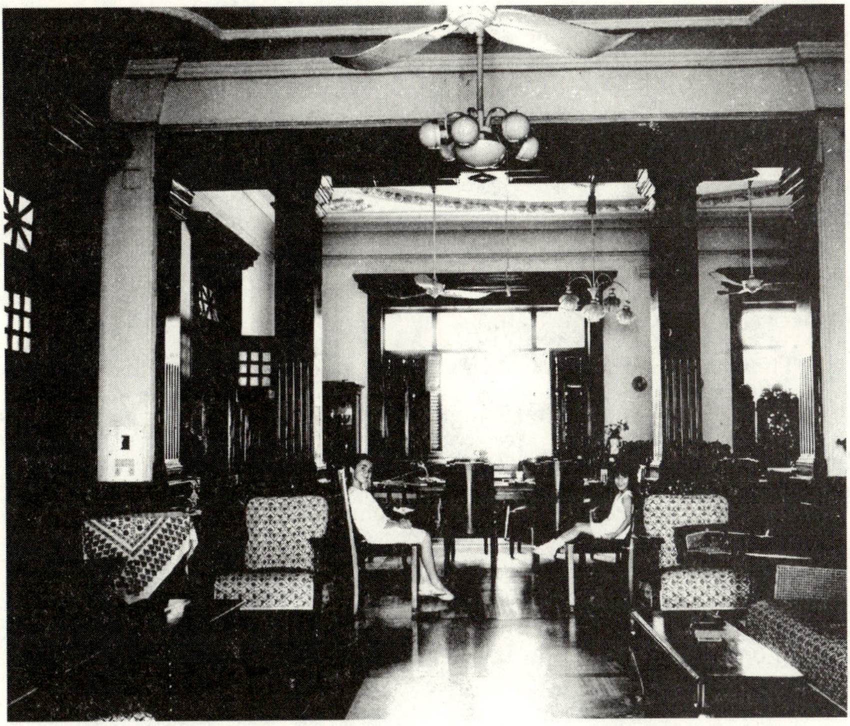

***The family home:** inside Kekee Manzil*

Look carefully at what he is saying and you will also see that this is not really a very meaningful remark. If we are talking about India in the 1950s, one might ask what kind of education would be available to qualify Kekoo for the very peculiar and specific role he played in the art world of the time. Would it have helped him to know what surrealism or futurism was? Or to discourse knowledgeably on the manifestos with which the twentieth century was littered, each fated, it would seem, to be the manure for the next bunch of radical young men?

What Kekoo had, instead, were his friends, his acquaintances, his ability to turn new acquaintances into old friends in the course of a single conversation. His was the classic case of it not mattering what he knew but who he knew.

And history, it would seem, was to bring a whole load of new acquaintances into his ken.

Well before the Nazis began to overrun Europe, some Jews managed to escape persecution. Some went to Switzerland, some to England, some to America and wherever they went, they were instrumental in bringing about a series of thought revolutions: think Freud in London, think Einstein in America. Some Jews came to India.

These included Rudolf von Leyden[10], a geologist by profession, who came from Germany; Walter Langhammer[11], an artist who would become the first art director of *The Times of India* who came from Austria, and Emmanuel Schlesinger[12], a rich hatmaker also from Austria who would start a partnership with a chemist in Mumbai and found a pharmaceutical company. In an undated biodata that was prepared for Kekoo Gandhy, they would be described as 'important teachers and patrons of the fledgling art movement'.

They would bring with them a sophisticated outlook, a cosmopolitanism and most importantly for our story, lots of slides of what European painters were doing. In this image-saturated age, perhaps it is difficult to understand how important those slides must have been. We live in a time when it is possible to summon up an artist's oeuvre at the click of a button or to go for a virtual tour of the Sistine Chapel, seated in the comfort of our homes. Seventy years ago, you had to rely on art books and it was for some reason assumed that the glossier the book, the better it was, never mind what the paintings looked like. It was not uncommon for many of these books to be in black and white so you had to imagine the colours and your imagination often got things wrong. (The sky must be blue, you would think, and then discover that it was a blur of yellows and ochres with hints of blue.) But even these books were few and far between because they were expensive and so unavailable to most impecunious artists. And so to look at good reproductions

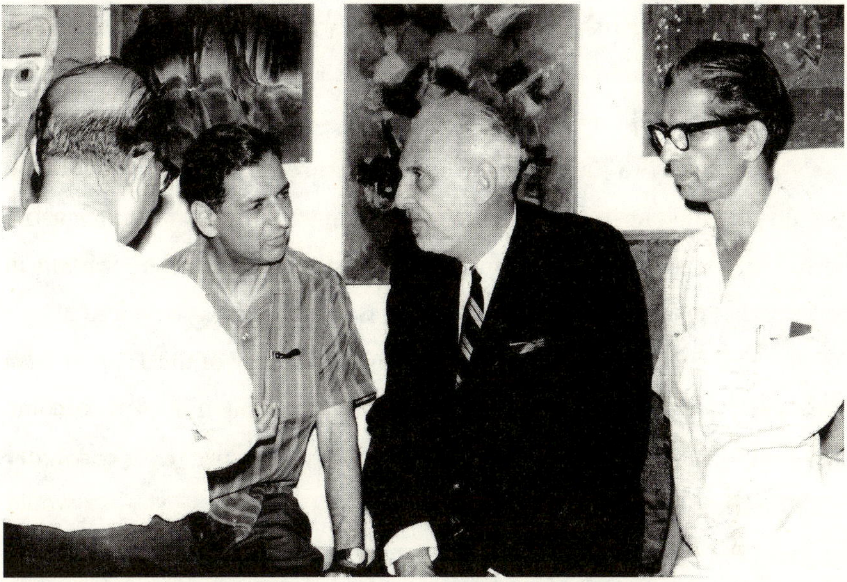

Early days: (left to right) Kekoo Gandhy, Rudy von Leyden and KK Hebbar

of works by Picasso and Schiele and Braque must have been life-changing for many young Indian artists who must also have been struggling to articulate the new age in which they were living. To have someone speak about these artworks knowledgeably, must have also been like being in an art class at a foreign university.

What fascinates me is the untold story of this encounter. How did these émigrés meet the painters they were going to nurture? You do not arrive in a city and get in touch with the painters if the art scene is as institutional and occasional as it was in the 1940s. Think about the Progressives for a moment and you see a motley bunch of men; most of them were poor, not all of them were recognized as painters. If you were a noisy painter who was going to '*épater les bourgeois*' as Souza was, you might be noticed. But the quieter painters needed someone to introduce them to the right people. Leyden was the best placed to meet painters because he was an art critic but there mustn't have been all that much work to do. He also had the good fortune to have his car cleaned by Krishnaji Howlaji Ara and when he discovered the man's talent, took him home and gave him a job as a 'houseboy' while supplying him with paint and canvas.

But it wasn't just the painters whom these three men encouraged. Kekoo Gandhy says that he had been content with doing frames by the strip until he went on holiday to Matheran and at Porcupine Point, met Herr Schimmel, an Austrian who was head of Kores India. Schimmel also introduced him to Walter Langhammer who summoned him to the office of the *Times of India* and demanded that he do a more aesthetic job of making frames. Kekoo was sceptical but allowed himself to be convinced and thus began his encounter with the world of fine art.

He was ideally located at the intersection of this encounter. The artists came to his shop to have their work framed (perhaps sent there by Langhammer) and found in Kekoo a friend. He, in turn, could connect them to the expatriate community and to the few rich buyers there were because he moved in those circles. Kekoo moved with chameleon-like ease between worlds.

Meanwhile, World War II had had another fallout. There were some Italian prisoners of war, captured in North Africa, interned in Bombay. Some of them were known to be painters and so it was decided that they should paint the messes and club rooms of the barracks across the country.

This scheme, called MURART, began around the time when the Chemould factory was running into trouble because wood was scarce. It had all been requisitioned for the war effort. Then the man who began MURART, a certain Captain Dust, according to Kekoo again, decided that the paintings the Italians were doing would need frames. They requisitioned the Shapur Baug bungalow for the war effort and Chemould began to work exclusively for them.

Once again, there was no distance between the home and the world. The

Italians became friends, they cooked together, they hung out together and Kekoo brought Indian artists to meet them. For more of this, see Part Two where Kekoo talks about the bread they baked with as much delight as he talks about the art they were making.

•

Some argue that the Progressives were born out of this cross-fertilisation between the Indian painter and the Jewish expatriate. That seems a little far-fetched to me. Modernism may need catalysts and the Jewish diaspora was good at this, rewriting the art and sensibility of countries as far-flung as India and Great Britain and the United States but modernism *is also inevitable.* Artists must respond to the way the world changes; if they do not, their art runs the risk of being repetitive and sterile. You cannot live in an age of machines and industrialization and still try to paint Renaissance sunsets and rural maidens at midnight though many would keep on trying. The arrival of Leyden, Langhammer and Schlesinger may have hastened the process but it would have come, sooner or later.

The problem is that for an art scene, it is not enough to have a college, an annual show and a handful of prizes. Artists must eat. And in order to eat, they must sell their work. Ila Pal has told us of Husain waiting for the last tram to pass so that he could spread out the film poster signboards that he was painting for a living. Other stories are equally dire; Krishen Khanna records in his memoir:

> Selling a painting in the 1950s was an event. It made not only the artist happy but all his friends. It was a kind of beacon of hope. When this happened to a person such as Ram Kumar, it was a major event. His pictures in those days were full of unemployed, bitter young men placed in the debris of urban slums. There weren't any takers. It happened one winter in

> Delhi that he actually sold a painting and the excitement of it broke through his usually reticent nature. He told me, he told MF Husain, he even told VS Gaitonde, and Bal Chhabda who was on his annual visit to Delhi, which also meant that we were meeting every day.
>
> On one of those days...Ram declared his good fortune to all of us jointly and said that this called for a cup of tea.
>
> 'TEA?' exclaimed Bal. 'I never drink the stuff and besides you've sold it for two hundred and fifty bloody rupees. A dinner is on the cards. And we don't want to eat at your house but at a suitable restaurant.'
>
> Ram's enthusiasm seemed to subside a bit. The same kind-hearted fellow, I think it was Husain, thought that a dinner might be overdoing it. Perhaps breakfast the following morning might be more appropriate. That's what was agreed upon[13].

If the Progressives were to survive, if they were to settle down to seriously work out what they wanted to do, they needed art galleries, preferably many of them so that there might be a bit of competition.

What they got was a storefront.

For when the Chemould Frame Company had stock on hand, and demand kept rising, it was decided that they should also get into retail. Two shops were set up within a short time, one in Bombay and the other in Calcutta.

One of the early managers was Roshan Kalapesi, the first of a line of people who would make their mark in other places. I met Kalapesi only late in life and did not know then of her association with Chemould. She struck me as one of those quiet forces of nature, a gentle stream that will erode boulders. It was she who would famously urge the painters to make small works so that they might fit in the shop window. (Later, she would be seen as the heir of those redoubtable women who worked tirelessly for the revival of handicrafts and tribal art, Kamaladevi Chattopadhyaya and Pupul Jayakar. Kalapesi would start Paramparik Karigar in later years, an organisation that showcases and supports artisans, carefully selected for their skill and integrity.)

•

The store front is still very much there, many decades after it began. It is still a framing shop and it opens out, in the manner of old Mumbai buildings, into a warren of small workshops and rooms. (I only found this out because I once asked to use the loo. Suddenly, I was out of the air-conditioned splendour of the front office and back in a world of karigars and glue and stretchers and piles of odd bits of wood. It has an artisanal quality to it now, as if indeed, the world has come full circle. What was once chemically moulded in faraway Andheri, an area where you could still go riding and fishing in the lakes on the factory property, is now made by hand and by skilled labour.)

A third generation of Gandhys now runs it. Kekoo and Khorshed began the store; they handed it over to their son Adil Gandhy and now his son, Riyad Gandhy, is often to be found supervising the selection of frames. It seems fitting.

•03•

A Womb with a View

'Gallery Chemould welcomes you to their inaugural exhibition. We will hold in our permanent collection paintings by the artists on display in the current show and also by other artists of our choice. It will be our special endeavour to discover and project painters of outstanding talent from different centres of India. We shall exhibit their work regularly through our galleries in Bombay and Calcutta and will also send the works of the painters we represent to important exhibitions within the country and abroad. Today there is a widening gulf between the painter and the lay public. Conscious of our responsibility in this field, we hope to make our own contribution through an intelligent choice of paintings that we hold in our gallery.'

—Text from the card for the inaugural exhibition,
Monday, 16th September 1963

'Gallery Chemould, on the first floor of the Jehangir Art Gallery, was the focal point of the Bombay art scene, but more. The Kekoo-Khorshed duo made Chemould an institution and a movement: they were protagonists of Indian modernism—from the Progressives to the most contemporary, including figural artists pushing at the edge, like Bhupen Khakhar. The Gandhys tried to understand the context of the art they showed, the way it would interact with the world around. Indeed the entire family—once the Gandhy children grew up—joined those many others in Bombay who were committed to envisioning the kind of India, the kind of society that would be supportive of the project of modern and contemporary culture. And, vice versa: the kind of art movement that would reflect the democratic aspirations of this nation.'

—**Geeta Kapur**, Art Historian and Curator

Bombay Gallery 1

Otherwise known as Gallery 59.

For a woman of many talents and avatars, Darshan Chhabda is remembered mainly as the poet Arun Kolatkar's first wife. I remember her as a member of The Poetry Circle, Bombay, a quiet presence with a distinctive poetic voice.

Towards the end of her life, she told Adil Jussawalla that she had some Poetry Circle papers that she would like to hand over to me. I began to visit her in a studio apartment in Colaba in Pushpa Bhavan, close to what was once the Strand Cinema. In a sunny room, bright with afternoon light and memory, we would sit and chat. I brought her Margery Allingham whodunits to read and news of the outside world. Her body was failing her but her mind was clear and her sense of humour intact.

Darshan had had a ringside view of the art world. She was a painter herself; one of her paintings was acquired by the Lalit Kala Akademi. She sketched and drew all through her life but she did not make a career of it. Her brother Bal Chhabda was one of the Later Progressives, as it were. She was the natural person to ask about Gallery 59.

'Bal wasn't an artist, I think, not a natural born one. But we were from a family that owned several theatres and we both grew up watching films. I remember falling asleep watching a film and being carried home and waking up the next morning, wondering what had happened to the screen. Bal got bitten by the cinema bug and directed a film called *Do Raha*[14] which was about the life of an artist; someone suggested he should meet MF Husain so he could understand what the life of an artist was like. That's how they met and became friends. Husain had a huge influence on him and eventually, I think it was he who encouraged Bal to paint.'

'He designed some furniture for Bal, no?' I asked.

'*Salle de* Bal,' she said. 'It was on show at the first Husain retrospective[15]. Bal began hanging out with the Progressives and he grew to like them and then he became one of them. Husain entered one of Bal's paintings in a competition and it won a prize. I think that was when he began to take art seriously.'

Husain and Chhabda probably spent a lot of time at the Bhulabhai Desai Institute at Breach Candy. The Institute was one of the magic moments in the history of Bombay. The space was meant for the arts; it brought in artists and painters and actors and theatre directors. So you have to imagine what it must have been like to hear Ravi Shankar at riyaaz on one floor while upstairs MF Husain was painting and outside Ebrahim Alkazi was directing 'The House of Bernarda Alba' while Satyadev Dubey nursed grim thoughts about the monopoly of English over the world of high culture in a multilingual city.

That kind of place.

The man in charge was the unlikely Soli Batliwalla. I say unlikely because one of the critiques of the Left as it existed in the city and in the state of Maharashtra was its near-criminal neglect of the cultural sphere. The argument was, I believe, that Indian cultural practice could never be clearly demarcated from Indian religious belief and since the latter was anathema to the Marxist, the former could be safely ignored. There were writers' associations and theatre groups but those were professional groups and professional associations and from this distance, they seem rather forbidding. If the mill workers wanted to act or dance or sing or find some way to express themselves, they were pretty much on their own as far as the unions were concerned, unless it could be proved that their artistic endeavours had something to say to the dialectic and the struggle for a classless society. This left the field clear for other actors to take over and enter stage right, the Shiv Sena. And yet it was this Soli Batliwalla, Communist, who was in charge of the Bhulabhai Desai Institute.

The artist Nalini Malani remembers both the Institute and its manager with a great deal of fondness: 'My first studio was at the Bhulabhai Memorial Institute [in 1964]; the building in which my parents lived shared a wall with the Institute and I was often over there as a child, for dance classes, for art classes, that kind of thing. On turning eighteen and being admitted to the JJ School in the fine arts programme, I went to Solibhai and he said he'd give me studio space. And so I got to be part of the unique magic of that environment. It was a great time to be an artist, a time of camaraderie and joy. I just needed a little money to keep me going and more than that for art materials. We all had the same idea: that we were not going to cheapen ourselves for money; that we would do what we wanted to do and see it through. As for everything else, there was so much in the air, so much you could take in by just being there. At the Bhulabhai Institute, for instance,

Annapurna Devi would be doing her riyaaz and you would hear her, like some legendary bird that was 'but a wandering voice'; and then there was Satyadev Dubey rehearsing plays and actors learning their lines or just talking; there were sculptors and painters in their studios. You could read art criticism in the *Times* and the *Express*; they covered the scene, such as it was, very conscientiously. On opening night, Rudy von Leyden would come to the show and then he would get on to his bicycle and ride back to the paper to file his copy. I asked him once why he did this and he said that the artist had worked so hard, put in years of time and the least he could do was make sure that they woke up the next day to find his review in the paper. Nissim Ezekiel, Gieve Patel and Adil Jussawalla would write too; so would Dilip Chitre and Eunice de Souza.'

And at the heart of all this was Soli Batliwalla. Malani remembers him as important to her development. 'Solibhai was inspiring. He helped me with my reading in Communism. He was not interested in the art that happened at the Bhulabhai Desai Institute; he was interested in managing the estate. Some people maintain that it was he who brought the Institute to an end but I don't think it was any one person's doing. It was a golden time and it had to come to an end. And I think it would have been the same utilitarian idea that would have pushed him to invite the Gandhys to set up a gallery on the top of Jehangir Art Gallery. [Batliwala was appointed Honorary Secretary of the Jehangir Art Gallery in 1963, in charge of administration and bookings.] He must have seen the space as wasted. At that point in time, Jehangir Art Gallery, specially the large auditorium, was often booked for weddings and functions; it was not being used for the arts. The architect (Durga Bajpai) had created galleries on the opposite side with French windows that opened out to a large patio so sculpture could be placed there and work could even spill out on to the patch of land outside, in the open air facing the Prince of Wales Museum. But since it was hardly utilised, the idea of a café seemed like a good thing and it added energy to the entire complex. It made sense to have an artists' *adda* like Samovar there.'

(Samovar was a café on the ground floor of the Jehangir Art Gallery. For decades it was where the art community went to meet and talk and gas. It was a remarkable place, an institution, and the Jehangir Art Gallery drove it out too. Now it's a narrow passage without a soul which pretends to be a gallery from time to time.[16])

Batliwala was thus the man on the spot. Narayan Surve, the great poet of the city, tells us he came from the Congress Party to the Trade Union Movement. He remembers the gift of a pair of trousers from Solibhai, a pair that he wore to go and hear Dr Ambedkar speaking. Batliwala was also the man whom Madhuriben Desai relied upon to keep the Bhulabhai Desai Institute going. For a while it is all right to imagine all these wonderful intellects and talents, working in harmony by the sea, I suspect reality was a little more challenging. You cannot put a whole bunch of seriously gifted people together and expect them to create a Utopia of Creative Energy. More likely an Arena of Competitive Savagery but let us assume that for a while at least the whole dream held together and those who remember it, have fond memories of their time there, or their experiences as audiences. Either way, we know very little of what went on except for these broad outlines and such oral histories as have been recorded over the years.[17]

But it came to pass that as the 1950s came to a close Bal Chhabda was seized of the idea that the Institute might be a good place to open an art gallery; it was in South Bombay, there were already artists in residence from the established ones like MF Husain to those who were beginning their careers then like Nalini Malani. Like all the other artists, he paid a nominal rent to the Institute. Gallery 59 began well and many artists held their first solo shows there. Akbar Padamsee and Prabhakar Barwe were among them. Gallery 59 organised a show for Tyeb Mehta but it was held at the Jehangir Art Gallery.

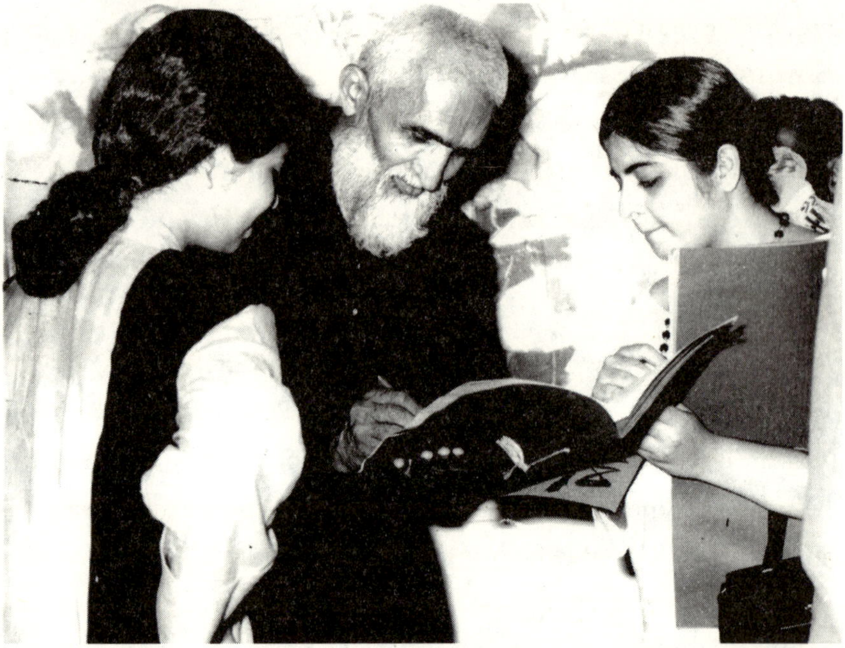

21 years of painting: Husain retrospective, organised by Gallery Chemould at the Jehangir Art Gallery, 1969

'He ordered the lighting system from abroad,' Darshan remembers. 'He was very proud of the gallery. Everything was supposed to be first class and he paid for all of it. But one day, someone told him about a rehearsal that was going on inside the gallery when there were also paintings hanging there. Bal had heard nothing about this so he went and asked Soli about it. I don't suppose he was very polite. Soli maintained that he could not see why he had to tell Bal. After all, the space belonged to the Insitute and as manager, he could use it the way he wanted to and the space was needed for a rehearsal. Bal returned later that day with his friends; they took down the paintings and then they smashed it all up with hockey sticks.'

So ended Gallery 59.

•

Bombay Gallery 2

Kali Pundole had a watch shop at the Flora Fountain which he turned into a gallery, which opened just before Gallery Chemould.

Adil Gandhy tells the story: 'Pundole had a watch shop, selling all kinds of timepieces but mostly wall clocks. When Kekoo befriended Kali, the Pundoles started a small picture-framing section in one part of their shop at Flora Fountain. Kekoo thought that because of the superb location the Pundole shop had at Flora Fountain, the picture framing business would increase. Pundole initially ordered our frames from Princess Street, then slowly set up their little workshop behind and we continued supplying them mouldings from the factory. It was later that Kali thought of setting up an art gallery and thereafter started Pundole Art Gallery. They discontinued framing later as their gallery grew and needed more space for display and storage.'

His sister, filmmaker Behroze Gandhy, sees the problem as spatial: 'Jal Arya was the architect[18] and he was the one who was responsible for turning the space we had been allotted from a dark booth into a gallery. And this was, I suspect, the reason that Pundole managed to scoop us. Theirs was a simple shop and changing it into a gallery didn't take much imagination or hard work. Ours was a slightly more complex space which, when you first looked at it, seemed like anything but a gallery. They were only months before us but I don't think Kekoo ever forgot or Khorshed ever forgave.'

'When Kali Pundole opened just a few weeks before Chemould, Papa was furious,' says Rashna Gandhy. 'He said, "Why didn't he tell me?" But he cooled down soon enough and then he would always maintain that competition was good for business, it kept you on your toes.'

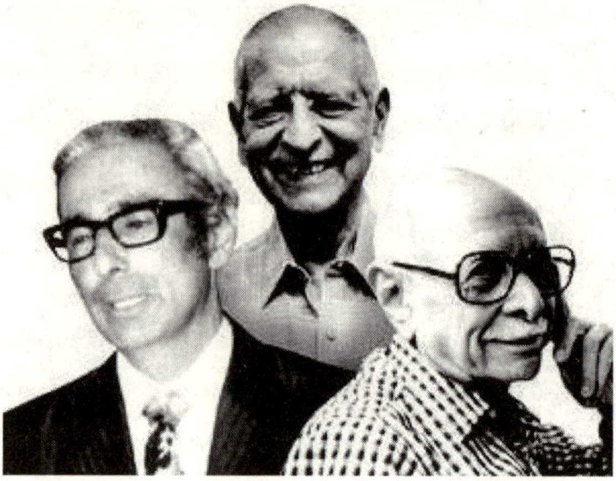

The triumvirate: (left to right) Kali Pundole, Kekoo Gandhy and Jehangir Nicholson. From the exhibition creatives for 'Kekoo, Kali and Jehangir: Framing a Collection', Sept 2014-Jan 2015; courtesy of the Jehangir Nicholson Art Foundation, Mumbai.

Bombay Gallery 3

The story of Gallery Chemould has several possible beginnings. Here is one of them. Nissim Ezekiel, Indian English poetry's first modernist, worked for a while as manager of the Chemould framing factory. His biographer, R Raj Rao writes in his authorised biography of the poet:

> After he chucked his job at Shilpi [an advertising agency at which he worked briefly], Nissim remained unemployed for just a short time. Within days of his resignation, as he was brooding over what to do next, he was approached by Kekoo Gandhy who dropped in at his house and made him an offer. It was for the job of manager at Gandhy's frame-manufacturing factory, Chemould. At Shilpi, he had already done some work for Chemould as part of his duties there; Gandhy was impressed by his work. Besides, he knew Nissim personally, as he frequently visited Gandhy's picture frame shop at Fort [sic].

> Nissim accepted Gandhy's offer and was appointed on a monthly salary of Rs 1200, which was high. One of the reasons why he took up the job was because the product was picture-frames; he felt he would be able to relate his work in the factory to his growing interest in painting and art criticism.
>
> The factory was situated at Andheri, while Gandhy himself lived at Bandra. His suggestion was that Nissim should go to Bandra, and travel to the factory with him in his car.
>
> Nissim liked the nature of his job at Chemould, although it was mainly routine administrative work that he did. He says he was happier here than at Shilpi even though his fellow-employees were not particularly friendly. Somewhere along the way he even seems to have got a promotion—to the post of factory manager. He could now discuss with Gandhy (on more equal terms) the various practical problems the factory was beset by. **One much appreciated suggestion that he came up with was that Gandhy should start an art gallery that would complement the activities of the factory (which existed, after all, to manufacture frames).**[19] *(Emphasis mine)*

Nissim Ezekiel, poet, the originator of the idea? It does not seem likely to me. Nowhere else is this suggested in the stories and legends of the gallery but it is entirely possible that Nissim also suggested the possibility and Kekoo greeted it, politely, as if it were an entirely new idea.

For it was a dream Kekoo was already nurturing, you can tell that. Kekoo was already thinking in terms of galleries, urging friends to set them up. He would have tired eventually of using the Metro Cinema or the Taj Mahal Hotel, both venues for early art shows. He would have thought of an art gallery.

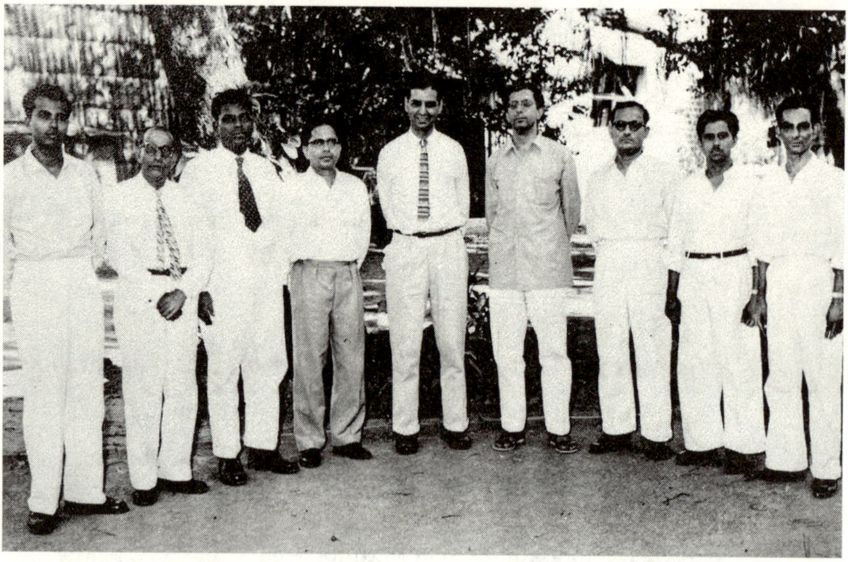

The poet and the gallerist: Nissim Ezekiel and Kekoo Gandhy with the Chemould staff from Delhi and Calcutta, early 1960s

We do not know exactly what Batliwala said or how this invitation was phrased, but my contention is that an invitation does not suffice to create an institution. It is built in tandem, between dream and sweat, between aspirations and quotidian book-keeping and challan writing. So here is where I think the Gallery Chemould, First Floor, Jehangir Art Gallery, started.

Not with Kekoo Gandhy but with Kekoo and Khorshed Gandhy.

Rewind now for a legendary Bombay romance starring Parsi eccentrics, tea dances and honeymoons that last for months.

•

If you go and stand at the Jehangir Art Gallery and look across the road at the building of the Elphinstone College, you can see a Parsi with a magnificent moustache in bas-relief on a roundel. Any resemblance to the painter Jehangir Sabavala is no coincidence. This is his grandfather, Sir Cowasji Jehangier as he spelled his name on the building he donated to the college. His daughter was the feisty Meherbai, renamed by her governess as Bapsey, the last of the great Bombay eccentrics. Bapsey's marriage to Ardeshir Sabavala failed

INAUGURAL EXHIBITION : MONDAY 16th SEPTEMBER 1963

GALLERY CHEMOULD

FIRST FLOOR

JEHANGIR ART GALLERY BUILDING

PHONE 252897

GALLERY CHEMOULD WELCOMES YOU TO THEIR INAUGURAL EXHIBITION. WE WILL HOLD IN OUR PERMANENT COLLECTION PAINTINGS BY THE ARTISTS ON DISPLAY IN THE CURRENT SHOW AND ALSO BY OTHER ARTISTS OF OUR CHOICE.

IT WILL BE OUR SPECIAL ENDEAVOUR TO DISCOVER AND PROJECT PAINTERS OF OUTSTANDING TALENT FROM DIFFERENT CENTRES OF INDIA. WE SHALL EXHIBIT THEIR WORKS REGULARLY THROUGH OUR GALLERIES IN BOMBAY AND CALCUTTA AND WILL ALSO SEND THE WORKS OF THE PAINTERS WE REPRESENT TO IMPORTANT EXHIBITIONS WITHIN THE COUNTRY AND ABROAD. TODAY THERE IS A WIDENING GULF BETWEEN THE PAINTER AND THE LAY PUBLIC. CONSCIOUS OF OUR RESPONSIBILITY IN THIS FIELD WE HOPE TO MAKE OUR OWN CONTRIBUTION THROUGH AN INTELLIGENT CHOICE OF PAINTINGS THAT WE HOLD IN OUR GALLERY.

***Birth of a gallery:** Invitation to the opening of Gallery Chemould, 1963* but she did not let that vanquish her spirit. She used her money—and she had a considerable sum—with a flair and inventiveness that is rare in the rich. She had a pet pig and the poet Adil Jusssawalla remembers how he and fellow prankster, Andrew Thompson, both schoolboys at the time, would telephone Bapsey and send her off on mad dashes across the city looking for blunt-nosed pigs. Animals were her thing and the painter Mehlli Gobhai took an endless series of homeless cats to her until he was instructed only to come back with tortoiseshells of the male persuasion. She threw an Animals' Ball at the Taj Mahal Hotel but it was for the four-legged and the feathered and she is said to have rode a horse up to his trough in the Crystal Room. She took part in amateur theatre and the dramaturge and director Satyadev Dubey remembers being overawed by her crystal-cut English accent. She held parades and floats went down the streets of a somewhat perplexed city. But she also started the Swabal Stores to help unemployed Parsi youth and raised considerable funds for causes dear to her heart, including famine relief. Jehangir Sabavala remembers a moment when she reduced a rather waffly and long-winded society lady to tears when she 'boomed—"Cut the cackle, is it a yes or a no?"'[20]

This time Bapsey was organising a tea-dance to raise money for some charitable cause and had roped in a young woman by the name of Khorshed Adenwalla to be her assistant. (Perhaps she felt an animal kinship; the Adenwalla family was said to have had a pet lion in their home in Aden.) She put down Khorshed Adenwalla, Kekoo Gandhy and Jehangir Sabavala at the same table.

'I had had enough of my mother's interference,' Jehangir Sabavala told me with a mixture of delicate glee and amused remorse. 'I simply cancelled their tickets so they found themselves with nothing to do and that afternoon, went for a film instead.'

So began one of the great romances of the art world. Khorshed and

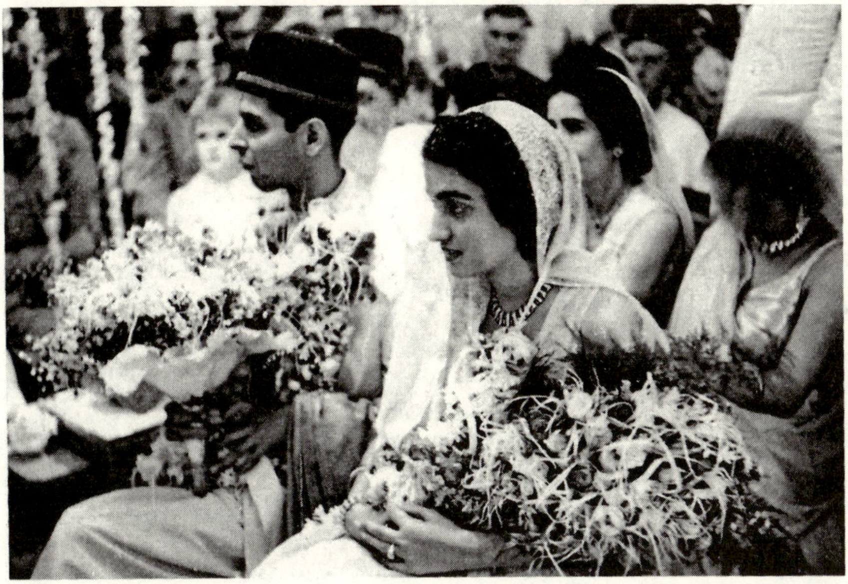

The marriage that led to a gallery: Kekoo and Khorshed Gandhy on their wedding day, 1944

Kekoo got engaged in 1943, and married in 1944 two days after the *SS Fort Stikine* exploded in the Bombay Harbour. For Khorshed, the Gandhys were a revelation. Her own family, she has said, were not very warm. In what may have been an attempt to write her memoirs while she was in bed at the Hinduja Hospital in Mahim in 2010, she notes: 'I came from a very unharmonious Adenwalla family in which brothers quarrelled….'

By contrast, her father-in-law seems to have been a loving and generous man.

'We were going for our honeymoon (which lasted for five weeks if you please!), Minoo Papa would remit the amount from time to time (bless his soul) and we kept on trekking from one spot to another—staying in Nedou's Hotel in Srinagar and Gulmarg and then in tents during the treks.'

Had Kekoo not wooed and won Khorshed, it is likely that Gallery Chemould might have begun but it would certainly not have become an institution. On his own, Kekoo would have run it into the ground, with his grandiose schemes and his complete refusal to consider the possibility that something might be impossible. It was Khorshed who made Chemould a viable gallery and who kept it going through the dark times. Gallery Chemould was their fifth child, says their fourth child, Shireen Gandhy.

•

The gallery began in high style in 1963. Behroze Gandhy, filmmaker and documentarist, says, 'When it opened there was this great energy in the air. Everyone seemed to be involved, everyone had a role to play. Part of this was my father's energy I think; he had a way of making you feel you were part of everything that was happening. But it was my mother who made sure the energy was focused and went in the right direction.'

Behroze Gandhy, the family tearaway, knew quite early that the gallery was not going to be her world even if there were artists like Ram Kumar, Husain and Gaitonde to whom she felt close. 'I have a strong memory of selling tickets with Shamshad Husain—I think it must have been Husain's retrospective. All I know was that we were on the counter; and that I got a salary for that. But I do remember making up my mind early that I was never going to work with the gallery. I think it was because I saw the work that my mother did and what she went through with each show. She would throw herself into it as if it were something she was creating—and in some ways a gallery show also needs a gallerist's time and love and attention. And then it would all come down off the walls and the process had to be started again, with another artist and another show. There was no slack time, no down time. You just had to keep at it and you had to keep ahead of the curve. I didn't know who was going to do it, Adil, Rashna or Shireen, but I knew it wasn't going to be me. I don't have the vision or the imagination or the combination of both that is required to run a gallery.'

It was lucky for everyone that Khorshed Gandhy did. It is unlikely that Kekoo would have even thought about who has going to manage the gallery.

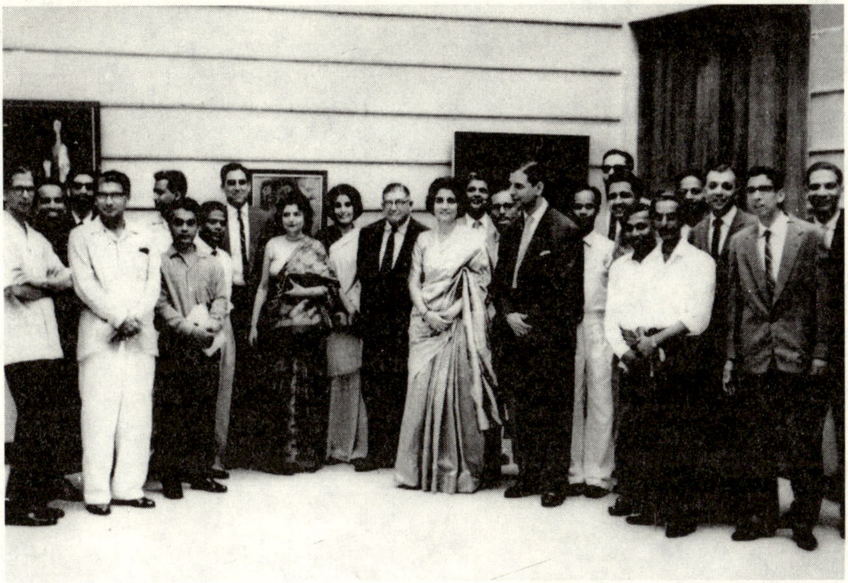

Opening of Gallery Chemould on 16 September 1963: (l to r) KK Hebbar, Laxman Pai, Jal Arya (Architect), Siaxes Chandan and Gaitonde, other members of the family and staff

But as Khorshed said, 'When it was being set up, I asked, "Who is going to look after it? Would you like me to do it?" Kekoo said, "Oh, fine, yes, good." That simple. I became the manager. I had an appreciative eye, but I didn't know what was good and bad art. I had to be taught what contemporary art was, and what to look for.'[21]

Both of them made this something of a mantra. They explained that they did not know about art but what they lacked in formal training, they made up for in sheer exposure. They had been part of the art world in such integral ways that their understanding of it went far beyond the academic.

Geeta Kapur, art historian and an old associate of the gallery, argues for another way of looking at the Gandhys, as protagonists of modernism:

'Chemould on the first floor of the Jehangir Art Gallery was the focal point of the Bombay art scene, but more. The Kekoo-Khorshed duo made Chemould an institution and a movement: they were protagonists of Indian

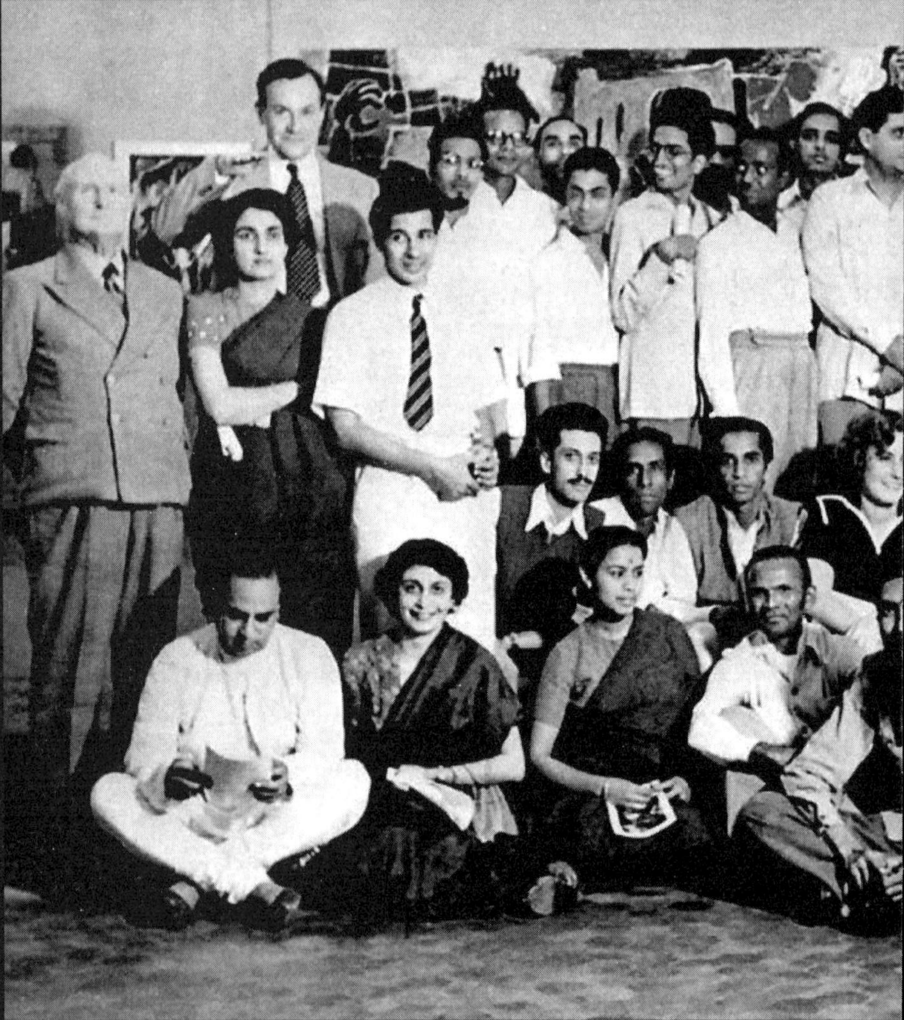

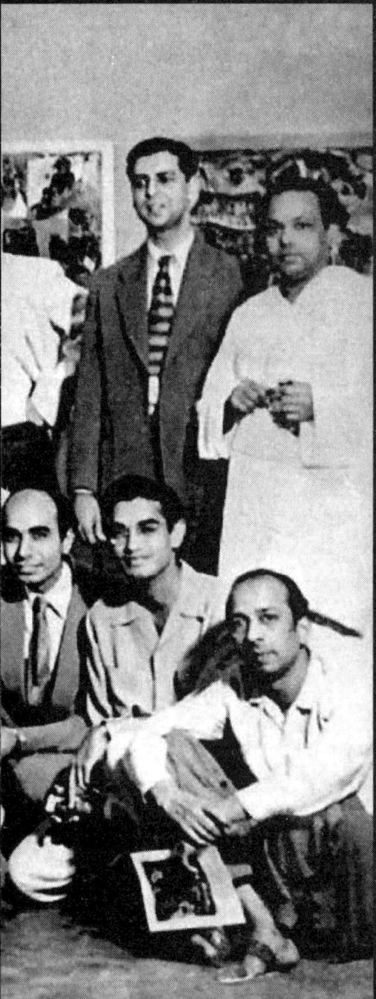

The Progressive Artists Group at The Bombay Art Society Salon surrounded by artists, art critics and patrons, 1940s, (l to r, seated in the front row): Mulk Raj Anand, K.H. Ara, M.F. Husain and others; (seated in the second row): Laxman Pai, Mrs Langhammer, Emmanuel Schlesinger, Bal Chhabda and others; (standing): Khorshed Gandhy, Krishen Khanna, S.K. Bakre, V.S. Gaitonde, Walter Langhammer, Kekoo Gandhy and others.

modernism—from the Progressives to the most contemporary, including figural artists pushing at the edge, like Bhupen. The Gandhys tried to understand the context of the art they showed, the way it would interact with the world around. Indeed the entire family—once the Gandhy children grew up—joined those many others in Bombay who were committed to envisioning the kind of India, the kind of society that would be supportive of the project of modern and contemporary culture. And, vice versa: the kind of art movement that would reflect the democratic aspirations of this nation.'

• 04 •

Chemould Goes National

> 'The first time I ever stepped in to Chemould, in the 1970s, it was a buzzing hub with Kekoo presiding over it. I had gone there for the exhibition of Nissim's Poster Poems and it felt like the right event in the right place. Nissim was ahead of his time (he might be on Instagram today), exploring a way to make poetry reach out to more people, and Kekoo was clever enough to see that the Poster Poems had a place in his gallery. I was a newcomer then, and looking at those poems on the walls of Chemould with people milling around to read them, I felt as if Bombay was a place where anything was possible, especially poetry.'—**Imtiaz Dharker,** artist and poet, via email

I was in one of the bedrooms of Kekee Manzil, sorting through a stack of papers when Khorshed, now nearing ninety, wheeled herself into the room. Each time she did this, I took it as a signal that she was willing to talk. I was allowed my questions but her answers were often crisp and succinct. 'I don't know,' she would say sometimes. Or even, 'I can't remember.' And once with a slightly mischievous smile, 'I don't want to remember.' If she did not want to answer a question, she would dismiss it with, 'Why talk about all that?'

This time I asked her about the two other Chemoulds, Kunika Chemould in Delhi and the gallery and shop in Calcutta. She thought about it for a while.

'There was never a time when Kekoo was satisfied,' Khorshed said. 'He was always looking at something only he could see. It lurked in his vision and it made him ambitious and it made him restless. He could not sit still; he could not trust what he had. I was different but then women are different, I think.'

She turned her sudden and strange smile on me. 'We are made to love what we have or how would we love our husbands?'

These conversations were all the more precious because it was Khorshed talking, not Kekoo. I never met Kekoo in Kekee Manzil, as far as I can remember. I knew him for thirty years and I didn't ever go over because that was not how our friendship had shaped. I don't remember ever planning to meet him; Kekoo just happened to you. Your paths would cross and the day would be altered because he had something he wanted to share, a new windmill he'd like some help tilting at. He never seemed to have something better to do than talk to you which was something rare in a city as self-obsessed as Bombay, in a life as crowded by event and people as his. If you had something you had to do, he let go of you regretfully but I always had the suspicion that he forgot about you as soon as another 'bakra' hoved into view.

Equally, it seems I never talked to Khorshed outside that house or even before the time that I undertook to do this book. When they were together in the gallery, there was almost no conversation to be had out of Khorshed. She was quiet to the point of being dour. At that time, I felt her silence was judgmental. I thought perhaps she just saw me as another person out to waste time. I had no money to buy art and no place to hang it. I did not even write about art regularly; I wrote only when the spirit moved me, if I saw a show I liked and thought I had something I wanted to say. Looking back now, I can see that all this was probably me reading my insecurities on to her responses. But even if she did think of me in that manner, I can empathise with her point of view.

As for Kekoo, I liked him instinctively and was pleased that he took to me. This wore off a little when I realised, his was a near-universal offering of friendship. That may have been why he was always looking over your shoulder at something only he could see. This could upset even his family.

In the latter half of 1970, it seems Kekoo visited Rashna and her husband in Zurich. On 18 November, Rashna wrote to Khorshed, what can only be described as a very Parsi letter:

> 'After lunch…Papa was busy writing more and more chitras [scraps]. Gosh, I tell you he bores me these days with all his art talk and dreams—he's become so one-track minded, only thinking of art and how it can be developed in Europe and the most ridiculous propositions on earth—as I keep telling him that all day he keeps blowing fuggas which are floating around in his mind, however each time he tried to tell me some of his future plans—I am like a pin who just bursts his big fuggas[22]. Now he wants to go on a German trip all over Germany to materialize his future plans about Germany, next year he wants an exhibition in Munich and Stuttgart and Bonn!! He keeps postponing his trip from day to day because he wants to fix appointments with people—however I hope something comes of it.'

Rashna remembers how Kekoo used to come and park himself at the Air India office where she worked in Switzerland. He would unashamedly use the

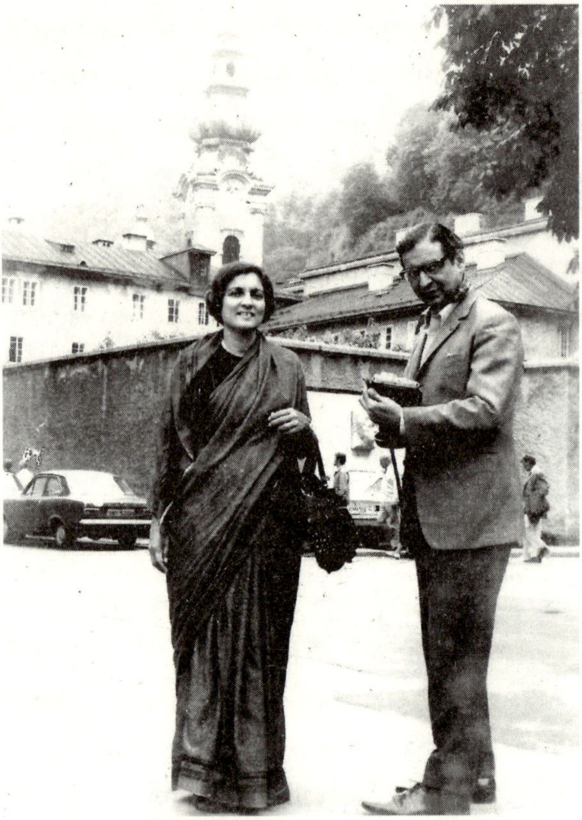

Going international: Kekoo and Khorshed in Zurich, 1970

telephone to make all his appointments. 'Every time I would protest that this was not his private property, he would say he was doing the government's work of making Indian art known to the West.'

•

Anyone who knew Kekoo would have known that he was not going to be happy with Bombay as a playpen. He was going national. Chemould was going national. It was meant to be. This was the way things were meant to work. He was not going to sit around and let his painters languish by the Arabian Sea. They were meant for better things.

From our vantage point, he looks like a seer. He was right. He was dealing with some of the names that would become legendary. He was talking about Husain and Gaitonde and Raza and Ambadas and practically anyone else he wanted. These are the names that dominate the art markets these days and whose prices steadily ratchet upwards as one by one they shuffle off the mortal coil and turn off the supply of 'originals'. But at that time, his was the lone voice crying in the wilderness.

Here is Rashna Gandhy's version of the Delhi Chemould moment: 'Pupul Jayakar[23] knew that Papa was really into art. The showroom of the Cottage Industries of India on Janpath, Delhi, had a small framing section which was run by Chemould and next to it was a gallery space that was used for things like saris and pottery and the occasional painting show by an artist. One day, Mrs Jayakar decided that it would be a good place to have a professionally-run art gallery space. And the logical person to run it was Kekoo. She knew that modern Indian art was his passion and so she asked him to start a gallery there.'

In the year 2004, which marked the fortieth year of Gallery Chemould's existence, Karin Zitzewitz interviewed Khorshed and Kekoo. There was a gallery at the Cottage Industries, Khorshed says, 'run by Richard Bartholomew with Ford Foundation money. They paid his salary. It was something that they [Cottage Industries] couldn't really handle.'

Kekoo took up the story. 'Richard was leaving so [filmmaker] Shyam Benegal and [art collector and founder of the Sanskriti Pratishthan that runs the Sanskriti Kendra Museum] Om Prakash Jain came and talked to us. They said that the gallery should be run more on a commercial basis, on good, sound ethical lines. The Ford Foundation could not just continue to pay the grant for Richard's salary forever. They had heard about all the group shows we had, so they invited us to run it in Delhi. We were interested, just as we were interested in going out in India and having shows in Kerala, in Cochin, and had a gallery in Calcutta and had early shows in Delhi. We realised we had to have good artists who were faithful. To make an artist loyal to his gallery, we had to serve them with outlets in different towns. Pupul Jayakar, OP and Shyam Benegal were the very special people involved in our activities at the time. It wasn't like dealing with them commercially. Occupying a bigger institution, the Cottage Industries, with Kunika as one space within, worked wonderfully.'

They opened with one of their own discoveries, a show by Bhupen Khakhar. Many stories are told about this show, and its opening, with Geeta Kapur and Nasreen Mohamedi in conversation, Bhupen Khakhar telling jokes on demand, and MF Husain filming.

But there was also a problem. One of Bhupen's paintings featured a male nude with a prominent and unashamed penis. You might not think that this should be a problem since nudity is a staple of the art world, male nudity as much as female nudity; and even in the US, the penis is not proscribed unless tumescent.

Here is Rashna's version of what happened. 'The first show was Bhupen Khakhar. The paintings were distinctly homoerotic in tone and content. The manager of the emporium was appalled. He told Papa: "Mr Gandhy, what are you doing? We are a government organisation. We cannot have all this." But Papa was equally adamant: Painters must have freedom of expression if they were to produce good work. Eventually a compromise was worked out because that was what Kekoo was good at: working out solutions. The paintings would be turned to the wall when the show opened. The press came, they saw the less explicit works, and the manager was relieved. But through the show, the paintings were displayed and nothing much happened. I think this was what he was good at: the art of the compromise. And this arose from his empathetic understanding of the other person. It would have been so easy to dismiss the poor manager as just another government servant with no vision; but Kekoo probably saw his very real distress and once he had had time to think about the issues at stake, he felt his way to a compromise.'

Here is Kekoo's version. He told Karin Zitzewitz that the crowd who had gathered for the opening was laughing but he was crying. 'Because I was in such a spot! Bhupen had a figure of a man with his penis exposed. And naturally, it wasn't my gallery, it was the Cottage Industries Emporium. No way would Bhupen relent...I had to find a solution because the show was opening and here was this tug of war. A lot of people had come. I finally told Bhupen, I have no say in the matter, this is not my gallery, it is the Cottage Industries and they are not allowing this painting to be shown and I'm removing it and that's that.'[24]

Perhaps it was restored the next day. For Bhupen himself never alluded to it nor seemed to have held a grudge. Consider this excerpt from an article by the old warhorse of the art world, Dnyaneshwar Nadkarni: 'I have had the happiest association with Chemould,' says Bhupen Khakhar, some of whose more sensational paintings have been uncomplainingly hung by Gandhy on the walls of his gallery.'[25]

I have told you both stories because they are both based on memory. They both look at the same event. They are told out of the same storehouse of family history.

Rashna did spend some time at the Delhi gallery because she was family and could be expected to step up to the plate when it was needed. The family had hoped she might make a life out of it. Adil was not interested in the frame factory—he wanted to be a jockey, he wanted to turn his very real passion for horses into a career. He spent some time in America because Annaita, his wife at the time, the mother of his two children Riyad and Roxanne, needed to be there. Annaita was half-American and could become a citizen at the age of twenty-one but needed to demonstrate she had spent some time in the country. Afterwards, Adil returned home and with great good humour, settled down to making frames.

Rashna was not so sanguine. She might indeed have wanted to be an artist in her own right because there was so much art in the air.

'We would be taken to artists' studios when we were young,' she remembers. 'We grew up with artists right from the beginning. I wasn't very good at studies. I used to be sent to Lady Temple[26] at Colaba for tuitions in art on Saturdays—she was quite a figure in Bombay, she used to be the art teacher at Cathedral School and a lovely water colourist. She told me: "You must never use the pencil. Take the paint brush and go straight at it." In my last year at school, I found that I had two things to do on the same afternoon. I had been entered for an interschool art competition hosted by the JJ School of Art and I had a date with my boyfriend. I wanted to be done with the painting as soon as possible so I used the Lady Temple method. I dipped my brush in the watercolours and went straight at the paper. Then I was free to go.

'And I won the first prize. But retribution was soon to follow. Someone at the JJ thought it might be a great idea for Kekoo to hand the prize over to me. I remember being terribly embarrassed because I had won that prize on my own talent and impetuous brushwork. But everyone was going to think that my father had wangled it for me.

'In my last year of school, my highest marks were in art. I got into the JJ for Fine Arts. I didn't even need my father's recommendation; I got in on my marks and my talent. But my parents refused to let me join. "We're supporting too many artists already," they said and insisted I apply for Commercial Art. I got in and I hated it. It ruined the free-flowing style that I had developed with Lady Temple and it curbed my freedom; you had to do things by the book, you had to recreate a font and design a box. I hated commercial art and graphic design. I had to work half day at the gallery where I helped Satish Panchal design the posters and cards; he was our in-house designer; he's now settled in Paris and is a painter in his own right. JJ really killed my artistic talent but Satish helped me with my homework during those four years. I also did other stuff at the gallery but none of it was very intellectual. I helped with the hanging of the shows, I addressed letters and cards. But I got to hang out with these people too.'

At one point in time, the manager of the gallery in Delhi, Mrs Kamala Sehgal, went on leave and Rashna was asked to take her place. 'My father said: "You go and run the place for the month she's away". I don't know if I was the right person for the job. I was very young but I might have been the only person they could think of. I think they were already overstretched. Papa already had galleries running at Bombay and in Calcutta, on Park Street.[27]

'I was sent to stay with Devyani and Kanwal Krishna, they were important print-makers in their own right and headed the art department and taught at the Modern School on Barakhamba Road; they had young daughters of their own and another young woman from Switzerland, Claudia Lutz, living with them. So we were quite a chummery. I took batik lessons with them. But to the art fraternity, I was a young woman on my own in Delhi so they took it upon themselves to make sure I was all right. The artists would come by and take me out for coffee at India Coffee House or to the shows. There was Swaminathan and Ambadas and Himmat Shah. They were all very protective of me; Claudia later married the artist Prafull Davé.'

Rashna had her own agenda. 'I had a boyfriend who migrated to London and I wanted to be with him. But there was just no foreign exchange available. You got something like eight dollars to travel with. Then Claudia said she would get me to Europe, to Switzerland; I could say that I was going to study graphic design but I went as an au pair to Claudia's uncle's boss who owned a large Persian carpet business. Hoovering, washing, cleaning—it made a change, I can tell you. But I was young and crazy in love.'

Kunika Chemould came into its own under the supervision of Roshen Alkazi who, both Khorshed and Kekoo agree, was the making of the gallery.

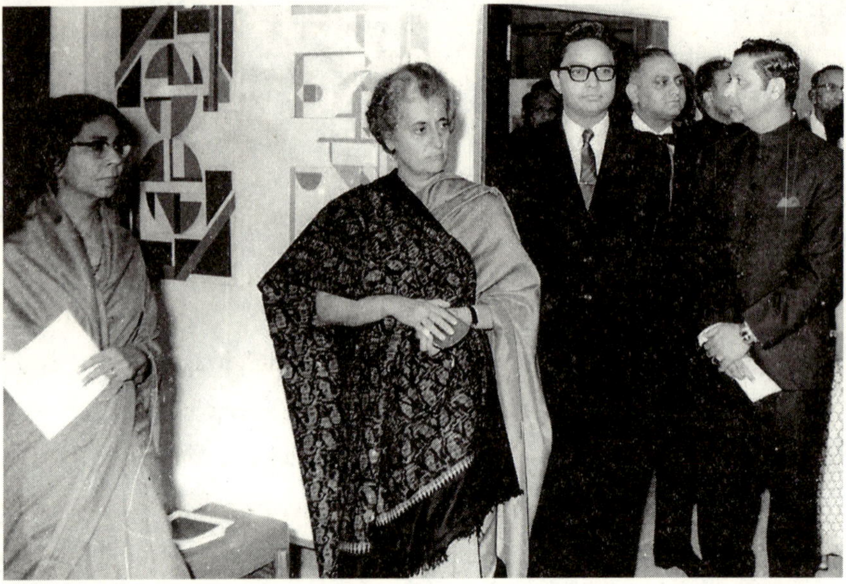

Indira Gandhi at Kunika Chemould, Delhi, Roshen Alkazi on left

Roshen Alkazi nee Padamsee was married to Ebrahim Alkazi, who had moved from Bombay to become the director of the National School of Drama in 1962, at the behest of the then prime minister, Jawaharlal Nehru. It was a Theatre Group romance, and so part of that whole Bhulabhai Desai moment. Roshen designed the costumes for all of Alkazi's plays, and earlier, for those directed by her brother Sultan (Bobby) Padamsee, the founder of the Theatre Group. She was an expert costumier and made the transition to gallerist with ease since she knew so many of the artists personally. In Bombay, the Theatre Group and the Progressive Artists Group had grown together, and the Alkazi home at Vithal Court was open house for Husain, Souza, Ara, Tyeb Mehta and others.[28]

'When Roshen was there, a great gift of confidence was built,' Kekoo told Karin Zitzewitz. 'All the artists knew her,' Khorshed added. But it wasn't always easy. 'The only trouble is that the artists we liked and she liked wouldn't always be the same. For example, Swaminathan and Ambadas. I

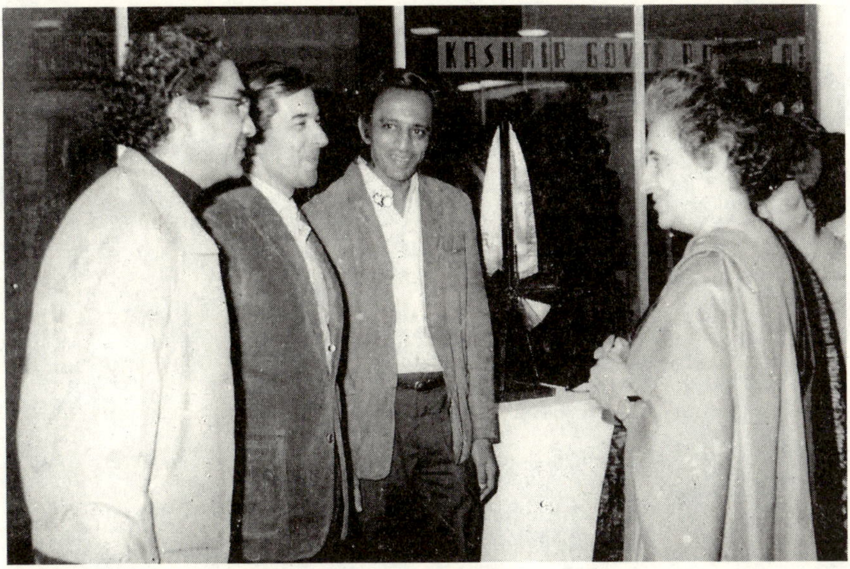

Akbar Padamsee, Krishen Khanna and Tyeb Mehta with Indira Gandhi at Kunika Chemould

found when I went to Delhi, I would get sick of hearing complaints from them. It was clear that Roshen had to have more creative control. So that's when she started on her own with Art Heritage.'

Kunika Chemould closed doors when the Cottage Industries Emporium 'shifted into a new building,' Khorshed said to Zitzewitz. 'They didn't want Chemould's name associated with it but we had it for over twenty years or so.'

But that didn't stop them from having a Raza show in Delhi when it was needed. Rashna explains how this came about. Claudia Lutz had indeed helped her to get to Switzerland but she could not get into the *Kunstgewerbeschule* [The Commercial Arts Academy] 'because I did not know German,' she says. 'So I signed up for evening classes where my teacher was a certain Bernard Imhasly. He was a student at the university and paying his way by teaching at these classes. We fell in love and I never went to England. The boyfriend was heartbroken; he was half-Parsi and half-British. My grandfather, Mota

Papa, was very upset because the right half of the boy, the male half, was Parsi and so my marrying him would not have counted as a mixed marriage, in his eyes.'

Rashna and Bernard married which caused the family some distress as we shall see but when their son-in-law went on to distinguished careers in journalism and diplomacy, they were reconciled.

'When Bernard came to India as a diplomat, the Cottage Industries space was lost because the shop itself had moved to a huge big emporium and Chemould didn't get the gallery space, only a framing shop. Mummy wanted to have a Raza exhibition in Delhi so we had it at our home, a lovely Charles Correa house. It was a sell-out show on the first night. She was very relieved because she didn't know the market in Delhi and she just wanted to cover the expenses. Using his considerable PR skills, my father had got Sonia Gandhi to come and see the show; that was a coup because she was the First Lady then as Rajiv Gandhi was the Prime Minister.'

•

Chemould began its Calcutta operations in much the same manner as in Bombay. They started with a shop selling frames which morphed into a gallery. The gallery launched with a Husain show, although the auguries were not good. Ila Pal writes:

> He [Husain] held his second one-man show at the Alliance Française in Calcutta. 'Bullock carts, village folks and festivals...painted in primary colours with rugged and innocent lines...That's how I would describe the show: OC Ganguly, the most eminent critic in Bengal at the time, dubbed my work as a "betrayal of Jamini Roy". Not a single painting was sold and I was left in Calcutta without money to buy a return ticket to Bombay.'

During the same year Husain participated in the inaugural show of Gallery Chemould in Calcutta, 'far more successful and satisfying'. 'There was a grand opening attended by luminaries...Even Jamini Roy emerged from his studio for the first time to be there...'[29]

The luminaries included the Prince de Ligne who served as the Belgian ambassador to India and who inaugurated the show. He was of course a personal friend of Kekoo's and you don't need to be an investigator to trace the one degree of separation between the minor European royal and the Gandhy clan.

But one good show does not a gallery make. Chemould needed a presence there, someone who could turn his shop into a gallery, someone who could connect with artists and with buyers. This is a skill set that would be difficult to find in most cities in India, and this was Calcutta.

And so Kekoo took one of his shots at the moon, hiring a young woman who had come to India, at a time when most of the young white people who fetched up were on the hippie trail, looking for nirvana and cheap hash. However, like so many of Kekoo's lunar (or lunatic) chances, it worked. She tells this lap of the story. It is almost as much hers as it is the story of Chemould's Calcutta operations.

'I was known as Cindy Hargate then,' says the soignée and self-possessed woman whom I met on the balcony of Kekee Manzil. 'I am now known as Cynthia Stroud-Watson, and if anyone should wonder where to find me, I live in Chattanooga, Tennessee.'

In a way, Cindy Hargate might well have found a surrogate family in the Gandhys. Cynthia's own father was killed in 1942 during World War II when she was six months old. Her mother remarried when she turned seven. It was then that a grim situation began to get worse. 'My stepfather began sexually molesting me when I was nine,' she says. Her mother developed breast cancer and died when she was thirteen. 'The molestation continued,' says Cynthia, her calm demeanour speaking of a survivor's hard-purchased inner strength, 'until he remarried, thankfully.'

The cumulative trauma of all this may have had some effect on her early education. The system was not designed to help. Cindy was not given much of a chance at a university education and after the ninth grade, became totally independent and began to live in lodgings. She worked as a florist's apprentice and then joined a mechanical engineering company. 'Recognizing my talent for drawing, they supported my education as a technical illustrator. In other words, I had to replicate in two dimensions the shape and size of a three-dimensional object.'

But there was a dissonance between her beliefs and her work. She sympathised with the Campaign for Nuclear Disarmament while working on the Blue Streak Missile which was being tested in Australia.

'When I met a man named Robert De Penning on a hitchhiking trip in Spain, it did not take much to persuade me to give up my job and join him and his family in Calcutta,' she says. 'His family traced its history back to colonial India; one of his ancestors had married an Indian; another had set up the first patents and trademarks agency, De Penning & De Penning, in Calcutta, in 1876. He was headed back to India after completing his law degree. I followed him a few months later when I received an invitation to stay with them for an extended period of time.'

That was her first stint in India. She left in 1961 but something called her back and she returned to Calcutta in 1963. This time, she found a way to get back to art education with classical sculptor Sarbari Roy Chaudhury. 'His studio was just next to the Ali Akbar School of Music. Visits to his studio were always so special because you could hear music being played by the students next door. He [Sarbari] loved Indian classical music and was generous with his time, encouraging me to attend any concerts that were happening.'

It was at this time that she met Kekoo Gandhy who had a successful frame shop on Park Street. Only Kekoo thought more could be done with it. A gallery could be created there and it would feed off the footfalls in the shop. All he needed was someone to run the gallery.

'My name was suggested to Kekoo as a possible candidate for the job of running the gallery. So in the spring of 1963, Kekoo contacted me and offered me the job of gallery director. I was not very keen on the idea at first, I loved my life as it was but Kekoo was a very persuasive man. He said I could continue with my art studies since the work was largely early evening to the night and I would have to go in only once or twice or week in the morning to do the books and attend to the administration. The other thing that persuaded me was the state of the art scene. The Bengali artists I knew were enthusiastic about the possibility of a new gallery with me in charge. Lady Ranu Mukherjee ruled the Birla Academy of Fine Arts with an iron fist. And there were many artists who felt left out.'

And so she took up the job and ran the gallery for the next three years. Without knowing it, she was taking the first steps to transforming herself from Cindy Hargate to Cynthia Stroud-Watson.

'Of course, it didn't work out quite so smoothly. I found I enjoyed the gallery so much that I ended up doing it almost full-time at a part-time salary which at the time was four hundred rupees, and no chance of asking for a raise because the gallery never made money and was always subsidised by the framing shop.

'Many of the industrialists' wives would come in with photographs or images of the Gods to be framed and I would approach them and encourage them to take a look at the art too. I saw it as part of my job to help them appreciate abstract art. Most of our customers were very traditional in their taste. I'd start out with the emotions, always a good place to begin: what does the painting make you feel? So I suppose you might say I was running a kind of art appreciation class on the fly.'

That was at one end of the supply chain. At the other was a series of interactions with artists: travelling with Meera Mukherjee into tribal areas, for instance, to watch the Muria tribals make figures through the lost wax process. 'We came back to Calcutta and hosted her first show which was a huge success,' Cynthia remembers.

'I was given a free hand to do what I wanted. Some shows would travel from Bombay or Delhi. Kekoo was anxious to have a gallery presence in all three cities. Kekoo had recently established an arrangement with Kunika Gallery to show Gallery Chemould artists there. Ram Kumar and Tyeb Mehta also had shows in Calcutta. I was given a free hand to mount exhibitions of the artists working out of Calcutta. I hung the shows and I cannot remember a time when I was told that I couldn't or shouldn't do something. Of course, I fixed the prices in consultation with Kekoo and Khorshed.

'Kekoo was also very keen that I should meet the artists and so I came to Bombay for two weeks and met everyone: Husain and Tyeb Mehta and Bal Chhabda. I have such magical memories of that visit. Khorshed had her music master visit very early in the morning and he would accompany her on the harmonium as she sang ragas. Waking up to that in the morning was quite something.'

Cynthia then went to Delhi and returned to Calcutta 'with a new sense of mission. There was so much to do, so much catching up. Developing a base of buyers was really difficult. The money was in the hands of traditionalists and they might go as far as buying Jamini Roy. There were however some exceptions. Lalit Thapar was a young industrialist at the time and he always brought some of his business contacts and friends to the shows. And bless his heart, knowing how important it was for me to socialize with the business community, he would invite me to all his cocktail parties. This certainly

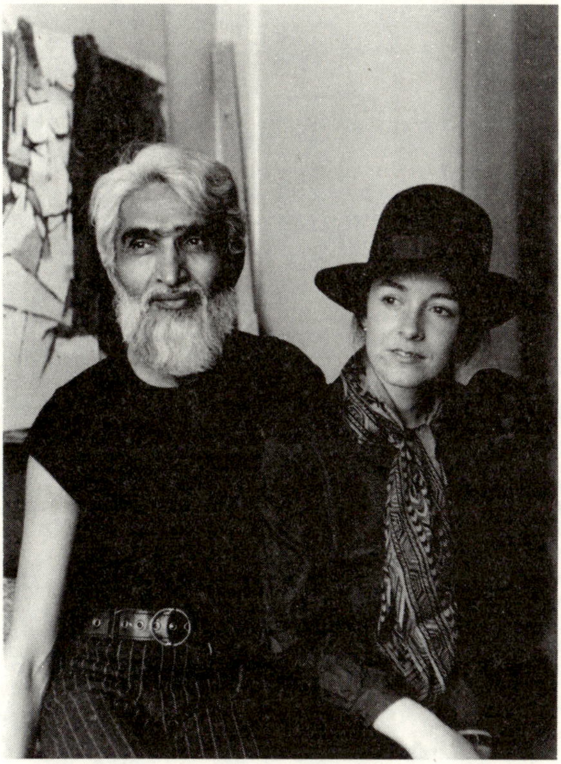

***Start of a journey:** MF Husain with Cynthia Hargate at Gallery Chemould, Calcutta in the 1960s*

helped grow our gallery audience. Paritosh Sen and Sunil Das had their first one-man shows at the gallery.

'Max Müller Bhavan was amazing at supporting the arts; they were facilitators, they had an office in Jamshedpur where Meera had her first exhibition. This was then transferred to Gallery Chemould in Calcutta. Satyajit Ray was alive then, beautiful man, he would come to see the shows too. The people who kept us going were the Ford Foundation people, the expat community, the diplomatic lot. They were our buyers and they were richly rewarded, I think.'

Cynthia remembers that a couple who were with the Ford Foundation bought a standing figure by Meera Mukherjee, it was about fourteen inches high. 'I think they paid about a thousand rupees for it. They gave it to their son who decided he wanted to sell. Shireen Gandhy was most helpful in suggesting the contact: Christie's in New York. It was sold for twenty-four thousand dollars, twenty years ago.'

Ill health forced Cynthia to return home. 'My doctors told me that if I wanted to fully recover I would have to return to a temperate climate so in the year 1966 I went back to England. That is when Adil Gandhy came to live in Calcutta to run the gallery.'

But it was the warmth of a family she took back with her. 'The Gandhys took me on as their fourth daughter. When Behroze came to England, it was at a time when India had so little foreign exchange that one could only get fifty pounds and you had to have a sponsor. So I was her sponsor and she came to live with me in Milton Keynes before moving to London.'

Cynthia's time in Chemould would cast a long shadow. Before she left Gallery Chemould, she met George Butcher and his friend Gustav Delbanco who had a long-established gallery in Cork Street, London: Roland, Browse & Delbanco. 'They had all escaped Nazi Germany and were early investors in Walter Sickert; this was at a time when gallerists did give artists stipends, so they had a stable of artists being supported in some shape or form.' George Butcher was working on putting together the first major exhibition of Indian Art to be held at the Commonwealth Centre in London in 1966. 'Kekoo had a lot to do with this, shipping many paintings to London. Through this chance connection in Calcutta, Kekoo recommended that I work with the Duchess of Bedford who had recently opened the Upper Grosvenor Gallery in London. Kekoo worked hard to create more international interest so several artworks from the "Art Now in India" show at the Commonwealth Institute were exhibited at the Upper Grosvenor Gallery along with many MF Husain paintings. The gallery was very large and there wasn't enough work to fill it. So Husain did a series of heads, quick flashy things. I didn't like

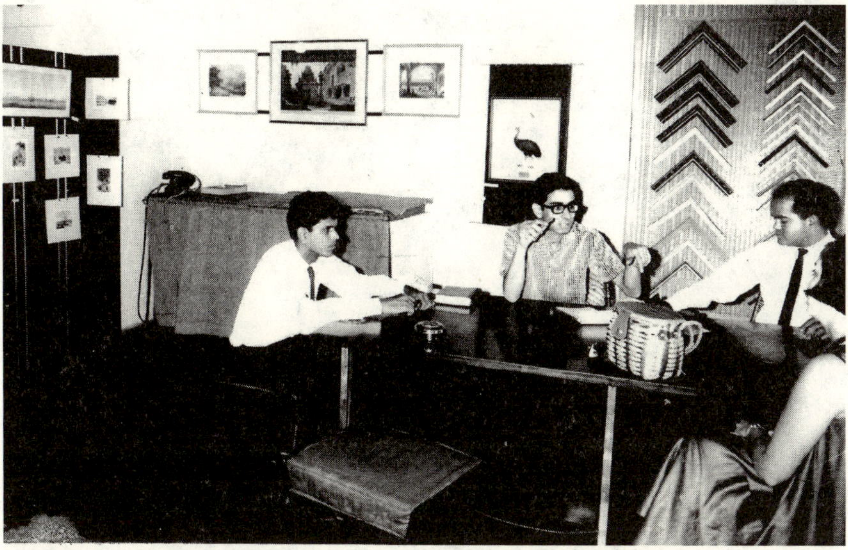

Chemould in Calcutta: Adil Gandhy at Gallery Chemould, Park Street, 1970

them at all but we framed them with big frames to give them some gravitas and filled up the empty spaces. I am glad to say they did not sell.

'He gave them all to me but he also gave me a beautiful drawing that was done with gouache and pastel, a wonderful piece. I never got it framed and when Behroze and Khorshed visited me in Tennessee in 1998, where I moved after my marriage, I asked Khorshed if she could sell it for me. The money was waiting for me in India in rupees when I came next and Behroze, Khorshed and I had a wonderful trip to South India.

'As for the other ones, the ones I didn't like, the Husain quickies, don't ask. That's history. When I moved, I had stored them in my assistant's attic and she had a bad divorce and so when I went to get them, her husband was in a frightful mood and he didn't even put the light on in the attic. I found some of my things and I kept asking whether there weren't any more but he was very rude and kept saying that there wasn't any more so I left. I sometimes dream of those pictures.'

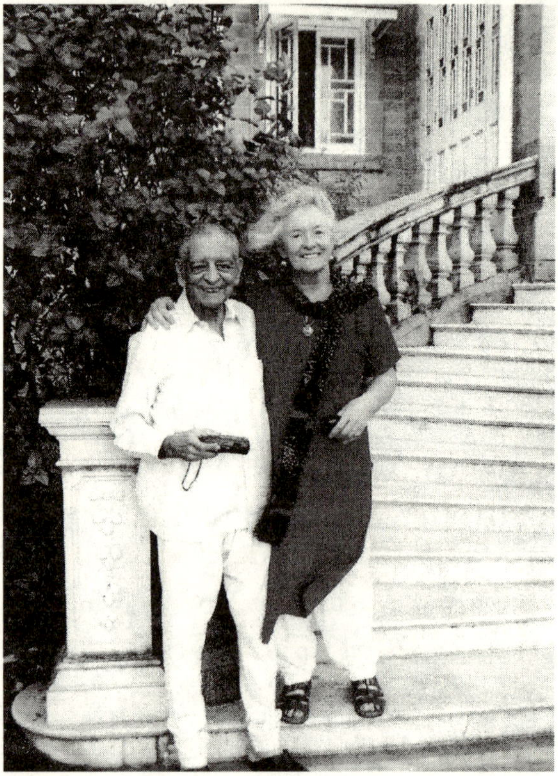

Enduring friendship: *Kekoo Gandhy with Cynthia Stroud-Watson nee Hargate on the steps of Kekee Manzil*

• 05 •

What the Letters Reveal

> 'Dear Mr Vimalchand,
> The bill no 2361 is cancelled because the painting of Bhupen Khakhar was lost from the car (it fell off its carrier as it was in a roll...)'
>
> **Signed: KK Gandhy**

Paper was once the record of our lives. It formed the matrix of our memory. In every way, it carried traces of our being. Our money was printed on it, our letters were inscribed on it, our records were thus largely paper.

Now things have changed although the paperless office that was envisioned in the last century has not yet materialised. These days our lives are recorded in pixels. Most of what Shireen Gandhy knows about her gallery is locked in her inbox[30], her WhatsApp (and Telegram) record, her cellphone's memory. The rest, the unwritten record, the spoken/unspoken record, is inside her head. I had access to some of this but the whole of it would have been useless. It would have been actually too much information.

Therefore paper becomes useful because it is the repository of the distillate of effort. In the pre-digital age, you had to think before you typed or else you had to clean up after yourself. Woe betide if you forgot that you had inserted a carbon paper and began to erase while your paper was still on the roller. The mess was incredible and I remember often giving up the desire to write a letter entirely because of a misspelling. You can do that if you're writing personal letters; if you're running a business, doing the letters was once an important part of the work world. Every manager—and secretary—dealt with the mail first thing in the morning. First the manager dictated the letters. Then the secretary typed out the letters. Then the manager corrected the letters and the secretary retyped them with carbon copies. The carbon copies were then filed. 'Mail and file' it was called; it was the kind of effort you did not put in unless you had to.

'I always associated Khorshed with carbon paper,' says Bernard Imhasly, 'because for years she would write letters to her children, spread out over the planet, in triplicate. Every time one of them would come back to Bombay, there was a standing order for thin "airline letter pads" and carbon paper. As post-stamps were expensive, KKG developed a kind of miniature writing style, packing loads of information—and opinion!—into a tiny space. Yet, her letters would regularly run to six pages.'

However there weren't that many other options either. Khorshed's stint at the gallery coincided with the time when you did not just pick up the phone and call Gorbio, France, for a chat with the painter SH Raza who lived there. Instead, you called up the telephone exchange and booked a trunk call. Most times you would be given an appointment for the next day although some leeway was possible if you explained that there was an emergency. (This generally meant that someone was ill and about to die; or had already died. I believe the term was 'compassionate grounds'.) Then you stationed yourself near the phone and waited for it to ring. This may sound counter-intuitive but the telephone exchange was calling a telephone exchange in Europe and that telephone exchange was connecting up the person you had called. Then the Indian telephone exchange called you up and put you through.

This would have been the sequence as it appeared to the layman:

Khorshed calls the Bombay Telephone Exchange.

She is given a time when the call will be made.

The Bombay Telephone Exchange calls its French counterpart.

The French telephone exchange in the area calls Raza.

Raza picks up the phone.

The French telephone operator patches through to the Bombay Telephone Exchange.

The Bombay Telephone exchange calls Khorshed who has been sitting by the phone waiting.

Khorshed picks up the phone.

Both parties begin yodelling 'Hello-Hello' at each other.

And it would seem like it was only a second later that the operator would cut in to ask: 'Three minutes over. Continue?'

You can see how many possible failures in the chain might happen. But you can also see how this might work well in certain circumstances. If you were calling someone in a terrible temper, you probably had enough time to calm down before you actually got to speak to that person. And you knew that the operator was listening in. Plus you were on a timer, repetition was going to cost you money. Letters were probably considered much safer and more effective. There was the illusion of privacy and as far as both parties were concerned, there was a paper trail on which everyone could rely.

Thus at the start of this enterprise, I asked for access to all the papers and files even though I didn't think there would be too much. Most organisations in India have a cavalier attitude to records. They store what the income tax authorities may need for seven years and then the paper makes its way to the friendly recycling man who bears it away. At the thought of this, the archivist blanches in horror. It is all valuable, it is all meaningful, every last document has something that will serve to flesh out the details of our time.

Adil Gandhy was in charge of storage. He looked a little perplexed at this request. 'What will you find there? There will be lots of letters about sending this painting here and talking to that manager there and so on.'

Shireen did not question my intentions or my sanity. She simply instructed that the godown where the files had been stored be emptied and the boxes be brought to Kekee Manzil. There were forty-seven huge boxes and although I love files and letters, I did quail at this mountain of paper.

But when I did get to work, it wasn't so bad. Most of the boxes were filled with copies of the publications Chemould put out. There were many boxes, for instance, of a book called *New Ways of Colour Print Making* by N Krishna Reddy, which did not seem to have much to do with Chemould because it had been printed by another gallery altogether. Perhaps they had simply done someone a favour. Or Reddy had asked them to store the copies for him. No one could remember.

I looked at every single paper and was amazed at how much the documentation could reveal. Here was a telegram saying that all the Warli paintings had arrived in Chennai (on their Alliance Francaise tour, no doubt) with their glass broken; they would need to be repaired but who was the insurer? Here is a bill of lading from the Swissair people and correspondence about the possible value of the works of art. As you can imagine, some of it was tooth-grindingly boring and a good reminder that behind every enterprise of this kind, someone has to make the challan, post the invoice, keep a duplicate copy, enter a notation, make a phone call, follow up again and again and again.

There were gems, of course and sometimes there were even the letters the family wrote to each other. This is Khorshed writing to Kekoo on 26 January 1966 about the death of Homi Bhabha.

Darling Kekoo,

I write this after my return from the uthamna of Homi Bhabha[31] which was held at the TIFR. My heart still feels heavy since we heard the dreadful news on Monday evening. 1966 seems to have started as a terrible year for India—first Shastri and before we got reconciled to the loss, another national calamity. In these two years since we had the Gallery, had you not come to admire the man immensely? At the time of Swami's exhibition, he had said he would come and see the paintings again one morning with Pipsy[32]. He didn't come that day but two days later he dropped in suddenly one Saturday afternoon and had a long look again. I was so impressed that if he said he would come, he always meant it.

The same letter mentions an increase in rent proposed and the possibility of a photography exhibition by Stella Snead[33].

From the family letters, it was clear that Khorshed was the maker of rules, the keeper of standards. There's a letter she wrote to her daughter Shireen when she was in boarding school which combines affection with an almost Macaulayan strain of advice.

Darlingest, sweetest Shiroon,

What a lovely letter you wrote this week—full of your responses and comments. You say you envy my and Rashna's gift of letter writing. I am sure you will soon develop it also if you remember certain points. For instance, when I sit down to write, I wish and hope that there would be no disturbances like telephones or visitors or servants to distract my train of thoughts. In other words, I want to give of myself fully to the task. Probably you have other exciting things you want to do at the back of your mind so that once letter writing is over, you could do that—is that correct? Then again I look at the writing page as only a small limited space in which I want to say so much whereas you look upon it as something so long which has to be filled up so you go—

Well I will end now bye bye and lots of love from yours ever Shireen Smile

[Khorshed wrote the last line in a huge script in imitation of her daughter's attempt at covering up the page.]

How's that?!! I think as you understand your attitudes—not just to the letter writing but to other things also—the quality will come out different. In fact it is already improving.

•

Kekoo was the star, Khorshed was the stage manager of the star. She made all things possible but it is a mistake to think of her as an administrator. This positioning was the result of a unique combination of forces, Kekoo and Khorshed, yin and yang, each occupying its own place, each complementing the other. If Khorshed seemed guarded, it was because Kekoo was wide open to encounter.

His granddaughter, Atyaan Jungalwala, put it well: 'He did not have barriers, the ordinary barriers that people put up when they meet new folks. He seemed open to every encounter, and open to every person he met. I think Kekoo Papa didn't do boundaries.'

Areesh Jungalwala, her brother, all of twenty-two at the time of writing, said that he remembered his grandfather most for those walks where he would, 'be talking to everyone. It would be some young artist who needed help or a child from the slums whose father was an alcoholic. He could talk to anyone and he would talk to everyone.'

(We will see that this will be not just the defining characteristic for him in the art world but in the many other encounters in the city.)

But one thing was certain: Khorshed was part of everything Kekoo did and she was often the person who made sure things happened. And when she thought one of her friends had stepped out of line, she could administer a sharp corrective. Even if that friend was MF Husain.

Ila Pal tells the first half of the story in her sympathetic biography of Husain:

> Prompted by the turn of events in the country, between 12th June, when a judgment of the Allahabad High Court unseated Indira Gandhi and 26th June, when she imposed a state of Emergency, Husain painted three 8 x 4 ft canvases. The first painting dated 12th June, depicted four hands (of opposition parties) pointing accusingly at a brooding innocent Sita. The second dated 24th June (when Jayaprakash Narayan urged the army to disobey unjust orders) showed Bharat Mata in turmoil, the national tricolour sullied, while the third dated 26th June had Durga emerging upon a roaring tiger, all set for battle.
>
> The paintings were his personal statement in support of Mrs Gandhi and the Emergency. Husain even titled the brochure: 'The triumph of good over evil'. [34]

Among Khorshed's papers, I found a letter she had written to her friend, MF Husain on 27 April 1975:

My dear Husain,

Your paintings on the Emergency are a point of view you wished to express. Though I may differ from this view entirely, I feel you have every right to express it.

However, I would like to point out that my right to express or convey my point of view has been taken away from me entirely. This is the true meaning of 'Emergency' as I understand it. Would you symbolize this aspect also in a painting? I am too unimportant a Mrs Gandhy to receive such a painting as a present from you but all the same I hope that you as an artist who thinks and feels would express yourself towards a problem which affects millions of Indians today.

Yours sincerely,

Khorshed

It is difficult, at this remove, I think to understand how much this letter must have cost Khorshed to write. She, more than anyone else, knew how dependent the gallery was on Husain's saleability. But it is to her credit that she had her say, wrote her letter and called out hypocrisy where she saw it.

•

Of course, the paper trail did not last forever. It began to peter out as telephony improved and email began to take over as a means of communication. But where I found them, I read them greedily. A letter from Shireen, one of the rare ones, revealed that Pushpamala N wanted her dates numerologically aligned. Alex Mathews sends a rude drawing...and 'everyone has a good laugh,' Shireen says. (No sign of the drawing.)

But in the main, the correspondence offered up the back-end of the business of the gallery, the bills of lading and the bills of sale, but they also told the story behind the back-end. For instance, if it had been decided to have a postcard made to accompany a show, then a transparency would be needed for the printer. That meant a competent photographer had to be hired for if the lighting were off or the colours not corrected, the painting could look quite different. (Indeed, it often did. I would walk into galleries sometimes and wonder what was wrong with the painting on the wall. Having seen it in print in a magazine or newspaper or invitation, the painting would look 'wrong'.) Then the transparency itself was a fragile thing, given to warps and scratches. When one faded, as transparencies did over time, it was a small disaster because this was often all that a painter had of a work he had laboured over for months.

Or here is another conundrum. Raza has a big show coming up. He thinks it might be nice to have a screening of a film which features him. It features three other Indian painters too but he thinks it might still work in his favour because he says he has clear views, he quotes nobody, his village looks lovely and yes, the gallery could go with the film. He debates the entire thing in his letter, a hand-written one. It was an exciting moment, Raza thinking aloud, thinking to his gallery, thinking to his friend, thinking of himself, all in one.

But there were weightier matters as well. Khorshed did not hesitate to weigh in on controversies. One of these began when Satish Gujral was interviewed by Madhu Jain who was then with *India Today* and said, 'Both Husain and Raza wasted talent on depicting a mythology which they were not brought up on. And if you forget the hypocrisy of our secularism, you can't deny certain characteristics about the Muslim and the Hindu cultures which give our society its plural character. But even artists like Chughtai, who was a revivalist, chose Persian and Mughal miniatures. Why did Raza have to take to Tantric art? He was trying to build up a false background. He said that a *maulvi* in his old school told him about all this. Would you believe it?'

Khorshed took him up in a letter.

My dear Satish,

This letter should have been written atleast [sic] a month ago—but I have been caught up in a lot of domestic events.

When I read the controversy over our statements regarding Husain and Raza's works, I was both sad and indignant. I had wanted to write a letter immediately to the press stating my point of view.

On second thoughts I felt that Satish is my friend, what I want to say is essentially to him of what my thoughts are on his statements, why do I want to get into the media? Hence I take up my pen to say what I have carried in my heart all these weeks.

1. The first point I wish to raise is that we in India are living through very precarious times where communalist forces are in the ascendency and what we say or do has to be thought through. Otherwise these forces jump in and make capital out of it for their own advantage. I am sure you had a taste of that yourself and must have been surprised as to what LK Advani had to do with your statement.

2. Raza's Bindu is a very meaningful experience for him which has taken him into his early childhood experiences and out of it has evolved a whole new dimension of thinking for this sensitive artist. Without going into the details of how a Brahmin headmaster taught him this simple exercise in concentration, I hope you will get to read Raza's own clarification some day.

> 3. As for Husain, I feel he is ingrained in the Indian culture where he thinks and acts in symbols all the time. For him to have wiped out Durga in Bengal was very meaningful, I feel, as he might very well do with Ganapati in Maharashtra some day! His is a restless spirit which cannot be tied down to norms or conventions and we have to allow him to be what he is.
>
> 4. Finally, one humble word: so many of you, our dear artist friends, have found your place in the 'Sun' (the blazing Indian sun at least). We are happy and proud as more of you get your place in that arc of recognition and honour as you carve out your own unique places. There is enough room for all!!

She sent copies to Raza and Husain.

Husain took the large view and in an interview with Madhu Jain which appeared in the next issue of the magazine, dismissed it all as a 'family matter', a matter of aesthetic disputation rather than anything communal. At this remove it is difficult to see it as anything other than the precursor of all that was to follow. But it would also be incorrect to think of what Satish Gujral said as the originator of the anti-Husain sentiment that would finally mean he would leave the country and die in exile, far away from the culture into which he was 'ingrained' to use Khorshed's word.

•

There's another Khorshed too on view in the letters. On 12 November 1986, she wrote to Amit Ambalal:

> One last thing I would like to mention about the reactions of the people to your paintings. It was lovely to watch a person going around the exhibition. By about the second or third

> painting, there would be a big smile on the face! On the whole, there was great appreciation from the public.
>
> However some of the artists were a little restrained in giving their unequivocal praise. It would be interesting for you to discuss with them your paintings for your own benefit.

I wonder whether she slaved over that last paragraph, phrasing and rephrasing it until she had found the right tone.

Ambalal took it well. He wrote back on 18 November 1986:

> 'I am happy to know the reactions of the people. I am aware of the mix [sic] reactions of the artists too. Still however, I am quite in the knowledge of what I am doing. As such I am consciously avoiding some of the established notions of the so-called artistic imagery, devices, techniques and ideals—which have made our art stale, repeatitative [sic], professional, heavy and to a certain extent boring. Yes. I do have my shortcomings and am trying my best to find a way out in my slow process.'

This does not seem to have affected the relationship and Ambalal continued to show with Chemould. In February 1988, he wrote to thank her for 'specially recommending Raza to stay with us. It was quite an enjoyable time. He is a very fine person.'

Most of the correspondence in the gallery is addressed to Khorshed. Kekoo gets a fond look in or a 'remember me to...' but when you wanted something done, you wrote to Khorshed. The family was not very far behind in this.

In one of the boxes, I found a delightful relic of another time and another way of manufacturing stationery. It was called a Duplicate Book and it was obviously constructed so that you could write in it and keep a copy. One of the last notes in the duplicate book is a letter by Shireen Gandhy to Rashna. Kekoo had asked her, Shireen writes, to choose some works for Rashna to keep in Delhi. After saying that she has selected some, Shireen ends with: 'If there are any works that you wish to return, please send them back with a note. Let's do this very systematically. (Keep KMG out of it in that case.)'

•

But it was not only Khorshed who was illuminated by these letters. There was the artist Sayed Haider Raza as well, writing in his distinctive handwriting, his signature a slashing pen stroke with a vaguely Japanese shape. Because there was such a great degree of trust, letters came through Chemould which were meant for other eyes and other hands. Here is Raza on Ara: on 30 July 1985, Raza wrote to Mr Clerk (perhaps SI Clerk who wrote on art for the tabloid, *The Daily*.)

> Your letter gives me the sad news of Ara's death. Something precious deep within me ceases to beat. And then, echoes and memories emerge in an endless chain: our association, youthful dreams, our collective action and our own individual work, in Bombay, during the years, 1943-50. I think I have shared with Ara, the richness of feeling in the kingdom of the heart, a certain emotional approach to life, where only the authenticity of MAN really mattered. There was no barrier of caste or creed or nationality. These petty prejudices which existed then in abundance and exist even now all around us. Our reactions were spontaneous, almost raw, dictated by animal-like perceptions and we painted and painted endlessly. It did not really matter if we were right or wrong, we did

make mistakes. But we lived and acted, responding to a mysterious life-force and this logic seems to hold good even today. Later I did realise the necessity of the participation of a thought process that should accompany natural forces in any artistic expression. I could not talk it over with Ara, involved as he was in a programme of active aid to artists, and I, myself, in search of my own equilibrium, between the treacherous domains of logic and knowledge and the fundamental human resources of instincts and intuitions. It is difficult to explain my quest and my present preoccupations but I know that this acquired knowledge of which our intellectuals are so proud and so anxious to exhibit in public forums is only a small thing in relation to the fundamental energy released by innate human forces.

Ara lived his life and he lived it completely. It has been pure, simple and beautiful. His 'colour' will glow with light and will reveal his truth for a long time to come.

On 22 July 1986, Raza wrote to Khorshed about the death of the sculptor Pilloo Pochkhanawala (1923-1986), perhaps knowing that he was talking not just about an artist but also a family member. (Pilloo was an Adenwalla, a first cousin to Khorshed): 'Life is generous and cruel both. I am so sad to know that Pilloo Pochkhanawala passed away. Yes! She was a courageous soul, a wonderful person and an excellent sculptor. The idea of the meeting at her sculpture at the Nehru Centre is most touching.'

•

There was a great excitement to handling these letters, many of them handwritten. Bhupen Khakhar writing from Gujarat, Ambadas writing from Europe. Often the wives would write too, making careful requests.

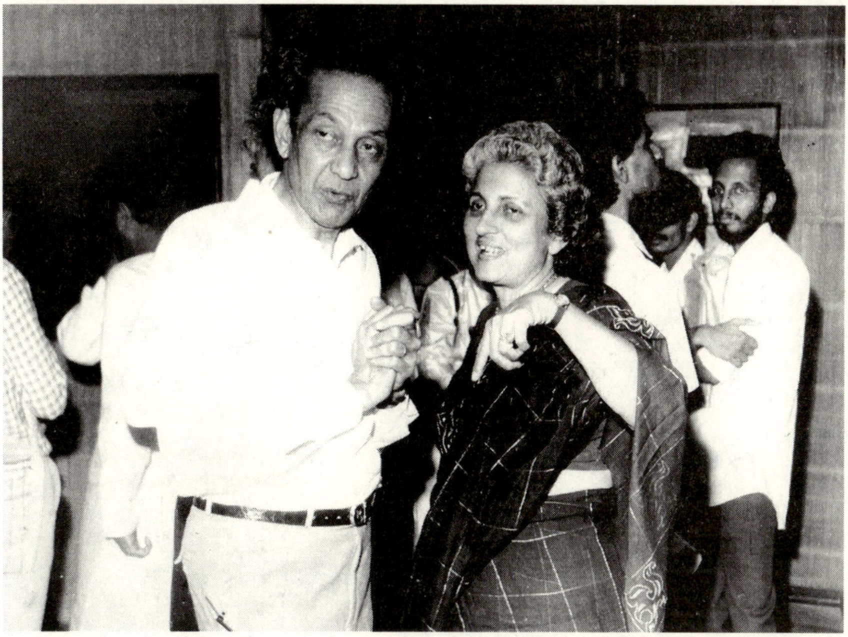

SH Raza and Khorshed Gandhy during Raza's exhibition at Gallery Chemould in 1984

But it became clear that the letters had already been sifted through. Krishen Khanna wrote to Khorshed to thank her when she found a whole bunch of his letters to Rudy von Leyden and sent them back to him. They were too late to be included in a monograph on him but he said, 'they brought back a forgotten piece of self.'

There were other reasons to write, and mainly this was to ask whether Gallery Chemould could be part of some scheme that the artist had thought up. Mickey Patel thought a collaboration with Cuba would be wonderful. When Nek Chand's Sculpture Garden was attacked in 1996, Georgia Beier wrote expressing her horror but suggesting that it would make much more sense if India were to protest sharply. There was a request in 1999 that Shireen Gandhy might consider putting together a show to raise money for a chair in the name of Rudy von Leyden by getting artist friends to donate paintings.

They were always ready to do their bit, helping in odd but important

Raza

Gorbio, 9th October, 1986 -

My dear Khorshed & Kekoo -

These are the last summer days in Gorbio. We have lived & worked well & we are now preparing to leave on the 13th for Paris - via Grenoble. Janine is presenting an exhibition of her paintings on the 15th at the Galerie Tête de l'Art. We should be in Paris on the 17th October - God willing.

It has been a period of concentrated work. I did about 15 paintings & two engravings. The theme is "अंकुरण" which means "GERMINATION". Its intimately linked up with the "Bindu" concept. I have had great moments of elevation, pleasure & pain, but the results seem good. Hewitts came over & picked up several - 6 - out of the recent. I am sending you a few photographs enclosed. I am planning to come over to India again 15th January - 15th February. What about reserving me a date - just one week early February. I think, something interesting can happen. The climate is such that we must make the most of it.

Patrick Bell sent me more reviews of the press following the evening of 27th at the alliance. I am deeply touched by the warmth & affection shown to me & my work. I have written to Mr Clark & will be writing to Nadkarni too soon. But I have been so busy this summer. Several months without work early this year, made it imperative that I worked. And I did paint. The photographs are an approximation, but still they give an idea.

Janine is showing, after Norway, in Grenoble & that inspite

to come. I continue to think that our book is excellent + a good example of a modern publication rarely printed in India.

Hope the first showers of rain will cool up Bombay soon. We are leaving for Gorbio next week for 4 months. I gave Mr. Beek some of my early prints – as Leena had asked. These are mostly <u>Offset prints</u>, done at the "Imprimerie Jack Renaud" but entirely supervised by me. They are a limited edition + these are the last prints. They are numbered + signed. Three of them are serigraphie – the red line drawings, a Bindu from the album. I have also offered to Mr. Beek a Bindu to thank him for his interest + I found that he was very pleased.

Now one thing is very clear that I will not like these to be shown at the occasion of launching the book. They are old + out dated – except the line drawing in red + the Bindu from the album. You can show these at Chemould without making an exhibition, but if you do something at the Alliance Francaise, please borrow original paintings, which will be a more serious effort than these small "estampes" in offset.

My letters are long, but please understand that I take every project seriously. Have you seen the weekly article. Do please send any other article if it appears. It helps me to do better next time.

Fond love to you + Kekoo from us both. Hope the film reaches in time + the programme is "à la Carte"!

Paris, 10th October, 1985

My dear Khorshed & Kekoo -

At last the books arrived, today morning from Satolas Lyon. Akbar had already given me 5. I hasten to say that it's a remarkable job & that I am so happy that I have the books in time for the exhibition. The custom clearance was difficult, but with the official documents I sent, everything was smooth.

Our book is beautiful, elegant, exquisite. Howsoever modest, it's condensed, charged with vitality & in extremely good taste. I assure you it will be a landmark in art publications in India - which will be forthcoming soon. Not that these do not exist, but the modern look & significant contemporary artists' monographs are rare. Vakils have done a good job, & I am delighted "Atal Soonya..." could be retained. Printing is absolutely 1st class & even the old blocks including "Oasis" are fine. The simple layout is revealing, unpretentious, the texts read well, & the colour sequence is as I had suggested. So we have every reason to be happy & I am delighted that we could make it.

I have shown it to several friends including Michel Troche who are all unanimous in praise.

My good friends, I am fully aware that it has been a lot of work for you, in fact for all of us including Vakils. Our only reward is the present good result. I am writing to Miss Cooper to thank everyone at the press & G.V. & Pradhan. Please see to it that they are paid in time.

Now, since the book will not be for sale here, & maybe people

(maximum)

will like to put an order to you. Let me know how much the price will be. As I wrote last a monograph of this kind can be priced for say 100 frances here – ie about 130 Rs. if exchange rate is 1 to 1.30. Plus we must know how much it will cost you to send it by air – well packed – say (~~40 Rs~~) ie 50 Rs. Please verify this – this is the maximum – as beyond this the book will not sell here.

Let me know how is the reaction at home. Is the Delhi editor still interested? Are you releasing it soon?

Yes, two remarks. I wish we had taken a cover almost ~~the~~ one & half times thicker. No 2 the page no 2 by Dheer. is over crowded... Pity. But well, we have so many reasons to be happy..... particularly that we could make it. Our resources were our imagination & will to do. I hope our industrials & govt can join in the common effort to promote contemporary Indian painting – which is one of the best in the world at the height of 20th Century. As my favorite hindi poet Kedarnath Singh writes, I can also say:

"शुरू हुआ दिन लो, मैं कोलाहल के पहले,
देश देशान्तर की, अनदेखी रूपहीन
खुलती हुई राहों पर हस्ताक्षर कर देता हूँ"

केदारनाथ सिंह

I was invited by the French President Francois Mitterrand to the Elysee Palace for a reception given to Parisian artists. It was fantastic. The film will be done at rue de Charonne. We are hanging the exhibition today. Ram is reaching Paris this afternoon. So its a grand, charged & happy life. More in my next.

Once again, a million thanks & fondest love –

Raza & Janine

P.S. – Akbar told me that you retains the slides for a film. Please try to get them as soon as the work is done by them. It's important that I am atleast represented by my paintings. But the transparencies are most precious – Rs 2000-each.. so please see to it that they are most carefully kept & send them after use to me by registered air letter. Thanks.

ways. 'Dear Keku and Khorshed,' writes Adil Jussawalla on behalf of the Students' Famine Relief Action Committee, on 21 January 1975: 'Thank you very much for loaning us your *chatais* for our exhibition. We collected Rs 2725[35] and the money has gone to famine-hit students in the rural areas. We appreciate your help greatly.' Those who went to the show might even have lucked out, buying Vivan Sundaram prints from his Machu Picchu series. And perhaps those chatais made their way to the show through Sundaram's good offices for he was already a 'Chemould painter' by then.

The Gandhys took advertisements in the books and magazines their friends brought out. *The Hill of Beauty; Matheran Centenary, 1850-1950* (New Book Company, 1950) by Dinoo Bastavala has a full page advertisement for Chemould Frames. I saw a similar small advertisement in one of the many poetry magazines Nissim Ezekiel edited.

None of this was really 'gallery work' but it was what Gallery Chemould did, stepping out of the confines of what a gallery could do and doing what a Citizen Gallery might.

• 06 •

Three Keys to Khorshed and Kekoo Gandhy

'The thing about K and K was that they were both one person and two distinct personalities. Simultaneously. At that same moment in time. Or so it seemed to me. You could if you tried hard tell the "apartness" of this "twinness"! Again, as the Americans say, momentarily. For without realizing it each protected the warmth, the generosity, the spontaneity and yes, the open-hearted hospitality of the other so that the idiot world out there didn't always succeed in exploiting these very human qualities in what was such a pioneering time in our art world, our art history, our art growth, our gallery system. Or to put it crassly, they were a team that instinctively did the right thing often more than the Right Thing but had the equally instinctive business sense to not be completely taken for a ride. Sharp when required. Astute. Businesslike. But always nurturing and able to suss out the real from the fake. Not paintings. People. Artists. So yes, eyes. They both had an eye for art. And behind that eye lurked a generous desire to help show, share, promote, even support artists. Artists that would go on to become household names in time. Legends, blue chips, artistically vital. All because at a particular time in their lives K and K became conduits of support. Or simply guardian angels that made it possible in their loft above Jehangir to showcase every single new artist who was headed for masterdom. Never as benign saints. Just as down-to-earth beings that had wandered into the world of art and found their life. And their life's work.'

—**Naveen Kishore**, publisher, Seagull Books

Everyone I met seemed to have a good word for Kekoo and Khorshed Gandhy. I had only to mention that I was working on their twinned lives and the way in which they brought Gallery Chemould into being and people as diverse as the novelist and columnist Shobhaa Dé or the industrialist Abhishek Poddar would have a story to tell.

What fascinates me is how they became who they became. One easy way to explain it is that they were 'like that only', the classic explanation for every foible or fancy Indians think of. But this is unsatisfying. Yes, they were rich but so were many other people, and many richer. Yes, they were educated but so were many others. What turned them into citizen gallerists?

When Laxman Shreshtha remembers Kekoo Gandhy fondly for encouraging his work even when he was a beginner struggling to find a foothold in the art world[36] or when Tyeb Mehta says, 'By ensuring a fixed income for me in the early years without pressuring me, Chemould helped me to remain independent and work my own way[37],' you could argue that Kekoo Gandhy was simply making an investment in the future of these artists. Perhaps he was. Perhaps he was acting out of some feudal instinct that was common to many of the entrepreneurs and industrialists of the

1950s. Perhaps he was seized of a mission, that he should be the intermediary between the world of those who could buy art and the artists, whom he often romanticized as gentle trusting souls who needed protection. (He said this so often, I suspect, he was reminding himself of his beliefs which were often belied by the behaviour of the artists.)

Ironically, his grandson Areesh Jungalwala, a new graduate at the time of writing, who was away for most of his growing-up years at a boarding school in Kodaikanal, remembers his grandfather in his later life as the one who in the eyes of the family needed protection. 'He was in a constant struggle with everyone in the family. They wanted to look after him and protect him and he wanted to be free. He just wanted to be who he was.'

But who was Kekoo? The variety and range of his interests defies description. His energy verged on the manic. The almost spontaneous hospitality he offered meant that there was a stream of visitors coming through the house. 'One of the great things about that time was that you never knew who was going to turn up; one day it would be Clement Greenberg [the American art critic] and another day it would be someone from the Moral Re-Armament. And I remember my grandmother sitting at the dining table through it all, being introduced to this stream of people and saying, "Sahibji" to each one with the same unfailing courtesy,' says Behroze Gandhy with a reminiscent smile.

This mention of Moral Re-Armament was the first key. As Rajmohan Gandhi points out in his foreword, Khorshed and Kekoo Gandhy were among the first evangelists for the Moral Re-Armament in India. The couple discovered the Moral Re-Armament on a trip to Switzerland. They had dropped in at Caux on an impulse.

Dara Gandhy believes that this serendipitous encounter was a turning point in Kekoo's life, defining who he would become. 'His and Khorshed's accidental contact with Moral Re-Armament (MRA) at Caux-sur-Montreux

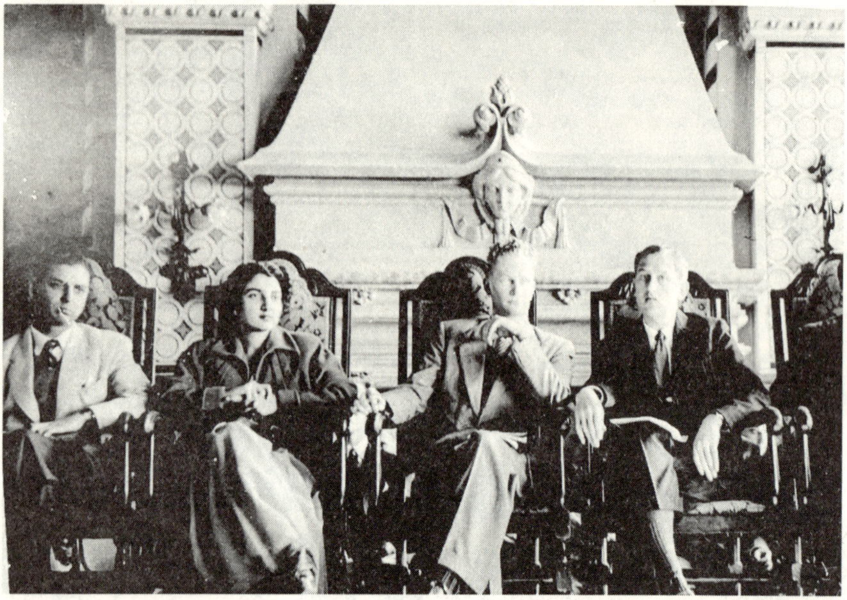

Defining moment: Kekoo and Khorshed Gandhy at Caux-sur-Montreux in Switzerland in 1951

in Switzerland in 1951 was an important happening. Never having heard of MRA myself, I asked him on his return what it was that enthused him so much about it. He replied, "Wouldn't you be if you saw Germans apologising to the French for what they did to them during the War, and in turn the French acknowledging the gesture by shedding their long-time hatred of Germans?" He then related his own experience. Before coming to Switzerland he had bought a car in England and since the car was for export to India, he was exempt from paying the heavy purchase tax as per prevailing rules. One evening, when he and Khorshed were at a theatre in London, their car was stolen. The insurance did provide a new replacement car, but as the stolen car would remain in England, he might avoid paying tax. In a moment of quiet reflection at Caux, he realised that this was an act of clever deceit, and to make amends sent a letter to the insurance company with a cheque refunding the excess value as he had falsely claimed. He later learned that the chairman of the insurance company was totally bowled over as never had he experienced such an act from a client. This cemented Kekoo's faith in a moral ideology which he endeavoured to live by and thereafter he actively pursued the MRA work in India.'

The Moral Re-Armament is remembered with some nostalgia and some suspicion. 'I know that the Moral Re-Armament was backed in India by the Tatas,' says journalist Sidharth Bhatia. 'They held camps in Panchgani, but they were one of the many youth regeneration movements around at the time, like the Yuvak Biradari, for instance. Students would gravitate in one direction or the other. A kind of Christian ideology if not theology was the backbone of it.'

The Parsis seemed particularly susceptible, it seemed, but the poet and archivist of the city, Adil Jussawalla says, 'The Moral Re-Armament probably thought we were pushovers, but they did not account for the mode of satire, and the savage satirical streak that the Parsis have when it comes to dealing with certain types of people out of the West. Since there was a stream of young people coming out of the West who were to be put up by local people, the MRA began to be known as the Maffat Rehvaanu Association (Free Homestay Association, in Parsi Gujarati), one of the many jokes cracked behind their backs. In some ways, the very things that attracted many—the high-minded obscurantism combined with bombast, the belief that the world's problems were being solved in Caux, that they could be solved in Caux, that this world leader had come and that famous person was coming—were the things that turned us off as well.'

Their son-in-law Bernard Imhasly believes Khorshed and Kekoo were ready for it. 'The spiritual underpinnings, remarkable for a Zoroastrian couple, had been nurtured early by the philosophy of Gandhi, and later, Siddha Yoga as practised by Swami Muktananda in Ganeshpuri, a village two hours from Bombay. MRA tried to be a Western equivalent of sorts to Gandhi's beliefs. Its mission was to reconnect to Christian core values after

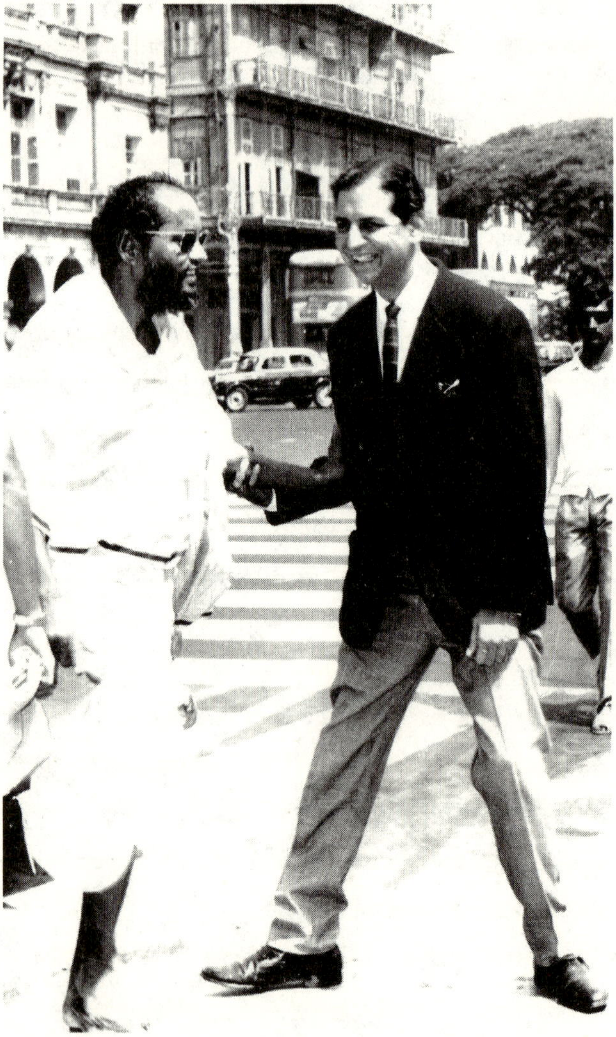

A gallerist and his guru: *Kekoo Gandhy with Swami Muktananda outside Jehangir Art Gallery*

the trauma of the Great Wars, which had not only destroyed people and countries, but also shaken their Christian ethics. Its founder, the American Frank Buchman postulated that individual ethical conduct enabled people to create peaceful solutions in society. In its Indian avatar, the links between Gandhi's ethics and the MRA philosophy was strengthened by the fact that MRA India was led by the Mahatma's grandson, Rajmohan Gandhi. Its finest hour came during the Emergency, when the weekly magazine *Himmat* was one of the few publications in which young journalists like Neerja Chowdhury and Kalpana Sharma, led by Rajmohan Gandhi, courageously wrote against the violations of democratic values.'

The Moral Re-Armament was something Kekoo shared with Khorshed. The second key to him was his association with Swami Muktananda of Ganeshpuri, something he did *not* share with Khorshed until the passing of the guru. These were the two poles of his spiritual and cultural formation. Both were of his own devising, both were lived in public but with private repercussions, as we will see.

I believe that if Kekoo lived his political ideals even at personal risk, worked tirelessly for the city and for the world of art, threw himself into projects with a huge zeal, wanted to build institutions, it was because of what he had learned at the Moral Re-Armament, the possibility that another world was just around the corner and we could all make it happen. His more intimate, more personal side, came out of his association with Ganeshpuri and the family encounter with EST. That he could look upon almost every man as a kindred spirit was probably something to do with the initiation, with his quiet time in the *gufa*. His was a mobile, malleable temperament and by all accounts, he was a good father.

'When I think back to growing up in Kekee Manzil,' Rashna Imhasly remembers, 'I feel that Papa was much more connected to our emotional issues. Adil and I shared a room and he would come there at night and share

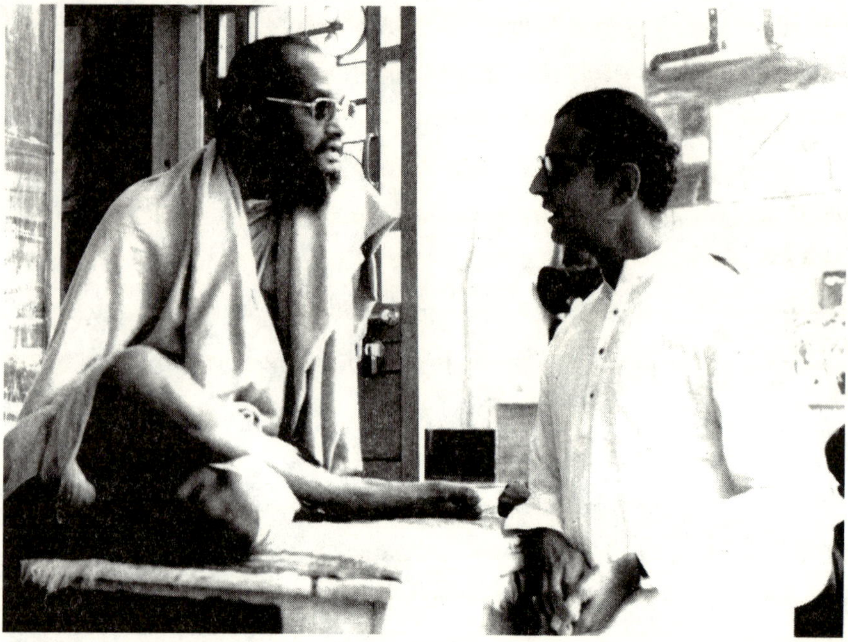

Kekoo with Swami Muktananda

his daily activities with us. He would tell us what had happened at the factory as he would massage our feet and he would ask us about our days; we would fall asleep to that lullaby. The room was supposed to be ours but we knew that when we got home, we might find someone else in residence: a painter from "outstation" for instance, who was staying with us. There was no guest room, you see.'

Khorshed and Kekoo might not have been too careful about the physical space their children occupied but they carved out emotional space for four children who grew up into markedly different individuals, always a sign, I would think, of good parenting.

But with four children came a variety of spouses and a cataclysm or two. The first happened when Rashna Gandhy decided that she was going to marry Bernard Imhasly. It is another matter that Bankie, as he is now known in the family, served as a Swiss diplomat to India before becoming a journalist and the correspondent for the prestigious Swiss German newspaper *Neue Zürcher Zeitung*. When it all began, he was a poor student and the Gandhys were a wealthy family. Bernard remembers the time well.

'When I first met the Gandhys, I was a student, a position of little or no power, no money and uncertain prospects. I came from a humble background and I wanted to marry their daughter, Rashna. They were polite and welcoming but they were also honest about the disconnect.'

This was the moment of truth for Khorshed and Kekoo. Their MRA ideals must have been sorely tested. Surely, they were supposed to accept this man as another human being as valuable as any other? But they were also Indian bourgeoise folk, caught in a class system that was invisible to them because it had never worked against them. (If a system works for you, you don't spot its functioning. That is why men find it so difficult to see the operations of patriarchy while most women can smell them a mile off.) However they did try their best and as we shall see, both the MRA and the Ganeshpuri connection, helped them get through it.

Imhasly continues: 'When you enter a new social network, you almost always land in a difficult spot. Looking back, I am amazed at how gently they handled me. There was the grandfather who was always breathing down their necks—he was distant. As far as he knew, Rashna had fallen in love with a young Parsi man. Now she had fetched up in Switzerland and now, here she was, with a young man who by all accounts came from a simple, if not poor family. All this they must have learned from her letters home. We came to India in 1968, sure of the strong emotional bond we had, sure that we were in love, ready to brazen it out. Again I got incredibly lucky that it was Kekoo, Khorshed and Dara waiting on the other side. I had no image of India inside my head. It seems odd now but it was true then. The country had never entered my mental landscape. And now suddenly, here I was, coming through Customs and Immigration into a whole new experience, on my own. I should say that Rashna had gone on ahead, to prepare the way, so to speak.

'I was staying at Dara's place which was also quite tactful of the family. It allowed me some space, and some distance from which to get a sense of the family. Again, I think we were both lucky that Kekoo and Khorshed—and more Khorshed I think than Kekoo—were attentive to the fluid dynamics of the family since Rashna and I didn't care. We were insensitive to family politics. We were in love and that was all that mattered.

'I think Khorshed did a marvellous job of it. She handled the entire situation with tact and charm. She was a 45-year-old woman at the time and she was being virtually turned into a grandmother but she bore it with no grudge or grievance against either of us.'

Rashna takes up the story: 'Mota Papa [her grandfather Minocher Gandhy] set his face against us. I didn't give a hoot. I was young and in love and I wanted to get married or else I would not have been able to stay on in Switzerland. My grandfather was absolutely against it. Papa, ever empathetic, said that he understood but explained his dilemma to us: "Mota Papa says I will have to leave the house if I give you permission to marry." And this is how lives intersect. Swami Muktananda was very important in Papa's life. We had a very close association with Muktananda; he was my father's mentor and guide; his ashram was my father's asylum and refuge. Moreover, it was a very turbulent time if you had a factory in Bombay with Datta Samant ruling the city. There were strikes and all kinds of protests. When it got too much for Papa, he would go to Ganeshpuri on the weekends to meditate and ask for advice. He would take anyone along who was willing, artists, friends, family. And so perhaps this was why I told Papa: "You go for all of your factory matters to Ganeshpuri, why not this one?"

'So Papa went to the ashram and Baba said, "Where is the boy? If I don't see the boy, how can I decide?" Papa said, "He is planning to come but I don't know what to do." Baba said: "Let him come first." And so when Bankie came to India, the first thing we did was to take him to Ganeshpuri.

'Baba said, "Don't look at the colour of his skin. His heart is pure."

'My father was not convinced. "But what do I tell my father?"

'Baba said, "Tell him I will bless them at the ashram."

'Though Baba wasn't his guru, my grandfather caved in at that. I think he had a very Indian respect for the holy man; he did not have to be a man of *his* faith; he just had to be a man *of* faith. Perhaps Mota Papa had also come to the bottom of his bag of tricks. He had tried everything. He told me he would disinherit me; I said I did not want his money; I just wanted his blessings. "*Bandook maara chhaati par mukhine maara aashirwaad lech tu,*" he said. (You will have to put a gun to my chest and take my blessings.) We were married at the ashram with only the artists in attendance. Ambadas, Husain who was filming it all on his small camera, Hebbar, Bal Chhabda, Behroze, my cousin Sherna Gandhy and my mother. We left for Switzerland after the wedding, and that was the end of my graphic design career. I started looking for a job. I had an uncle, Jal Cawasji, who told me to go and meet the manager of Air India in Zurich, "*Patrel lei ja* and give it to Homi Dubash, and ask him to give you a job." Homi was the manager there. So I took the *patrel* and I got the job, can you imagine? They were very happy to have someone who could wear a sari, who didn't have a visa problem and who could speak English and Hindi and some German too.'

Eventually, Rashna discovered Jungian analysis and became an analyst and a writer of books such as *The Psychology of Love—The Wisdom of Indian Mythology* and *Emerging Feminine—Discovering the Goddess Within.* Bankie, the young and impoverished student, took a Ph.D., became a university lecturer and later a diplomat and a journalist.

'Eventually Mota Papa was won over. He even apologised to me, on the verandah here,' says Bankie as we drink tea at Kekee Manzil.

He was magnanimous enough to apologise to both. Rashna remembers: 'He said: "I was trying to protect you. That was why I made some mistakes." He was very proud when Bankie came to India as a diplomat.'

Swami Muktananda saved Rashna's marriage and Kekoo's home life but some might say that Kekoo's association with Ganeshpuri was part of the zeitgeist. In the 1960s and 1970s, the counterculture had not been tamed into decals and repurposed as nostalgia. Many did want to drop out of the rat race and tune into another way of living. Many intellectuals would seek to walk away from urban living. Some chose the commune life with Bhagwan Rajneesh (as he was then known), some went off to Ashishda's Mirtola ashram. Kekoo made his practical; a drive away from the city he loved and the life that could sometimes get on top of him. Rashna Gandhy explains the Baba phenomenon in the Gandhy family's life. 'When Kekoo had union problems at the Chemould Frame Factory and he couldn't cope with that stress, he would go to Ganeshpuri to ask for Baba's advice. Baba would send him to the *gufa* to meditate in order to get his answers. And in his enthusiasm, he tried to get other people to go. He would invite all the artists there. He would take us there on weekends, I was the only one who would willingly go.

'Papa was really into Baba; he felt peace and tranquillity and really loved him. Yet he did not spurn bodily comforts. He would go to the Kothawala Baths in neighbouring Vajreshwari, run by a Parsi, and soak in the thermal waters. Needless to say, he tried to intervene when there were problems between the owner of the baths and Baba.'

Through all this Khorshed held aloof. And then came the night of Baba's death. 'Three different people called saying that Baba is asking both of you to come to Ganeshpuri. My mother thought it strange that she too had been summoned but she went anyway. My father, my mother and one of the couples who had phoned were travelling to Ganeshpuri. They asked her, "Is

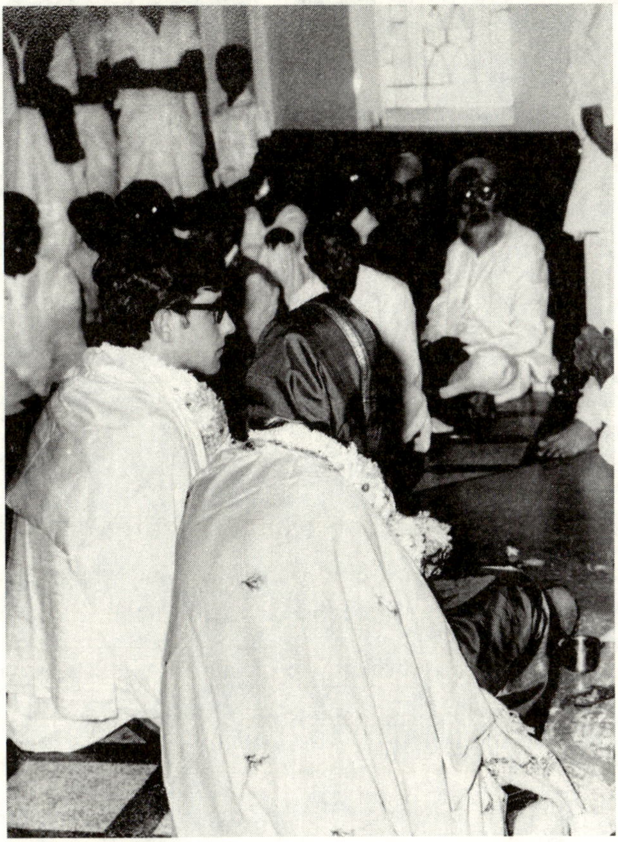

With the blessings of the guru: *Rashna and Bernard's wedding at Swami Muktananda's ahram, (l to r, seated at the back): KK Hebbar, Bal Chhabda, MF Husain, 17 December 1968*

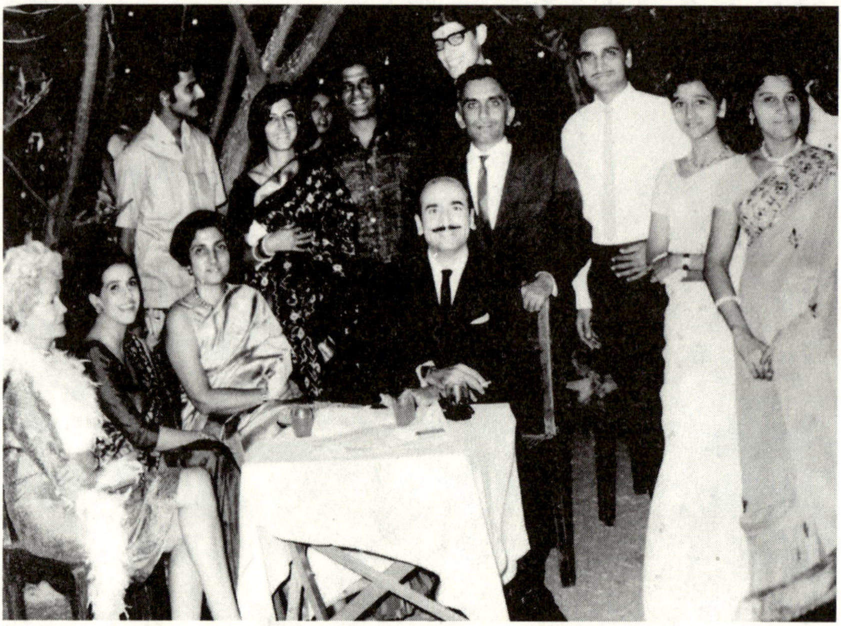

After the wedding: (Seated, l to r) Stella Snead, Shirin Sabavala, Khorshed, Jehangir Sabavala; (l to r, standing) Rashna, Ambadas, Bernard, Homi Patel, Satish Panchal at the wedding reception on 17 December 1968 in Pilloo Pochkhanawala's garden in Bombay

he your guru?" She said, "No, he's my husband's guru but I sing for him." This was true. She would sing for him in Ganeshpuri and when he was having heart trouble in Bombay, she sang to soothe him.

'Baba called them in and told them of the trouble he was having with Kothawala. Kothawala was spreading stories about the American devotees who were guarding the ashram and not allowing the local folk to enter. Kekoo was sent to deal with him.

'Kothawala was adamant. "Who is this man? Nityananda was my guru. I am not dealing with him," he said. Kekoo tried but when he saw that he was making no headway, he came back. That night, at 12:30, Baba had taken *mahasamadhi*. Kekoo went back to Kothawala and said, "He has gone, it is time to come now and make your peace and pay your respects."

'Kothawala came and paid his last respects that very night. When Baba's last rites began, Kekoo and Khorshed were called into the room where they had seated Baba quite close to the site. Khorshed was shocked, she could not understand this honour because she had never thought of herself as his disciple.

'Later, she told me that when she was sitting in the courtyard outside and meditating and began to think about him, she thought to herself, "If you were my guru, give me a sign" and a small coconut seed fell into her open palm. She then thought about the story that the couple who had driven down with them that day to Ganeshpuri had told her, when she had admitted to them that Baba was actually her husband's guru: Draupadi had called out to Lord Krishna, seeking His protection when she was being disrobed on the command of the Kauravas. The Lord had intervened in the nick of time but Draupadi wanted to know why he had been so tardy. He replied: "By what name did you call out to me?" She said, "Dwarkanath." He explained, "Dwarkanath is the one who lives far away. Had you called me Hridayanath, I would have been there immediately."

'The story now made sense to her. Her guru had been close but she had kept him at a distance by calling him her husband's guru. She had the coconut seed mounted in gold and wore it as a locket.'

To Rashna, these influences are not contradictory at all but work in tandem with each other. 'With us, our religion is ancient and far away from us. The connection is lost. It is anyway an austere, stripped-down religion with nowhere to hide. For ninety-nine per cent of the Parsis, their entire faith can be summed up in *Humta, hukta, hvrashta* or "Good thoughts, good words, good deeds". This leaves something of a spiritual vacuum and the combination of the high purpose of Moral Re-Armament and the practical karma marga in Hindu spirituality served Papa well. The first gave him a moral compass by which to judge his actions and even to step back from himself and take stock. My mother and he put great faith in what MRA called "quiet time", the moment when a spiritual audit has to take place and you have to account for yourself and your own actions, getting in touch with one's "Inner Maker" for answers. This may have, in turn, led me to Jungian psychology, which had a similar process of turning inwards to get in touch with the "Higher Self", when caught in the outer conflicts of life.'

•

Bernard Imhasly has an interesting take on this pairing:

'Kekoo did not process things in the same way as Khorshed did. He didn't have to. He got lucky that way. He had Khorshed and his father and Dara to cushion him, he never had to wean himself away from his father and such Oedipal sufferings as he had were comparatively mild. This meant he could negotiate family spaces without too much care. But Khorshed could see how much the family had given her and she was careful not to disturb the dynamic too much.

'When Rashna and I announced our decision to get married, Khorshed took us to see her sister Aimee Wadia, who lived in Poona at the time. She wanted someone else to tell us what she could well have said herself: "to take it easy, not to rush things, to be sensible and think things through". I remember her sitting with us at a table and talking about love with a clear-headedness that I can admire even at this distance. She told us how she too had felt these ferocious pangs of love, whenever she touched Kekoo's hand; and how after a while, they died down. I remember her looking at us and saying frankly: "Now I touch his hand and I don't feel anything. So what you're feeling, what you're going through, it's not going to last forever, but other things surface and strengthen the bond between you." She was, I think, at that point, the only person who was fully aware of all the tensions that arise in a family such as theirs as a new generation begins its struggle towards selfhood. She had a ringside view of Kekoo and his father, who must have been alternately perplexed and disappointed by his mercurial son. I think Minocher was often clear about how his son was a failure, fooling around with painters. Khorshed knew her figures, she was attentive to accounts and that gave her a connection with her father-in-law, the benefits of which Kekoo must have also enjoyed. He had no care for money. He often did not even carry a wallet. Or if he carried a wallet, it contained a few nominal rupees and a picture of Swami Muktananda.'

•

Many people called the Gandhys socialists, meaning the label in the broadest sense of the term, as people who thought social inequality was wrong, who had some fellow-feeling for the underprivileged, believed that the government's job was the amelioration of injustice. But they also belonged to the Moral Re-Armament which saw the Left as inimical to its project. Adil Jussawalla remembers being introduced to some young people from Kerala when he was visiting Caux in 1960, a backpacker hoping for some free meals and perhaps a bed for the night. 'They seemed friendly enough at first. But then they told me that there were some "converts" from Kerala, young people who had been Communists and now had seen the light. I was seen to be talking to them and this was not liked; so I was told politely that the authorities did not want me to stay on at Caux and so I left.'

By the 1970s, there was PROYOM, Progressive Youth Movement, which caught the imagination of young intellectuals as well as artists. Navjot and Altaf Mohamedi for instance were members and the Left welcomed the artists so long as they turned their skills to propaganda and made posters; or used their art to convey messages that would raise the consciousness of the working classes.

Of course, this could not be a satisfying project for too long and when PC Joshi, one of the few Communists who had a feeling for how the political and the cultural might be natural allies, was sidelined, the artists moved on.[38]

And yet, until very recently, the intellectual life of the country has been Left-leaning. Did the Gandhys see themselves as intellectuals? I think not;

there was too much of the British in them to be comfortable with that kind of self-conscious self-labelling. But they felt part of the world of ideas, not just the ideas that informed the arts, but also those that underpinned the nation that was being built around and by them.

Did the Gandhys see the contradictions in their monotheistic faith and their acceptance of Swami Muktananda as a guru? Did they see the contradictions in their belonging to the Moral Re-Armament long after it had peaked and having Leftist sympathies? My guess is that they would have but that they would have also understood, perhaps instinctively, that one has to make sense, make a life, make a personal theology, out of these negotiations. I believe the incessant social work, their preoccupation with the state of the city and the nation, were part of their exculpation of privilege.

Dara explains: 'Kekoo was a socialist by nature because socialism for him was not that of the politician brand, but the simple desire to care for those around him. Money, in which he never wallowed, was there to be given away to those who he perceived as needing it, even arranging for it through other sources if he did not have it himself.'

•

Some of the stories I heard about Kekoo made me wonder. When he saw that his daughter's marriage had given him a base in Europe, a base from which he could go tell it on the mountain, evangelise for Indian art. At this remove, it all sounds very amusing but his spirit, always incandescent with possibility, could also take its toll. Rashna tells the story of one of those trans-Europe excursions. 'One of my not-so-happy memories is a family vacation with Mummy-Papa and Dara, Behroze and her ex-husband Martin, and our three-year-old daughter, Anisha. We were all supposed to go to the south of France to see Raza. We rented a van and drove. I was a working woman, a wife and mother, looking forward to a holiday with my family. Papa raced us from one exhibition to another without any hotel bookings.

He had a different agenda from mine; I wanted some rest and relaxation; he was looking for art, for connections. Thanks to his art contacts, I remember being stuck in the south of France at St Tropez for a show. We arrived early, and parked our van in the front of where we were supposed to see the show. Later, we came out and found the van neatly hemmed in with no place to move, cars blocking us in place for miles. So we had no choice but to camp in the garden. Even Mummy had to curl up in her sleeping bag. Our next appointment was in Menton where Raza's show was opening so the next morning we were off to see that one, again without a hotel booking. That was when I freaked out. I said I was going back right then. "I have a child, I can't do this without a hotel room," I shouted. And so we got one and my mother and Anisha and I used it. The rest of them had to go off and roll out their sleeping bags in a meadow somewhere. At first light, along comes the farmer to flood his field and so they had to hop it. One by one, they crept into our room for baths and to use the toilet. It was a nightmare for me, not at all the holiday I wanted or needed: this manic trundling about, making do, without shelter. But all this ended in a wonderful village, Gorbio, where we visited Raza and Janine, and we had a lovely time in their enchanted home so all was well again.'

This kind of behaviour, to believe that you could pull off a trip across Europe with women and children in tow, seems, well, a bit mad, to put it mildly. Even though the Parsis have a reputation for eccentricity, this was a bit much. There were often times when I wondered whether Kekoo was bipolar. He seemed to have the same mad energies and then there were other times when he would simply vanish. I thought the best way to answer the question was to ask it.

Was Kekoo bipolar?

'Can there be any doubt?' asks his daughter Rashna, the clear-eyed psychotherapist. 'He had clear patterns of manic and depressive phases.

During the manic stage, he was all that he could be: a dreamer, a visionary who could see what no one else could, a bull-dog when it came to projects close to his heart. When he was depressed he didn't even want to leave the house. He once told me, "It's like having a snake wound around my head, constricting every thought, every feeling, every movement." We did take him to a doctor and he was put on Lithium but he did not take to it. The pills left an odd dry after-taste in his mouth and so he became adept at avoiding them.

'In his manic phases he would have no control over money. He would go down to Jehangir Art Gallery and buy painting after painting, none of them very good. He knew that they weren't but he would say: "What does ten or fifteen thousand (or whatever it was) matter? It will help the poor artist. How can he live? He has sold practically nothing." Khorshed—and later Shireen—would protest, "There may be a reason that he has sold nothing. He may just be a bad artist." Sometimes, they would send them back downstairs, sometimes they would keep them to see if anyone else might be interested in them.

'His depressions were also part of his tool-kit. In a way, he could let himself spiral downwards because he knew Khorshed was there to take charge of things and to keep everything going. But it was also a way he had of opting out of her control. You can control energy but what can you do when a person is completely passive and will not do anything? How can you control the void?' says Rashna.

But when he was in his productive phases, it was easy to love him because he loved so well. Even his sternest critic, Khorshed Gandhy, could see this: 'In everything he did, his love of people was there.'

•

But he wasn't just a lovable old man; he was the man who believed in modern art, the man who had kept the faith, the man who had put his money where his mouth was, the man who had been there when it was all happening and the man who remembered it all.

What was magical? He was open-handed with his memories. He wanted you to share them, to know what it had been like to live in his city with his friends.

As any journalist will tell you, information is hard to come by in India. Our information economy is to hoard it. Libraries are guarded, archives are defended against researchers in the best cases; in the worst cases, they are destroyed by indifference, disinterest or malice. And so, it is hard to underestimate the importance of Kekoo as a living archive.

Yashodhara Dalmia, art historian, independent curator and author of *The Making of Modern Art: The Progressives* remembers him as 'one of the few people who was not just interested in his gallery and his show. He was an initiator and a promoter, it is true, but he was also interested in the development of art.'

Dalmia arrived in the city in 1972 and almost immediately found a friend in Kekoo Gandhy who would spend hours talking about art with her. 'For him, the beginnings of modernism and the Progressives were lived experience. In the 1940s and 1950s, the intellectual ferment was at its peak in Bombay and he didn't just have a ringside view, he was part of the movement. He was their friend, their patron, their sounding board. He listened as they debated, he stepped in to comfort and to counsel and to help.'

This was extended to Dalmia too when she began to work on her book on the Progressives. 'I think he, and to a certain extent [Ebrahim] Alkazi[39] got me interested in them and he was delighted when I undertook to write a book about the Progressives. He was my chief informant for the Progressives and for the beginning of Modernism. I was living in Brady Flats in Colaba at the time and he would come to see me every week simply to talk to me about that time. He knew everybody and he had seen all their work. He was a living archive and he was generous with his knowledge and that is rare.'

When Dr Priya Maholay-Jaradi wrote her beautiful piece about her time with Khorshed and the 'Portrait of a Community' [see Chapter 10], the landmark exhibition on the Parsis in 2003 that was Khorshed's brainchild, she followed it up with another email: 'Kekoo was a vital oral repository when it came to the post-War art scene in Mumbai. His oral history archives contributed to my own research on the history of collecting by the House of Tatas as well as research conducted by Karin Zitzewitz, now at the University of Michigan. Both Karin and I were starting out our careers as young scholars and relied immensely on Kekoo for documentation of lesser known aspects of the art world.'

But it wasn't only PhD students who came to those oral history archives. Dolly Thakore remembers when she was arguably the first art auctioneer we had. 'Kekoo was my go-to guy for everything. He was very keen I should write on art, specially catalogues, because I was the first art auctioneer in India. I would have lunch at the Samovar every day; I had just arrived from London and was working at SH Benson's, the advertising agency. The only art gallery I knew of was the Jehangir and of course, Chemould. Kekoo was the nicest, gentlest person I knew. Whenever I had an art auction to do I would go to him and he would tell me all that I needed to know about the artist, all the stories, all the cues. And that made my spiel as an auctioneer very special, very different. I never did get around to writing those catalogues; I was too distracted by other things in my life.

'Kekoo was a member of my Rotary Club. And I suppose in a way, I got invited to become a Rotarian because of those art auctions and Kekoo's help with them. I did an auction for the Rotary Club of some artworks in the late 1980s or early 1990s; they had set a target of eight lakhs that they wanted to raise for charity. I got them twenty-four lakhs and they invited me to join.

By the time I began to attend those Tuesday meetings, Kekoo was showing some signs of slowing down; he was already ailing but he would still make it a point to attend.'

That he would attend points to another role that the pair had; they were part of the social fabric of the city. Shobhaa De, columnist and author, was in school with Rashna and so knew the family well. 'The Gandhys really represented the best fine Parsis of that generation, never a wrong word, never a step that was even remotely inelegant. Look at the talent they nurtured, look at the way they worked with Bhupen Khakhar back in the day when to be gay was to be considered "sick"or "perverted".

'They created a space for conversation, for adda. You could walk down from Chemould to the Samovar or just sit and talk endlessly in the gallery itself. I enjoyed talking to Kekoo, he was remarkably observant and he had a wonderful sense of humour; his wife was more taciturn. They used their respectability, their position in society to great effect, with brave and wonderful initiatives that never over-commercialised the art they were supporting, the art ecosystem they were helping to build.'

The artist Nilima Sheikh did not show with the Senior Gandhys—she shows with Shireen Gandhy now—but she puts it well when she says, 'With Chemould, the Gandhys provided a valuable cultural ambience. It was reassuring simply to know they were there, that there was such a space. Though I didn't show with them, it felt as if they were there for me in some way.'

•

In the Chemouldsphere, art might be likened to a contagious disease. Prolonged contact with Kekoo Gandhy might bring on an attack. It happened to many people including Abhishek Poddar. He remembers meeting Kekoo first 'in 1987. A year later while I was working with Standard Chartered Bank in Mumbai, we spent a lot of time together. During that time, about twice a week, after work, I would go to Gallery Chemould and he was kind enough to introduce me to all the artists and the art scene in the city. I was deeply touched when he threw a party for me at Kekee Manzil, his home in Bandra, and introduced me as India's youngest collector to all the denizens in the art world. He helped sharpen my eye for art and it was in fact, through him, I bought my first Gaitonde and Tyeb Mehta. He visited me in Calcutta and stayed with me on a few occasions. Both he and his wife Khorshed have always been extremely hospitable and I've always been grateful for their friendship and kindness in my life. I owe a lot to him and his mentoring me, and it's possibly all the hand-holding he did in my formative art years that have helped me get to now starting MAP—the Museum of Art and Photography [in Bengaluru].'

•

I stumbled on the third key almost by accident, towards the end of the writing of this book, when I was reading a new cache of letters. I discovered that EST or est, a movement founded by Werner Erhard who ran it between 1971 and 1984, had been an important factor in the lives of the Gandhys. This was a sixty-hour self-improvement programme that ran over two intense weekends. What you hoped to get out of it was a transformational experience of the kind its founder had on the Golden Gate Bridge when he discovered that his life was meaningless. This is the kind of thing that happens to most of us at a certain point, only we push through it and make some peace with the lack of meaning. Erhard did not. He broke through the sadness and discovered that he was 'free to choose, free to create a life that was worth living.' He devised a series of workshops that would help others to do so and for a while in the 1970s, it was dizzyingly successful

Those who remember EST training think of it as a boot camp, intense, physical, insomniac, partaking perhaps of a cult mentality. Kekoo and Khorshed went in and were transformed. They 'got it'; getting it was crucial and released you from your bondages to others and their expectations, from your history and your past. The Gandhys, who were evangelists at heart, urged their children towards EST. 'We all had to do it,' Shireen Gandhy says, rolling her eyes. 'I was sixteen but I wasn't excused. I didn't understand a thing but I did it anyway.'

So did Rashna on whom it has had perhaps the most transformative effect; it redirected her path but it was not all happy going in the beginning. 'I remember after the first flush of EST and "Getting It", I found that it lacked the essence of what I was seeking. The six-day experience in the Catskill Mountains, a course that was called "Getting You Ready for the Rest of Your Life", left me cold. So cold, in fact, that Bernard and I almost broke up.'

Then Kekoo and Rashna went to the US to Swami Muktananda's Southfallsburg Ashram. This was where Rashna had her breakthrough. 'I would call it a Transpersonal Experience. It had a lot to do with the fact that I happened to be sitting next to Stewart Emery and Joan, who happened to be at the Ashram too when we arrived. Stewart Emery was almost a co-founder, you may say, of EST with Werner Erhard. They broke away for reasons best known to them at some point. I told Stewart about the bad experience, and he urged me to write a letter to my trainer and ask for a refund. I did write that letter and got a stupid reply. I remember feeling very sorry for myself at the ashram and walking down the aisle to meet Baba, thinking that until then he was "ours"; he was my father's guru, the saviour of my marriage to Bernard but now we had lost him to the Americans. My poor victim ego was afraid he wouldn't even recognise me! As soon as I did my pranams, Baba saw my confused state and pulled me up with my head on his lap and thumped me on my back several times telling me, "*Sab kuch theek ho jaayega*" (Everything is going to be all right). He told me to attend the silent meditation course that was just beginning and not to speak to anyone during the course. So I sat for the first few days feeling very sorry for myself, cried my head and heart out, but by the third day I had a revelation.

I suddenly discovered, for the first time in my life, that I BELONGED TO MYSELF. That was what started my spiritual journey.'

This led to her involvement in the Transpersonal Association and a career as a Jungian therapist.

In the letters, there is clear evidence that Khorshed Gandhy 'got it' too. But history was also impingeing on all of them. In 1980, Indira Gandhi swept back into power when the Janata Party's government failed; this should have devastated Khorshed Gandhy but it did not. Instead, she wrote to Werner Erhard:

> I want to acknowledge that my est training worked for me on the morning of January 8th in such a fantastic way that I felt catapulted into space in which I am still floating!
>
> Millions in India woke up that morning feeling elated or utterly crushed and dejected, depending on which side of the fence they were, in having to accept Indira Gandhi as their Prime Minister once again. For me, an ardent Indira loather, this was such a THIS IS IT experience, such an experienced experience that I just threw back my head and roared with laughter. On that morning I believe I completed my training!! Fourteen months after I took it.
>
> Werner, I also believe that in that instant I just barely fathomed the Universal Mind with which Indira is in touch and which is the source of her power. When I sensed that, her literally rising from the ashes and making such a phenomenal comeback within three years, makes sense. I can also see that at the level her opposition reacts, she would make mince meat of them. Which she has done again and again—individually and collectively.

> However what I cannot reconcile in my mind is that her Being and her Doing run in two separate streams. If one is in touch with that source, should it not produce integrity in one? Of course, Indian mythology is full of the stories of the 'Devas' and the 'Asuras'. Should I look upon Indira Gandhi as a 20th Century asura? These are the type of puzzling thoughts that buzz around in my mind.
>
> One thing I do know with certainty—that I will be able to come off it every day, ten times a day and that I will be able to hold my upsets of the new political scene instead of the upset holding me as it did so completely during the nineteen months of the Emergency.
>
> I also do not want to wait for a Deva to appear. I want to live so as to make that source of power available to me every day. It is a strange coincidence that the seminar series 'est & life' has just started in Bombay. I am participating in that series and I am sure that it is going to push us forward into something totally new.

With the fervour of which she was capable, she 'cleaned her house'. In a letter dated 14 December 1979, she harked back to the time she found she was pregnant with Rashna when Adil was only nine months old and she was just beginning to enjoy her first-born.

> There is one very special sharing I want to do with you, my darling Rashna, so that I complete this relationship between us. When you were conceived Adil was just nine months old, I thought it was a definite intrusion when I was just beginning to enjoy Adil and I didn't want another child. Dr D'Silva's son

> Leslie had agreed to curette me and I even lay on the table. He fiddled around, asked me to get up and then made his confession that he had not done anything because his father had made him realize what a sinful thing he was doing as a Catholic. I was shocked but then and there decided that God wanted me to have this child and I was going to stop fretting. I can't tell you how many times I have blessed the old Dr D'Silva for invoking the conscience of his son so that we could have our beautiful daughter. I have just realised that God has made us repay our gratitude to the old doctor by our granddaughter being born into the Catholic faith! Isn't it all mysterious but beautiful?

When Karl Imhasly, Bankie's father died, her letter reflects her newfound beliefs:

> Death is cruel but at the same time it also uncovers within each one's heart a lot of the beautiful things which are the things nearest to the self such as love, tenderness, feeling of togetherness as a family, and above all the positive qualities of the one who has just passed on. Suddenly you see the person in a new light, feel gratitude for all his wonderful qualities and remembering them, the pang of separation seems even deeper perhaps...but only for a while—specially if the relation has been completed and is beautiful.

Of course, the family was not convinced. Dara Gandhy, the faithful third of the Gandhy triolet, did his est training but did not 'get it'. He and Khorshed would have words later over her new attitude to Indira Gandhi but this was surface static in a deep soul relationship.

Having watched her daughter Behroze 'live from reaction to reaction' as she put it, Khorshed wanted her to try est but was stymied by her daughter's dismissal of it as 'pseudo-American junk'. She asked Bankie, perhaps as the family intellectual, to offer his feelings on the course. He wrote on 5 November 1981:

'I enjoyed the course very much. Although not choosy in its methods I felt I for one needed quite a bit of shaking up to get in touch with my trying to control my life from an intellectual base, with all the emotional tensions and fears tucked away behind my act.'

Eventually Behroze did go through the two weekends while Khorshed waited and watched and worried about how she would take the lack of sleep. Behroze says, 'I never got it, always resented it and hated being blackmailed into doing it by my mother. My father who did it with me a second time, slept though it and one of their attendants had a full-time job keeping him awake.'

Bankie sums it up: 'The training employed fairly invasive methods of coercion to surrender, but the Gandhys survived it—Kekoo by sleeping through it, Khorshed by being able to separate the chaff from the precious wheat.'

Did Kekoo sleep through the violent enthusiasms of those encounters? Quite possibly, though his letters, not very many of them, do acknowledge a debt to the est training.

•

It is odd how the good father Kekoo became the eccentric grandfather while Khorshed as mother and Khorshed as grandmother seemed to be much the same person.

Atyaan Jungalwala, twenty-five at the time of writing, remembers her grandfather as being non-standard issue. 'I was his acknowledged favourite grandchild. In that, he was very different. Most other grandparents I know say they have no favourites but he was clear: I was his favourite. So when I was little I would go and sit at his desk and play with his things, I would scribble in his diary and he would never complain. In fact, he always said they were wonderful even if they were only childish doodles. I think it was because I didn't have building friends, I simply hung out with my granddad.

'I don't remember him ever telling me much about the art world but I do remember him telling me at great length why JRD Tata was a great man. I suppose we thought he was a little crazy but we were very fond of him. He would come for sleepovers in our room and fall asleep on the sofa with his left arm over the back of the sofa.

'But I don't think he was the kind of person who knew what he was doing with kids. He was lovely but he was also the kind who would take you along with him and forget about you as soon as he got to a place. He wasn't all about hold-my-hand and look-both-sides or anything like that. He was very *laissez faire* as a grandparent. You could do your own thing with him. I had some of my most memorable times hanging out with him.

'Khorshed was very different. She was strict and she was clear about things being done in a certain way. She wanted us to be neat, systematic. She was all about where-are-your-chappals and did-you-wash-your-hands? So obviously, I went and hung out with him a lot, when he was working on his restoration, I would be allowed to sit there and help him with stuff or I would just be scribbling.

'I do remember the bad times though. I think there were times when he would get really bad, I remember once in Matheran when he wouldn't eat, he wouldn't get out of bed. And I would be sent to coax him to come to the table. I remember going downstairs and feeding him. One of the caregivers would come and say, he's not eating, come and feed him and I would coax him like a child.

'That floor is unused, empty. It's weird. We don't hang out there any more.'

• 07 •

God's Good Man

'Moral Re-Armament trained me to treat opponents not as enemies but as human beings who have been brainwashed. We have to cultivate them and have a good relationship with them if we are to have a better world.'

It was intriguing nevertheless for former Shiv Sena MP, Mr Madhukar Sarpotdar, who played a controversial role in the Bombay riots, to encounter Gandhy's earnestness. 'When we met Mr Sarpotdar at Behrampada, the scene of major rioting in 1993, he thought we were not going to listen to his point of view, only that of Shabana Azmi and others like her, who, according to him, only dabble in grassroots social work,' says Gandhy. 'So I said Khorshed and I would visit him at his house for a talk.' When they did go—an elderly elegant couple—Mr Sarpotdar could only ask in some amazement, 'Why are you doing this?'

Khorshed has an answer when she remembers the Emergency. 'When something is imposed on me like this,' and she brings her hand down on the table, 'I go berserk. We just had to fight it.' Gandhy's best friend, Sadanand Varde, Minister of Education in Maharashtra in the 1970s, was put in jail, as were many others. 'We harboured Mrinal Gore, leading social activist, in our son Adil's room, for over fifteen days,' Khorshed says, her face animated by the memory. Her father-in-law did get suspicious and was worried the police would come. Ms Gore was safe at the Gandhys but was arrested soon after she left them. Another warm memory Khorshed has is of organising a 'prayer meeting' during the Emergency since no other kind of meeting was allowed. It was a Saturday afternoon. Sarvodaya Jayaprakash Narayan was very sick then, having to undergo frequent bouts of dialysis. Rajmohan Gandhi, Gandhiji's grandson, was with us. They put out an announcement in the newspapers about a meeting at Sophia Wadia's home at Theosophy Hall. About hundred people gathered, she recalls. Prayers from every religion were chanted. It was our way of adding a subtle political colouring to the meeting.

'I have Khorshed, four lovely children and Kekee Manzil,' says Kekoo. 'The least I can do is to work for those less privileged. I feel you don't deserve all this until you put in your bit.'[40]

—**Nandini Bhaskaran,** Journalist

By its own narrative, the city of Bombay had no time for God and by extrapolation, no time for communal disharmony. The story that we had been told—and which we told ourselves—was that the city was full of people who wanted to make a living, who wanted to get ahead and had no time to concern themselves with the problems that racked the Other India, from which news came of riots sparked by religion. In December 1992, various Hindutva forces came together to wreak havoc upon the historical fabric of the nation; in this case, it was the Babri Masjid in Ayodhya, Uttar Pradesh, which was said to stand on the birthplace of Lord Rama. If ever we needed any evidence of the potency of symbols in the sub-continent, here it was. The Bharatiya Janata Party had started with two seats in the parliament of 1984 but its fortunes were to change when Lal Krishna Advani got into a Maruti van that had been dressed up as a *rath* (chariot) and drove across the country, arousing a new sentiment about an old issue. (Nearly fifty years had passed since the dispute began.)

The day after the mosque came down with surprising rapidity, riots broke out all over the country. Again, Bombay was held to be immune by virtue of its lack of interest in matters of religion; most of the city went to work as if it were just another day. But that terrible month, December 1992, ripped through the myth. Some argue that the riots were politically motivated and politically supported; the common people were 'not like that'. Some argue the riots were the doing of vested interests who suddenly saw a way to clear slums and settlements off what had become prime land. But neither explains how neighbour turned against neighbour and areas in which Hindus and Muslims had lived together for decades suddenly became battlegrounds.

Suddenly no place was safe. In this new dispensation, the old defences came down. The poor suffered the most, of course, and suddenly the city was not recognisable to many of those who had lived in it and prided themselves on its record of communal harmony.

To Khorshed and Kekoo Gandhy, this was a turning point. They had grown up during the dying days of the British Raj but their loyalties were clear. They were for independence although this was not a position that the Parsis of their class espoused. Rashna Gandhy remembers: 'My parents were extremely Gandhian but that was not a popular position with my grandparents who also lived with us. We used to have these heated conversations at the Kekee Manzil table since my grandfather was a lot more conservative—he wouldn't allow my grandmother to go to weddings of mixed marriages. He did not like Gandhiji or his politics; he found all the strikes and protests and marches extremely distasteful: "*Aa tamaaro Gandhi, jaw soo karech*!" (This Gandhi of yours, see what he's up to) he would say. I suppose they had made their money under the British Raj and were unsure of what might happen in an independent India. But my parents also had a strong point of view and they were not loth to speak. This made the discussions powerful and we grew used to the notion of dissent. You were entitled, we could see, to your own opinions and you could stand up for them. We never grew up thinking that we had to think in a certain way.'

Khorshed and Kekoo had lived through Partition, that bloody birthing of two nations, but there had always been hope, there was always the dream that the new world had been born but was simply taking its time to show up. Theirs was a world that was cushioned by privilege, it is true, but they were in touch with the realities of India. Pandit Jawaharlal Nehru had been their prime minister and they felt empowered enough to walk up to him at Bombay's Santacruz Airport where they were all waiting for a flight and hand him a letter.

As Khorshed had once done.

'Did you really?' I asked her.

'What is so "really-really" about that?' she replied with some asperity. 'I had written Pandit Nehru a letter and it was in my handbag. I was going to post it to him when I saw him so I thought I would give it to him directly.'

She paused a perfectly timed beat and then added. 'Kekoo was the only person who was not surprised. He said, "You must have thought you would save a stamp".'

The Gandhys knew they were privileged but they did not see this as a license to ignore the realities around them. Their children were brought up in the same way. Behroze Gandhy remembers: 'I was very conscious that I had been born with privilege. I also had it dinned into me that you had to earn it. In this city, I was always going to be Kekoo's daughter which may be why I put seven thousand miles between me and my family and tried to make my way in England.'

It was when she came back to the city of her birth to make a documentary on this city, wracked by forces of communalism after the fall of the Babri Masjid, that she realised exactly how he had used his position to build a network of people so that he was never very far away from anyone, whether it was the Governor, the head of the Shiv Sena or the police commissioner.

For the Gandhys had joined the fight against communalism before the mosque in Ayodhya was brought down. The Safdar Hashmi Memorial Trust (SAHMAT)[41], decided to bring together Artists Against Communalism. This was how writer and activist Rajni Bakshi encountered the Gandhys of Chemould.

'Ashish Rajadhyaksha was my next-door neighbour and he said that SAHMAT was desperately looking for volunteers so I went ahead and offered them my services for two weeks,' says Rajni Bakshi. 'Shabnam Hashmi came down to Bombay and set up a command centre in a small room off Gallery Chemould; the idea was to have a twelve-hour concert of classical Indian music at Shivaji Park and that was what I was going to help with. And Kekoo, of course, was in the thick of it. So was Khorshed, because it was music and that was her love but also because it was music deployed in the defence of something that she believed was truly Indian.'

Bakshi would go on to write books such as *Bapu Kuti: Journeys in Rediscovery of Gandhi* and *Bazaars, Conversations and Freedom: For a Market Culture beyond Greed and Fear*. She is also a trustee of CRY (Child Rights and

24th Oct. 1961.

Dear Prime Minister,

I write this letter to you not just as an Indian citizen but as a mother. Last week I took my children to a cinema and the "Story of Kashmir" was being exhibited as a side show. The effect on my children – to say the least – was alarming. It invoked a deep hatred in their hearts towards Pakistan. Is this what we want to see in our rising generations? Is this how we will establish good relationship with our neighbour?

You, Sir, are seeing this film to-night at the Regal Cinema. I do not know whether it is for the purpose of giving endorsement to this film or whether you are seeing it for the first time. It may be presenting India's case very well but by whipping up so much hatred in Indians' hearts towards Pakistan will it help to bring the solution any more or actually make it more distant?

Whether it is the problem of Pakistan or disintegration in the country or anything else, we can choose either

Letter to a Prime Minister: *Khorshed Gandhy's letter to Jawaharlal Nehru and (overleaf) Nehru's reply to her.*

to live in the realm of self-righteous blame or help one another to find faith, love and an answer. Because I am concerned about our youth and their thinking, I take the liberty of putting my thoughts before you.

Yours loyally,

(Smt) Khorshed Gandhy.

Prime Minister
Jawarlal Nehru
New Delhi

No. 2185-PMH/61.

PRIME MINISTER'S HOUSE
NEW DELHI
27th October, 1961.

Dear Mrs. Gandhy,

I have received your letter of the 24th October.

I saw the documentary "The Story of Kashmir" in Bombay recently. I had seen a part of it only before. My own view of this film is that artistically it was very good and factually it was completely correct. In fact, it was based on admitted statements and documents.

It may be that people who see it might develop strong feelings against Pakistan's policy in regard to Kashmir. If you happen to read the Pakistan press and statements made by Pakistan leaders on this issue, you will realise the vicious character of this Pakistan propaganda. It is not our wish to cultivate hatred against any country or people. But the fact is that Pakistan continues to spread entirely false accounts about Kashmir. We have to put the records straight and to state what the facts are. I do not quite see how we can escape this duty without doing grave injury to our own case and to the people of Kashmir.

I hold strong opinions about Pakistan's policy although I express myself with some moderation. This policy has caused misery to large numbers of people and is based on the quintessence of hatred. Our response to it has been on the whole restrained and moderate. But it would be odd if we were to refrain from placing the facts before our people and others.

We have to distinguish between a policy which a Government follows and the people of that country. We fought British imperialism for many long years but we did not encourage any hatred of the British.

Yours sincerely,

Jawaharlal Nehru

Mrs. Khorshed Gandhy,
Kekee Munzil,
B.J. Road,
Bandra, Bombay.

You). Her vision is an inclusive one; she was a natural fellow-traveller for the Gandhys.

An inclusive India to which we were all heir was non-negotiable to the Gandhys and they fought to restore normalcy to a city that seemed to have run mad at the end of 1992 and the beginning of 1993. Julio Ribeiro, who was one of the seagreen incorruptible policemen of another era, was one of their fellow workers at the time. He had retired but the force of his personality could still make itself felt and he joined the Governor's Peace Committee. (This was the time when governors of states actually felt responsible for calming communal tensions.) Ribeiro joined the Indian Police Service in 1953 and was Commissioner of Police, Mumbai, between 1982 to 1985. He was promoted to Director General of Central Reserve Police Force, then to Director General Police of Gujarat. He runs two NGOs now: the Public Concern for Governance Trust and the Mohalla Committees.

He first met Kekoo Gandhy in 1958 when he was in charge of Parbhani District in Marathwada. 'There were two Parsi brothers, Soli and Phiroze Parakh. Phiroze lived in Parbhani itself; Soli in Sailu, a sub-division of Parbhani. In 1959, I got married and Soli, who was also a bachelor decided to tie the knot in the same year. He married Kekoo Gandhy's younger sister. Kekoo was also the cousin of my classmate, Dara Gandhy.'

Kekoo and he did not cross paths when Ribeiro was Deputy Commissioner of Police but Ribeiro does remember meeting him as Commissioner of Police. 'When the riots broke out in Bombay, I was in Romania as ambassador. I returned to Bombay in the last week of December 1993. It was in February 1994, that Kekoo phoned me. He asked me to come to Kumaram, the home of Rajmohan Gandhi, who was deeply involved with the Moral Re-Armament Movement. His flat was often used as transit accommodation for international guests. There I met Sushobha Barve[42], a Hindu and a Brahmin. I had heard of her work, she had gone into the slums of Dharavi and tried to bring about some reconciliation and some healing there. She was an MRA worker and very active in the movement. Kekoo was by that time a little older but he was active in trying to protect the Muslims. Sushobha Barve had started mohalla committees and Kekoo was attending them; so was Khorshed. He was particularly interested in Behrampada which had a large Muslim population. When there was a big fire there, Kekoo immediately rushed to the spot. He also gave them monetary aid.'

•

Meher Pestonji is another of those Bombay people who has worked tirelessly for the city of our common imagining. I remember the tenacity with which she covered the Justice BN Srikrishna Commission, tasked with investigating the Mumbai riots, for a daily newspaper, turning in a report every week that the Commission sat. She too had an old association with the Gandhys.

'Kekoo would encourage me quite a lot and pushed me forward. Perhaps there was some sense of the Parsi connection because he introduced me to many of the luminaries of the community, or at least, the important people, like Rustom Jeejeebhoy. He was very encouraging, very supportive and tried to get me involved in all his schemes and plans. He was deeply involved with many causes, not just the art world and perhaps that is why I grew to like him. He tried to get me to work with the Bombay Civic Trust.

'I got to know Khorshed as well. They were both regulars at all my parties; and with them, Dara Gandhy would also come along. Kekoo also encouraged me to come along to the Moral Re-Armament. This was around the time that the communal build-up was beginning. He had a long-standing association with them. I had heard of the MRA of course, in college. There were some performances, I think, and I attended some, but these were things we flitted in and out of. Kekoo and Khorshed suggested I come with them to

Panchgani and I had a wonderful weekend there; it is a very beautiful centre. But I was not interested in that kind of thing. Sushobha Barve was also part of the MRA and did some great work during the riots.

'Governor C Subramaniam had a Peace Committee and I was on it with Alyque Padamsee, Shabana Azmi, Kekoo Gandhy. Shabana asked for a curfew pass because the city was under curfew. She wanted to go into the slums to work. I asked, "Can I tag along?" And so Shehnaaz Sheikh, the feminist activist, one of the founder members of Awaaz-e Niswaan, who was staying with me at the time, Suma Josson, a journalist, poet and filmmaker, and I went with her and those visits were some of the most intense experiences of my life. We began with Madanpura, then Dharavi and on to Govandi, Mankhurd and Jogeshwari.

'Khorshed was worried about the effect on the children. She decided that it would be a good idea to have an art camp for them. We went into Behrampada with a whole load of paper, colour pencils, felt pens, that sort of thing. On a wall there, we found this slogan had been painted by what looked like a young hand, "Don't hait me" it said. Khorshed wondered aloud at what this painter had meant. I thought he might have done something and was asking for forgiveness. But equally there was the possibility that he might have been the victim of violence and this was a plea.

'The two-day workshop broke our hearts. The children painted and painted but they only wanted black and red. They ignored the blues and greens and yellows; those bright colours that children love had been wiped out of their minds. They used so much black and red that we ran out. But that was all they wanted and so we sent out for more black and red paint.

'There were meetings afterwards at the Worli MRA hostel. People would come there, activists, concerned citizens, some politicians, to discuss matters. Kekoo was always present; Khorshed would come sometimes.

'Kekoo also played a vital role in the mohalla peace committees. Julio

Ribeiro, Satish Sahney and local people from the areas all took part. Kekoo was not very vocal at these. He took a backseat and it seemed sometimes as if he were dozing. But when discussions got heated, he would suddenly open his eyes and say something that would act as an icebreaker. Everyone would start laughing and we could resume discussions again. I don't think it would be any use to remember what he said; it was the way he said it that was unique to him. I think it also was because everyone in the room knew that it was said without agenda, that he was speaking for some ideal of the common good which he held to be central to our work there.'

Rajni Bakshi adds, 'Kekoo struck me as one of the nicest people I had ever met. He was a kindly man and felt strongly about the values we were espousing but he would not froth at the mouth about what was happening. Perhaps he did have moments when he was upset but I never saw them. I only saw someone who represented the best in common humanity, basic human decency, kindness to strangers. That was who he was. The other thing that I must say: I never got the feeling that Kekoo was an activist or worked alongside activists because he was an ethnic minority. He was doing it because this was what he believed in.'

Rashna Gandhy also traces this back to his work as a Rotarian. 'As a Rotarian, he did a lot of community work. That was where he began to get involved with Behrampada. When the area flooded during the rainy season, drains would fill up and infectious diseases would spread. When Kekoo heard of this, he would get the Rotarians to bring the doctors, go to the Municipality and pester them to clear the drains. We used to call him Bandra *ka dada* [The Boss of Bandra]. When the Sea Rock Hotel was coming up, he heard that the dhobis were protesting for they washed their clothes on the rocks, there was a sweet water spring there. He took up this cause and he would go to the MLA, the police, to the political parties, to everyone. In his quest, he became single-minded and he would use whoever he could. We would sometimes ask: how can you make friends with a person from *that* political party? He would say: "They're also human beings. We must learn to get on with everyone."

'That was why I think he could play such an important role in the 1992/'93 riots, mediating between the police, the army, the people. He knew them all, he had known them all, he had nurtured his relationships with them; he had kept his social network strong. When the mohalla committee was started, Kekee Manzil became its meeting place. I did attend a few of the meetings, Muslim rep, Hindu rep, MLA, Police Commissioner, they would all be here and everybody knew Kekoo and could talk to him even if they couldn't talk to each other.'

This was Kekoo's finest hour. He did not seem to be motivated by anything except his belief that we all belonged and that every citizen was important. But this was not just Kekoo-in-the-moment; it was who he was.

'I see my father as representing the Hermes archetype[43],' Rashna says. 'He could deal with the highest and the lowest. We had a sweeper who would look after our road in Bandra. Papa used to chat with him in the morning when he went for his walk. When he retired from his job, the Municipal Corporation was having a farewell to which he invited Papa. Of course, Papa went. He couldn't find parking so he sent the driver off. There was a stage and speeches and the local Member of the Legislative Assembly was expected to make a speech. But he didn't show up, so Papa was garlanded and taken to the podium and he used the occasion to make a fiery speech and protested about how it was amchi Mumbai, how terrible it was that people from other parts of India could not see it as their home. He demanded to know who these people thought they were, denying Indians their rights. Everyone was applauding and he was happy: he had turned it into a medium for his message. The sweeper was so overwhelmed, he brought Papa home in an auto and then Papa invited him for lunch. The man was a bit embarrassed but Papa was having none of it. "I was your guest there. Now you are my guest here," he said.'

Sidharth Bhatia, long-time friend, who has been watching the city develop for decades, says, 'I do not think either he or Khorshed ever thought of what they were doing as something they could milk, as something from which they could gain social capital in any form. They did what they thought was needed to make their world a better place. I believe they also wanted to distance themselves from social and political dirt; but this did not mean that they would not get involved. They would look for a clean alternative and they would push for it, throw their energies into this clean alternative and try their best. This was their commitment to their moment and to the kind of nation they thought we should be building.' (For another example of how Kekoo could turn a private event into a public one, and even a movement, see Part Two.)

•

The last word should be Julio Ribeiro's: 'Kekoo Gandhy was earnest about bringing about a change in society and was eager to help in whatever way he could. He was God's good man.'

• 08 •

Kekoo and the National Gallery of Modern Art, Mumbai

'Till the Fifties, C J Hall was the city's premier location for concerts, political meetings and art activities but fell into disuse after the construction of Jehangir Art Gallery and air-conditioned auditoriums like Tejpal, Birla and Patkar Halls which had better acoustics and lighting. Neglect led to deterioration and in the Sixties and Seventies it would be hired out for boxing matches, trade union meetings, wedding receptions and discount sales of leather goods and readymade garments.

The artist community, led by the eminent sculptor, Pilloo Pochkhanawala and the doyen of art, Kekoo Gandhy, protested against the deterioration from culture to bazaar resulted in the decision to convert the hall into a museum for contemporary art.'[44]

—Quoted verbatim from the website of the National Gallery of Modern Art, Mumbai.

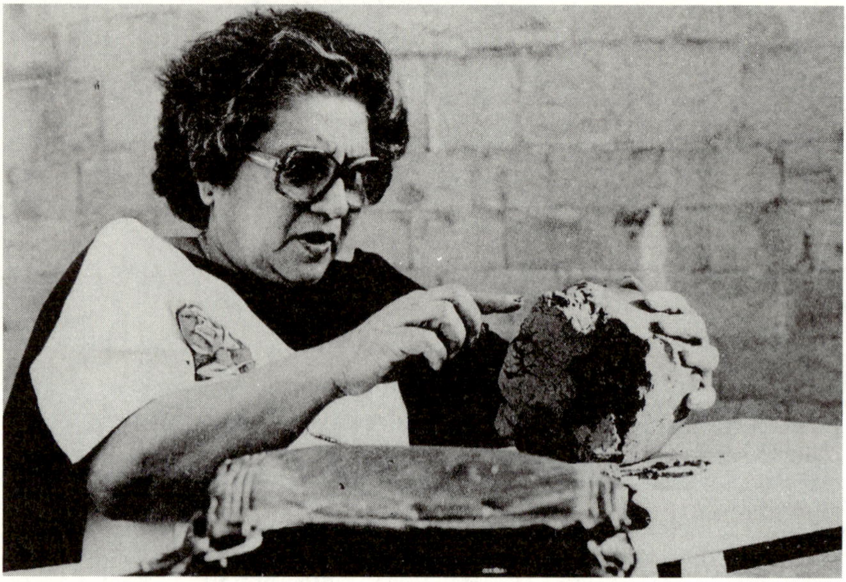

Pilloo Pochkhanawala

Ever since I have known him, Kekoo Gandhy believed that Bombay was the epicenter of the modern art movement. I greeted this pronouncement with incredulity when I first heard it, then I came to believe it cautiously and now I think it has a grain of truth in it.

A very large grain.

In the 1950s, Bombay was the Dreamnagri of artistic experiment, the Mayaville of cosmopolitanism so much so that the Urdu poet Kaifi Azmi referred to it as the Temple of Arts[45]. If you are the kind of Marxist who believes that art is the handmaiden of capital and draws nourishment from places where it gathers in excess, where else but Bombay? If you are a socialist and believe that art flourishes in community, think of the Progressives, think of the Bombay Group, think of the communes that both sustained and constrained the Progressive Writers, think of Akbar Padamsee's experiments in Worli, think of the Vakil Sisters, Hilla and Dossan Vakil and their Three Arts Circle, think of the Poetry Circle, Bombay, that ran for ten years on volunteered energy and the need for poets to be able to hear themselves in the cacophony of the city, and the shorter-lived Poetry by the Bay; think of Prithvi Theatre and Sanjna Kapoor and Sameera Iyengar's Junoon which ran for nine years, bringing artistic passions to the city, think of Bhulabhai Desai Institute and the Walchand Terrace and finally the Chabildas School in Dadar, think of Meher Pestonji's Wednesday terrace hub and Kamala Das's Bahutantrika, which she described as a club of sorts, Gopal Dutia's film society Anandam to which everyone in the intellectual community seemed to belong. Prabhakar Barwe's paintings might have been dreamscapes but he found the time to conduct a study group, Astitva, that met at the Milk Bar between the Elphinstone College and the Institute of Sciences which included the likes of painters like Lalitha Lajmi and Prabhakar Kolte. Nissim Ezekiel made The PEN All-India Centre a place to discuss the world and the arts, and lassoing in the USIS across the street for events, think of *Chauraha* at the National Centre for the Performing Arts co-authored by theatre doyenne Vijaya Mehta and the poet Arundhathi Subramaniam, think of Parmesh Shahani and his experiments at the Godrej India Culture Lab, Vikhroli, think of Adil Jussawalla's Tuesday poetry readings at Loquations, think of the resuscitation of the Chhatrapati Shivaji Maharaj Vastu Sangralaya by Sabyasachi Mukherjee and the Bhau Daji Lad Museum by Tasneem Mehta, think of how Satyadev Dubey catalysed modern Indian theatre by demanding autocratically that plays be translated, think of the Maharashtra Mitra Mandal Library in Bandra run by Vibha Kamat, Vaishali Shinde and Sonal Bimal who turned an empty space into a vibrant community centre...This is not an attempt to make a case for Bombay's exceptionalism. But contrary to the clichés about the city, it does have spaces for art; they are hard-won; they often do not last long; they take some finding but they are there.

If you look closely at any of the above, you will see the figure of a private citizen, working at doing something, contributing in some way, organizing or getting people together. Institutional support is much more hard to come by since governments all over the world are not particularly comfortable with criticism and art without a political critique, a connect to the now, can become sterile.

It should be well-known now that we have a National Gallery of Modern Art in Bombay because of the devoted work of the sculptor Pilloo Pochkhanawala and Kekoo Gandhy. With Adi Davierwala, Pilloo was one of India's most important sculptors. (As with most things that should be well-known, it is not. Pilloo's work, pioneering, electric, abstract and powerful, has been forgotten as has her commitment to the arts.) She was, of course, related to the Gandhys; she was Khorshed's first cousin. Her career began on a trip to England, where, she told S Vasudev, as she walked around the art galleries, the sculpture seemed to speak to her. She came back to India and took some lessons from NG Pansare, whose most famous work is perhaps the equestrian statue of Chhatrapati Shivaji Maharaj at Shivaji Park. Soon, she would move to working with other materials and with other forms. Her house was an adda for the arts; the poet Arvind Krishna Mehrotra remembers visiting it and hearing Adil Jussawalla's poetry there for the first time; it was being read out by Nissim Ezekiel[46]. Pilloo believed that Bombay deserved a National Art Gallery and a Bombay Arts Festival.

After she died, Kekoo became a one-man army who waged war for the dream they shared. Perhaps that was because no one else could believe that you could get your city a National Gallery simply by pushing away at a reluctant bureaucracy and an uninterested government. But there was no stopping him. Whenever I met him, he would urge me to support the cause of the National Gallery of Modern Art, adding often that it had also been Pilloo Pochkhanawala's dream. He would bemoan the fact that such a beautiful and architecturally interesting building as the Sir Cowasji Jehangir Hall was being used for marriages and other functions. He would point me to the Jehangir Art Gallery across the road and tell me the story of its birth and how it made perfect sense for the NGMA to be there, thus turning the whole area into an art district, with the Prince of Wales Museum (as it was then known) and its famous Ragamala collection (many pieces donated by his friend Karl Khandalavala), its magnificent sculptures just across the road.

Then he would suggest that the area be pedestrianized so as to create a hub of art and quiet in the noise of the city. It did not matter in the least that at the time this was the heart of commercial Bombay, where bankers and bureaucrats rewrote our histories. He could see a National Gallery and simultaneously bull-headed and dreamy-eyed, he was going to get one for his city. (Today, his plan seems a lot more doable. The city's epicentre has moved away to the north and South Bombay is beginning to look like it could be pedestrianized without too much difficulty.)

When his daughter Rashna had lived in Switzerland, he would visit and track down the buyers of his old friends, the Progressives, many of them businessmen who had worked for Swiss companies in Bombay, and try to persuade them to gift the paintings back to the country of their origin. Often he came away with promises—that a painting would be left in a will—but ever the optimist, Kekoo was undaunted. Now Rashna had moved to Delhi and so he made her home the base for his campaign for the NGMA.

'When he came to Delhi, he would use Rashna as his secretary,' says Bernard Imhasly who by this time had moved from diplomacy to journalism and had been posted to India.

Rashna nods. 'He was hellbent on getting Bombay a National Gallery of Modern Art. He had worked on everyone, on the heirs of Cowasji Jehangir; and on the Parsi Panchayat and he had got the building turned over to the Maharashtra Government. Then they said they didn't have the money to convert it into a gallery so he began a lonely fight for the money. For fourteen years, he waged this battle, between two cities, all at his own expense. I remember picking up the phone once and the voice on the other side said, "I'm speaking from the Prime Minister's Office. May I speak to Shri Kekoo Gandhy, please?" This was during Atal Bihari Vajpayee's tenure as prime minister. When I asked Papa what the call was about, he said he had written to the Prime Minister's Office about the National Gallery and given our number for them to call back.'

'He would knock and knock and keep on knocking,' says Bernard. 'Most other men would have given up, saying "This is like banging my head against a wall" but not Kekoo. He was the kind of person who would break down the wall at the risk of his head.'

This can be seen as an extension of his drive to make sure Indian art found a place in the international sun. In 1966, he went to London and stayed there for six months for the Commonwealth Art Exhibition, 'overstretching myself on all fronts. I neglected my factory and gallery in Bombay, to ensure that Indian art got proper representation...'[47] You know that when BC Sanyal, secretary of the Lalit Kala Akademi, New Delhi, writes in the brochure: 'I wish to take this opportunity to offer our sincere thanks to Mr Keku [sic] Gandhy, for the numerous responsibilities undertaken by him on behalf of the Akademi, but for whose unstinted cooperation this exhibition would not have been possible,' you know this is not mere boilerplate.

•

Pinakin Patel, the Alibaug-based designer, art collector and friend of the family says: 'Kekoo was the one-man crusade who made the National Gallery for Modern Art happen in Mumbai. He spent his own money to fly to Delhi. He worked at it for fifteen years and it is a crying shame that there isn't even a plaque in that building to commemorate the work he did to make it happen. It didn't just happen, Kekoo made it happen.'

But as importantly, Patel believes Kekoo was not power hungry. 'I think Kekoo was such an effective gallerist because he never wanted to be the king.

He wanted to create institutions, he saw the need for them, he saw how these spaces were needed if Indian art was to grow but he had no desire to dominate them.'

The painter Mehlli Gobhai sat on its board for several years. He remembers that through the time Kekoo was pushing for the National Gallery in Mumbai, he did not seem to have a personal agenda, a personal ambition. 'I never got the feeling that he thought of himself as running the National Gallery of Modern Art; though he probably saw himself advising it and having all his advice taken. Perhaps he even dreamed of it as a stage that would be larger than Chemould and unconstrained by the women in his family.'

By the time the National Gallery of Modern Art was coming close to becoming a reality, Kekoo probably knew himself too well to know that a formal role could straitjacket him. Far better to be loosely attached, a gadfly, an advisor. He also certainly had ideas about who should run the NGMA. And when Saryu Doshi was announced as the gallery's first director, Kekoo made no bones about telling his friends about his disappointment. But there was a bit of history to this.

Mulk Raj Anand was an old friend of Kekoo Gandhy. One of the earliest articles in *Marg* was a piece by Kekoo Gandhy on the proper way to frame pictures. He wrote, 'The frame should enhance...the picture, without overpowering the subject. It should act as a sort of impresario, the picture always remaining the star performer, whether it be an original Botticelli or a Gaugin print.'

When Saryu Doshi was brought in, Dr Anand resigned and left the magazine. This may have affected Kekoo's response to her selection as the first director of the NGMA for he was nothing if not a loyal friend. He contended that she was a specialist, an academic and had no real connection with modern art. But he was also the kind of man who could change his mind when confronted with the evidence.

For Kekoo evinced a paternal interest in the early stages of the workings of the NGMA. He would drop in every morning, intent on ensuring that nothing went wrong. Saryu Doshi says, 'Within a few weeks, however, his initial fears about me as director of NGMA were dispelled. In fact, he found our discussions stimulating and concurred with me in the manner in which I organised and curated every exhibition—its concept and display. He stood by me and supported each one of the projects with enthusiasm and creative suggestions. For me, he was my *guru* and I benefitted from his vast experience in the field of Indian modern art.'

Doshi continues: 'Mine was an honorary post; I valued my freedom and my family life too much to accept a salary that would tie me down to government regulations.'

Perhaps, it was this voluntarism that helped or it was Saryu's openness to ideas and innovations. She has nothing but praise for him in this phase when he would drive in with either his daughter or his wife, and then spend hours at the gallery interacting with the various members of the staff.

Everyone was invited to the party that was the National Gallery of Modern Art. One of these was Roshan Kalapesi, daughter of the man who invented the chemical recipe for the taste of Mangola, old MRA hand, and one-time manager of the Chemould Framing Shop at Princess Street.

Pinakin Patel remembers the Paramparik Karigar show at the NGMA. 'Kekoo called me in to design the show. There he introduced me to Roshan Kalapesi, that meant one teacher took me to another. In doing that show, in sitting with the craftsmen and understanding what they were doing and what they would be bringing to the show, I learned so much about tribal arts and crafts.

'But all that we did, we did without hype, without histrionics. We did our work with the quiet assurance that things would happen, that the show would matter. So what happened in those times didn't just happen because

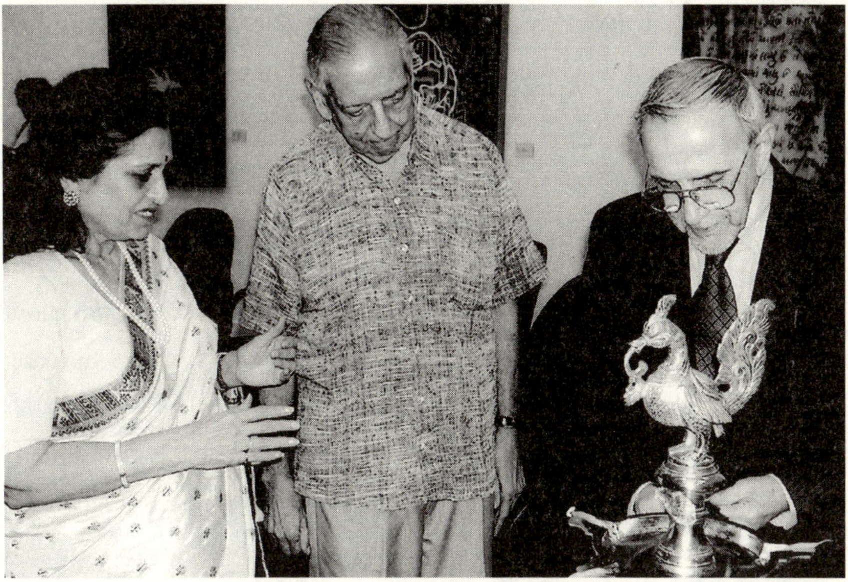

A dream takes shape: (l to r) Saryu Doshi, Kekoo Gandhy and Ebrahim Alkazi at the NGMA, Mumbai.

of the people; it also happened because of the settings in which we worked and in the times. There were no agendas, there were no hidden political ramifications. So much has changed today; I don't know what of all that could happen now.

'Dashrath Patel's retrospective came to Mumbai. I went to see it and was deeply moved by his art, by his concerns, by his commitment and his contributions to India. Kekoo was also very angry that Dashrathbhai Patel was ignored, that the younger lot had no time for him or for his work. I remember collectors saying they weren't interested because it was paper and it would not last forever and they were interested in posterity. As if they would live to see posterity. I wanted to say: an artwork will change your life in the here and now. It will give you almost all it has to give you in the first four years of your life with it. It will feed your soul now; why are you worried about what happens when you're dead?

'Dashrathbhai and I began to talk and within six months, he had moved into my house in Alibaug. Kekoo and Khorshed would visit as we were planning the museum for him and the conversations would be lovely because I was learning and I was laughing at the same time. It was all so rich, so much larger than life. So much information, so many ideas, some were so magnificent, some were grandiose: what is China, we can defeat China at any time, that kind of thing. It was all about design and it was about world domination too. But that was Kekoo, he was not capable of thinking in miniature.

'Today when we have access to so much information, when we can verify so many things, we seem to have reduced the scale of our dreams. They were dreamers, they were thinkers and they did not allow the thought of failure to terrify them into paralysis. They went ahead and did what they dreamt and thought.'

• 09 •

Chemould and Non-Traditional Art Forms

The monsoon in Mumbai is part of the city's myth and legend; it is also a mixed blessing. Coming after the terrible humidity of summer, the first showers are greeted with delight; children dance in the street and the minds of adults turn to chai and pakoras; perhaps even to the joys of Raga Malhar. But it is also culturally speaking a dead time for the city. You could choose to hold 'an event' but you know you are running the risk of it being washed out, literally. Your lead speaker might end up stranded at the airport, your interlocutor stuck in a water-logged part of the city but worst of all your audience might stick its nose out of the window and think, 'Better not.'

For the art galleries of Mumbai, this has always been a challenging season. For many years Gallery Chemould had a Monsoon Show which was meant as a launch pad for younger artists or for those who were out for the first time. Then in 1979, Khorshed Gandhy began to use the season to host tribal and folk art shows. Karin Zitzewitz records that the first exhibition was 'of Kalamkari paintings, the centrepiece of which was a single large painting. MF Husain, to Khorshed's delight, bought the large work and posed for a picture in front of it with the Kalamkari artist, J Gurappa Chetty of Srikalahasti. Later on Khorshed asked Gurappa what he thought of Husain buying his painting, and the artist shyly admitted that he had no idea who Husain was.'[48]

There was likely to be ignorance across the spectrum from contemporary modern artist to folk and tribal artists. With only a few exceptions, artists lived in cities; the tribal artists lived away from the city. They were supposed to. Because the most important criterion for judging a work of tribal art is not aesthetic, it is biographic-ethnographic. The question is: Is it 'authentic'?

This is a word that has haunted art practice in every sphere and it has often been used without much thought as if there were ever anything 'pure' about art. However, the word persists and one source of its danger lies in the patent desire of its users to create pigeonholes and to confine artists to them. And when we talk of 'tribal art', we are often guilty of othering. We want our tribals to conform to the notion of the noble savage; we want them to be untutored and unlettered geniuses; we want them to be silent producers of the material we would like to take from its setting and into ours.

How much of an 'authentic' tribal life can a tribal of today lead? When you put a tribal artwork on the wall of an air-conditioned gallery in a city that has been built by systematically erasing a tribal past, how far from its home is it? When it is acquired by an industrialist who might be trying to acquire tribal land to exploit its mineral resources, how authentic is his response to the work he now surveys as he sips his single malt and plans his next assault on some bauxite-rich hill?

There are no easy answers to these questions. Because we have not worked out these questions with care, the interface between the art world and the tribal artist can often end in tragedy as it did with Jangarh Singh Shyam.

For those who came in late, Jangarh Singh Shyam was a Pardhan Gond. This means that he was a tribal but what he created was uniquely his; it was not, while he was alive, shared by the community. It is now known as Jangarh kalam (literally, the Jangarh pen) which came to be read as the Jangarh style.

A group of talent scouts from the Bharat Bhavan is said to have discovered him by seeing a mural he had painted on his hut. The painter J Swaminathan took the young Jangarh under his wing and brought him to Bhopal and found him a job at the Bharat Bhavan where it has been argued he developed into the painter the world knows and loves. His work was the opening show and he went from strength to strength. Eventually, he was invited abroad and did two residencies at the Mithila Museum in Japan.

It was during the second one, in 2001, that he hanged himself, at the age of 39.

We don't know why.

One of his collectors, Mitchell Crites, talks about his friend who painted the devis of the Gond forest and who wondered aloud if they would come after him for he had not taken their permission to depict them.[49] Or was it simply that Jangarh Singh Shyam was depressed? That he was far away from home? Far away from the objects and memories Jyotindra Jain talks about which fuelled his painting? Was it precipitated by his stint at the Mithila Museum? Was it the loneliness of the adivasi in another culture, being turned into the prize exhibit? Was it a personal thing, as Jain argues? Was it because of a lifetime of slights, of being asked to take off your shirt when a photographer wanted to make a picture of a tribal painter—how could a tribal painter wear a shirt and 'look tribal'?[50]

We will never know. Nor do we look at Jangarh Singh Shyam's works as clues in the way we would examine Van Gogh's last paintings before his 'suicide' or the poems in Sylvia Plath's *Ariel.* Whenever I hear Jangarh's paintings being discussed, they are seen as if they simply happened. This is not an argument for biographical criticism; it is only an observation that our lens is very different when we look at the tribal artist.

But what we do know is that the tribal artist is invaluable to us and to our art. Many modern and contemporary urban artists have used them as resources. I am not suggesting that this is plagiarism or even co-optation. It is what artists do. All over the world. They take what they need and they reuse it. Picasso takes an African mask and makes it his own, Van Gogh raids Japanese prints for his motifs; Atul Dodiya finds inspiration in Bollywood posters, Manu Parekh reworks Leonardo da Vinci's *The Last Supper.* [51]

But here's a question. Would we extend the same courtesy to the tribal artist? If a tribal artist were suddenly to want to deploy some varietal of abstract expressionism, say, would it be 'authentic' enough for us? I was once at an exhibition of Jangarh Kalam and someone asked Bhajju Shyam, one of the best known of today's Jangarh Kalam painters, whether he used traditional materials.

'Yes,' said the artist briefly.

'And what are those materials?' the young man asked, hoping no doubt for some esoteric weeds and roots and stones.

'Rotring pens,' said Shyam.[52]

Tribal art is a part of the archive, part of our visual memory, part of how we experience ourselves. It is invaluable to us as a resource until it comes to paying for their work. Then something in us turns cheap and it is difficult for us to take tribal art as seriously as its city-bred and Anglophone counterpart. (Of course, art has no language. If you believe that, *ce n'est pas une pipe.*)

The urban/e Indian artist also looked at tribal art as a resource. Perhaps this was occasioned by the post-colonial predicament of locating oil painting. Was it an import from the West? Were those patrons who had been so central to the experience of the Progressives and modernism merely part of the colonial project, an expansion of the Neo-Company School? How was the notion of canvas and oil to be integrated into our experience of the making of pictures? Remember Dr Moti Chandra's remarks on the art of the Progressives?

Tribal art, assumed to be unfettered by notions of a viewers' gaze, unrestrained by market demands, already imbued by notions of the sacred and the occult so dear to the Abstractionists, was a ready source of material. The forms were also startlingly 'modernist'. Consider Warli art's reduction of the human form to its basic shapes. Here you have the triangles, the circles and the lines of the cubists.

Flattening the plane of the painted space? Tribal art had been there and done that.

Simultaneity of perspective? Tick.

Sacred geometry? Tick.

The human figure as mnemonic? Tick

No wonder a painter like Mehlli Gobhai was in awe of the tribal artist. 'It's more than awe,' he said to me as we looked through his collection of tribal art, which included some Warli work as well. 'It borders on terror. It seems sometimes as if modern art is reinventing the wheel simply because it was born in the city and most of us didn't see enough tribal art when we should have.'

But while tribal art was welcome, the tribal artist was a peripheral and shadowy figure. His or her work was anonymous, and that was part of its allure. It lived outside time, and that made it even better as a resource to be mined.

•

In some ways, there has always been an organic link between the Parsis of Bombay and the tribal communities of the Western region. It is possible to see some elements of this in Gieve Patel's 2008 masterpiece, *Mister Behram,* a play in which the eponymous Parsi lawyer adopts a tribal boy, Nanu, who becomes a lawyer as well, marries his benefactor's daughter and at the beginning of the play seems to be the perfect Galatea to Mr Behram's Pygmalion. However, in a key scene, it is revealed that the old stereotypes are never far from the surface in the head of the benefactor. Mr Behram asks Nanu to strip down and appear in his tribal 'costume' and to move a heavy cupboard to demonstrate his strength. It is a startling scene both for its homoerotic content and for its revelation about the politics of our encounter with the tribal Other. Nanu may be a lawyer who speaks English and has even married Mr Behram's daughter; but he will always be, at some level, the tribal of the magnificent physique; he will always replay some version of the myth of the Noble Savage in the head of his putative father.

It was this encounter that the Gandhys rewrote in their association with the Warlis. I like to think it was the belief that they might be the people who would try to rewrite that old script that drew someone like Bhaskar Kulkarni (1930-1983) to them. Kulkarni seems to have been a brother-in-spirit to Kekoo.

He was 'an unparalleled guy,' the artist Manu Parekh who was a close friend of Kulkarni, says. 'He joined the Weavers' Service Centre[53] about a week after I joined. I was immediately impressed. He was a total vagabond. He had travelled all over India on a bicycle and seemed to know everything and have a fund of stories about everyone.'

Then there was a famine in Bihar and Pupul Jayakar asked Bhaskar Kulkarni to go there and see what could be done. 'He said it was a terrible situation. He had to walk over dead bodies to get from place to place,' Manu Parekh remembers. 'And there in two villages called Jitwarpur and Ranti, he found that women painted on mud walls, in a style that he thought was magnificent. And so he pinned paper on to the walls, and got them to paint on that and brought them back with him.'

Manu Parekh and others saw these and were immediately impressed. You owe that Madhubani on your wall to that moment.

•

Kulkarni built long-lasting relationships with the artists. It was he who in a way 'discovered' Warli art and Jivya Soma Mashe (1934-2018), its most famous exponent. He set up house next to him and lived there, digging in deep to understand not just the art but the way of life from which it had emerged.

'Once Bhaskar Kulkarni took me and the poet Arun Kolatkar off to the interior of Maharashtra, into the tribal belt,' Manu Parekh continues. 'I don't remember where it was exactly but it was somewhere after Karjat-Kasara. It was a Warli festival and as night fell thousands arrived to dance in a circle. They danced all night and we watched all night until the first rays of the sun cracked the dark shell of the night and they began to leave for their villages. Bhaskar had thousands of photographs of Warli paintings...'

A network throws up its own energy and new ideas. The Gandhys were in contact with Swaminathan and the atmosphere of Chemould would make it a pitstop for someone like Kulkarni. No one remembers when he first blew into the gallery but he was soon a fixture. Khorshed says it was he who took her to her first Warli village and introduced her to the art form which they did as murals on their walls. Just as Chemould would build familial relationships with the artists, they would also work with the tribal artist.

And when Jivya Soma Mashe came with an extraordinary and somewhat ground-breaking piece of work, Khorshed formed the idea that she needed to do something more than a show.

She told the story to Jayati Vora of *Man's World* magazine: 'One day Jivya's son brought a whole lot of paintings to the gallery. I saw one painting which was distinctly different. You know, the general style tends to be a little repetitive—sowing, reaping, dance, village life.

'So I said, hello, what's this? He told me this story, which was like a myth. This was startlingly different, so I said, "Keep it aside. This painting is not to be sold." And the next time I went to the village, I took it along. I told Jivya, there must be other myths and legends. Make me other paintings like this.

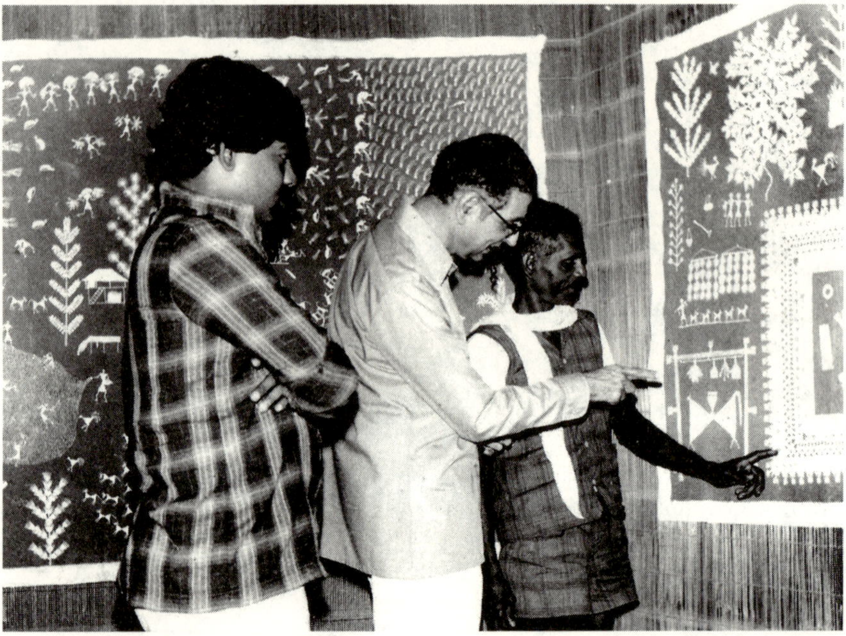

***At home in the city:** Jivya Soma Mashe with Kekoo Gandhy at his solo exhibition at Gallery Chemould, 1975*

'The whole concept of their painting changed once they started thinking about myths and legends. Within 10-15 days, Sadashiv, his son, brought a whole roll of paintings to the gallery. They were so excited; they had begun that very night. I said, "I can't sell off these paintings; then they will be gone, and no one will know these stories." So then I thought, "Why not have a book?" That was when I started Chemould Publications as a trust, not knowing it was so expensive. Warlis danced at the show, and people were clamouring for the paintings. I had to, I was obliged to sell a couple of them, and I sent the rest as a donation to the Craft Museum at Delhi.'

The book is called *The Warlis: Tribal Paintings and Legends* by Jivya Soma Mashe and Balu Mashe. No record exists of Pupul Jayakar's speech at the inauguration but the poet Nissim Ezekiel reviewed the event:

> Chemould has also printed greeting cards, reproducing a number of Warli tribal paintings, commissioned for the purpose. Sales of these will support the Bombay Civic Trust in its rural employment schemes. The cooperation of Bombay Rotary Club and Air India has been obtained for the sale of these cards in many parts of the world, through the network of Rotary Clubs. Also involved is the Society for Folk Arts Preservation in New York.
>
> The exhibition is enjoyable and the cause it represents may be supported without conceding the exaggerated claims sometimes made for their artistic weight and significance. Mrs Pupul Jayakar tends to do this, glorifying the culture which produced it as being "uncorrupted by knowledge." This seems to imply that the Warlis would be well advised to remain uncorrupted in their idyllic rural setting, perpetually poor and cut off from the rest of the world so that they may endlessly demonstrate their "creative powers for our benefit". That is not, in my view, the message of the exhibition.[54]

The legends were retold by Lakshmi Lal, an art critic who would go on to publish books about art and about religion in general. (In an odd way, this, her first book, would bring both preoccupations together: the aesthetic and the sacred.)

'I would often go to their art gallery and once there was a show of Warli art on. I think I bought a painting and gave it as a gift to someone. Jivya was sitting there and in the course of the conversation, I learned that they lived not very far from the city. I decided that I would like to see these paintings in situ as well so I went out there. And there, I learned that some of the paintings told a story.[55] I told Khorshed this and she said, "If you will write the stories, we can do a book." I had a Canadian friend, Stan Walsh, who was visiting India and he said he would design the book. I was so excited, I forgot to ask Chemould to pay me. But when the book came out, I was delighted.'

The preface to the book states that Khorshed was the President of a newly constituted society, the Chemould Publications Trust, formed specifically for this endeavour and registered under The Indian Societies Act. This was only natural, for 'This was where Khorshed took the lead,' says Bernard Imhasly, 'Kekoo accepted that as far as tribal art went Khorshed was the expert and he followed her lead.'

The preface says: 'It is a trust formed expressly for the promotion, through publications, of Indian contemporary and folk art. *The Warlis—Paintings and Legends* is our first book, a companion volume to a special exhibition of paintings by Jivya Soma Mashe, the celebrated tribal painter, and his son Balu Mashe.'

By this time, Jivya had had some taste of international fame as well. His paintings had been exhibited at a special presentation at the Biennale de Menton, France, in 1976; at the Institute of Papua New Guinea Studies, Port Moresby in 1977 and at the Festival of India in Britain in 1982 and he had already had three successful exhibitions at Gallery Chemould.

The Gandhys and the Mashes shared a lifelong friendship and both sides benefited equally from it. Kekoo was once asked: 'Would you agree that the promoters of Warli art are party to the exploitation of the Warli artists?'

His reply: 'There are a number of Warli artists now who have become well-known. Particularly because this tribal art form is appreciated all over the world and many people want to be promoters for that very reason. We (at Gallery Chemould) deal with Jivya Soma Mashe and his son Balu Mashe with whom the Warli phenomenon began. We are concerned with their promotion only and my answer to your question will be in relation to that.

'When these artists bring their work, they demand a price which we pay

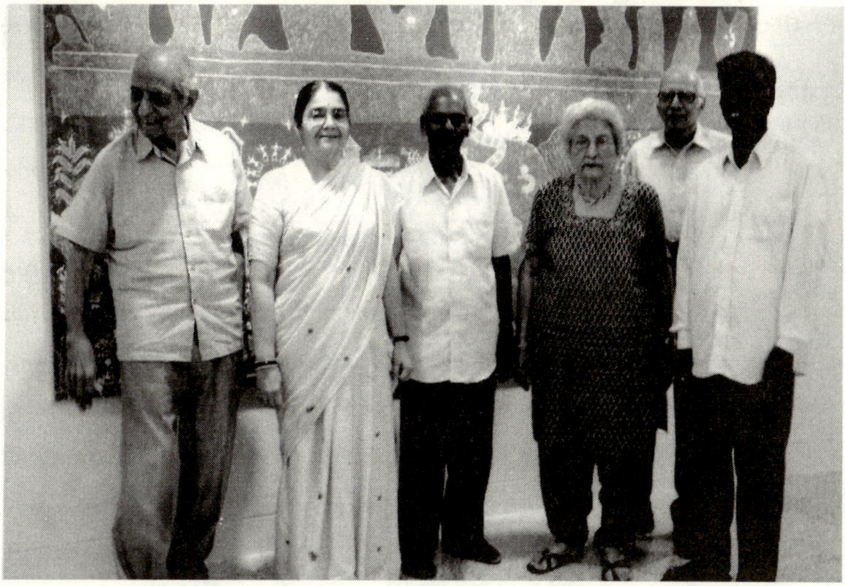

Farewell Exhibition of Gallery Chemould, 2007: (l to r) Kekoo Gandhy, Sita Setalvad, Jivya Soma Mashe, Khorshed Gandhy and Balu Mashe

them. Later, the selling price is fixed taking into consideration the promotional costs involved which are immense. We not only hold exhibitions (which is a temptation since we run a gallery) but we have brought out a book of the Warli paintings. By this we avoided the damage done to the paintings while they were being transported from one exhibition to another. We stopped ourselves from indulging in that.

'Our relations with the Warli artists are friendly and not business-like. We don't disturb their normal routine life or demand anything out of them. Whenever they have something to sell they come to us. They even have an accountant who handles the financial aspect very well on his own. We help the artists in all other ways that we can. Like, we built a well on Jivya's request in their village with funds from Bomanji Wadia Trust. In fact, we are not party to any exploitation.

'Let me tell you that this form has caught on worldwide because it is not in the tradition of the Indian art as it is generally known to be. These

Warli paintings fit into any modern or contemporary ambience. They have a particular sensibility which they communicate. The public and the private sectors should collaborate to promote this art form without self-interest, because trade follows culture and such wealth of folk art is nowhere existent in the world, except in India and Mexico.'[56]

Afterwards, the British-born artist Richard Long would come to live in the village with Jivya and create art out of sand and ash and the footsteps of children which would travel the world. It would be shown in Padiglione d'Arte Contemporanea, Milano and in Dusseldorf.

Towards the end of their lives, Khorshed and Kekoo were housebound by the increasing frailty of their bodies. 'One day, Jivya and his son Balu came by to the house,' Shireen Gandhy remembers. 'I think they were saying their farewells. They didn't say much; it isn't the Warli way to talk much. They just came and sat there. All four of them sat out on the verandah in silence and thought back over the years, to the book and to those shows, to the phone calls and those conversations, to the roads travelled and not travelled.'

•

Besides Kalamkari and Warli art, there was also Khovar and Sohrai painting which was done by the tribal women of Hazaribagh. The existence of these paintings was brought to the attention of Bulu Imam, a researcher and activist who worked in the area. His father was Indian and his mother was French and it is said that he got his name Bulu from the fact that he had blue eyes. In 1996, he brought khovar and sohrai paintings to the city.

The term 'khovar' comes from the word 'kho' or cave, and 'var' or bridal couple, he explained. These were the paintings done when a woman got married; the women of her family and her female friends got together and painted the marital bedchamber with images that were rich with suggestions of fertility and reproduction: animals suckling their young, trees laden with fruit. He told journalist Gunvanthi Balaram: 'It is an overflowing stream of symbols, designs and images which are connected both to the prehistoric rock art of the Hazaribagh region as well as to local folklore. The style changes subtly from village to village and is thus a mosaic of the area's rich tribal heritage.'[57]

Sohrai was an art form that was practised during the harvest when a wall would be layered with dark mud and then covered with a thin layer of white. After this was dry, a sharp instrument, sometimes a hair comb, would be used to scrape the white and show the dark mud underneath.

'"Soh" means closing and "rai" means stick. It means herding the cattle into a stable and shutting the door with a stick. These paintings are done on the day after Diwali and are symbolic of the domestication of cattle. The colours are red, black and white,'[58] he told the press.

Another clipping noted: 'Animals are brought into an enclosure, bathed and decorated with corn in their ears followed by a bullfight the next day symbolising their capture from the forest. Suprisingly sohrai images are not of goats, sheep or buffaloes but of snakes, wild boar and tiger, using the same techniques and pigments as the khovar works.'[59]

The show, at Gallery Chemould, was rendered even more urgent by the degradation of the area in which the art was produced. Indiscriminate mining was threatening the Karanpura Valley which was home to many caves which contained Mesolithic paintings.

Imam believed that the art bore a resemblance to the 'characters of the Indus Script. Further research can perhaps open doors to the past which is currently locked up in the as-yet-undeciphered script of the Indus Valley Civilisation.'[60]

Imam was also concerned about the possibility of commercialising the art form: 'We do not want to commercialise the art form, as has happened in the case of Warli and Madhubani paintings,' the activist stresses. 'The idea is not to turn tribal artists into businessmen, but to sustain their sense of pride in their art and culture.'

•

Santokba, the Gujarati self-taught artist from a village near the Gir Forest, was another regular at Gallery Chemould. Meher Pestonji remembers the first time she saw Santokba: 'My marriage ended in 1975; I began to work as a trainee journalist in 1976 and began to become aware of Kekoo Gandhy. He was the only Parsi I knew in those days who wore a kurta; the other male Parsis of my acquaintance were corporate types, they were all suited-booted-tie-wallahs. I didn't have the courage to talk to him although I saw him often at the Samovar, where we would often have lunch. I was at the *Eve's Weekly* at the time, the office was somewhere near Lion's Gate and we'd walk down to lunch sometimes and then to the galleries. One day, I saw a tribal woman sitting cross-legged on the watchman's seat. He did not seem to mind much nor did he ask her to get up. Then a car drew up and Kekoo got out and greeted her warmly and began to chat to her. Then he took her up to Chemould. Intrigued, I followed, for no reason other than a journalist's curiosity. That's how I got to know Kekoo. This was Santokba Premjibhai Dudhat.'

Santokba discovered painting through her son, the painter Bhanu Dudhat, who told art critic and curator Georgina Maddox[61] that his mother's artistic roots lay in her embroidery.

"My mother learned how to embroider before she started painting. It's a tradition that the women of Saurashtra engage in. However transferring that skill to paper was her own initiative.'

He brought her to the city to see his work at an exhibition, he says, and she took one look and decided that this was something she would like to do.

Meher Pestonji interviewed Santokba who said that her family had once been rich and she had worn gold earrings so heavy that they had distended her ears. But their land was mistakenly confiscated during Partition.

Santokba was widowed young and left with four children. She married her daughter off, sent two sons to an ashram and kept the youngest with her. She worked as an agricultural labourer and when that was unavailable, as a road construction worker. In the evenings, after a day in the sun, she would mix kaajal with cowdung and paint on cloth; then she would embroider the material and sell it to the wealthier farmers of the area.

Her son Bhano wanted to study fine art at Baroda University, writes Pestonji:[62]

> 'It did not occur to her that he could be taught a profession more lucrative than art. As he saw how much effort went into paying for his education, he resolved to make it up to her. In 1976, on his first visit to Bombay after graduation, he insisted on bringing her. "I wanted the satisfaction of showing her Bombay before she died," he says simply. "Then in 1980, I took her on a pilgrimage to holy places of north India. We hired a Matador van and the whole family went. We saw Hardwar, Rishikesh, Banaras, my mother had never thought she would see these places in this lifetime. Even I was surprised at how devout she became, how much it meant to her."
>
> 'It was during the visit to Bombay that Santokba entered an art gallery for the first time, and it changed her life completely. "An artist called B Prabha was having an exhibition," she recalls. "I thought she is also a woman like me, if she can have an exhibition, why can't I? So I went to Ram Chatterjee who was in charge of the gallery and asked if I could hold an exhibition and he said yes, but the gallery is booked till next year. So I booked the gallery for a future date. Then I had to go back and learn how to paint."

> 'KG Subramanyan was her son's professor. When Bhanu showed him some of Santokba's sketches, he realised in her he had a promising student. In 1977, Santokba painted on paper for the first time.[63] Under the tutelage of Subramanyan and Bhanu, she learnt to draw the human figure in all its moods and postures. Animal figures came to her naturally because of her familiarity with Gir animals. She prefers using natural colouring agents to paint. Black is obtained by combining kajal, cowdung and oil; yellow ochre comes from haldi; and blue from crushing the pulp of a wild berry. Synthetic paints are used but minimally. In December 1977, she had her first show in Baroda and her sponsor was none other than KG Subramanyan himself.'

Santokba's masterwork is the 1,200-meter painting of *The Mahabharata.* It was, it seems, a challenge to herself as much as a challenge to Lord Yama, the god of death. It was shown in the Jawaharlal Nehru Birth Anniversary Celebrations in 1991. She was ninety-three at the time of the exhibition and was still at it, though she now had her son and daughter-in-law fill in the colours under her supervision. The work was still as lively, and as vibrant, full of colour and light.

Like so many other painters, she was not appreciated during her lifetime. Meher Pestonji recalls, 'When Santokba came to Bombay, she would visit me at home. We grew to be friends. Ulli Beier[64] was the only person who seemed interested in her work at the time. He bought a lot of it. I remember her leaving wads of paintings with me in Bombay and over the years, I gave them away as gifts to friends. Now Shireen tells me they are worth quite a lot.'

•

In the absence of a complete list of exhibitions, it is difficult to say whether these represent the totality of Chemould's interactions with the tribal and folk artist. There was a handicrafts shop for a while. Rashna Imhasly remembers: 'My mother had what she called the "Art Shop" that was for many years run by Geeta Chakravarti, in the room behind the Gallery where my mother used to personally collect the most beautiful bedspreads and crafts from her travels around the country. I had the opportunity of travelling with her to Gujarat. The women used to come out of their village houses and spread their bedspreads, shawls and other handicrafts for sale. It was a memorable experience as there were no hotels in those days and we used to sleep on the charpoys of the villagers in their courtyards.'

In 1990, Gallery Chemould closed its handicrafts shop to repurpose the space for a wing that would sell watercolours and graphic works.

•

I did ask whether Shireen thought that this aspect of the gallery was at an end.

'I hope not,' she sighed.

• 10 •

Khorshed's Last Hurrah

'Khorshed never did anything without a committee,' Shireen Gandhy said to me in passing once and I remember thinking that it was an old-fashioned word, an old-fashioned idea. Perhaps this was because we had just come out of a meeting to plan the retrospective of an artist friend, Mehlli Gobhai, and we had taken to calling ourselves Team Gobhai. The idea was to draw on the hive mind of the group: Shireen Gandhy as gallerist; Ranjit Hoskote and Nancy Adajania as the curators and experts on his art; Sheetal Gattani and me as friends of the painter. (Needless to say roles overlap, Ranjit and Nancy and Shireen were also Mehlli's friends.)

But the principle of the committee was pretty much the same; you brought people in; you used their skills and knowledge; you wove a web of contacts and contracts to support your project; you offered the positive reinforcement of association with the project which becomes a group effort. But you always need someone at the centre, making things happen, the holder of the dream.

I believe that is what happened in the case of the Bombay Arts Festival of 1987 which the Gandhys seem to have put together in memory of Pilloo Pochkhanawala; she had been taken by cancer a year earlier. The artist Nalini Malani says, 'My relationship with the Gandhy family and the gallery

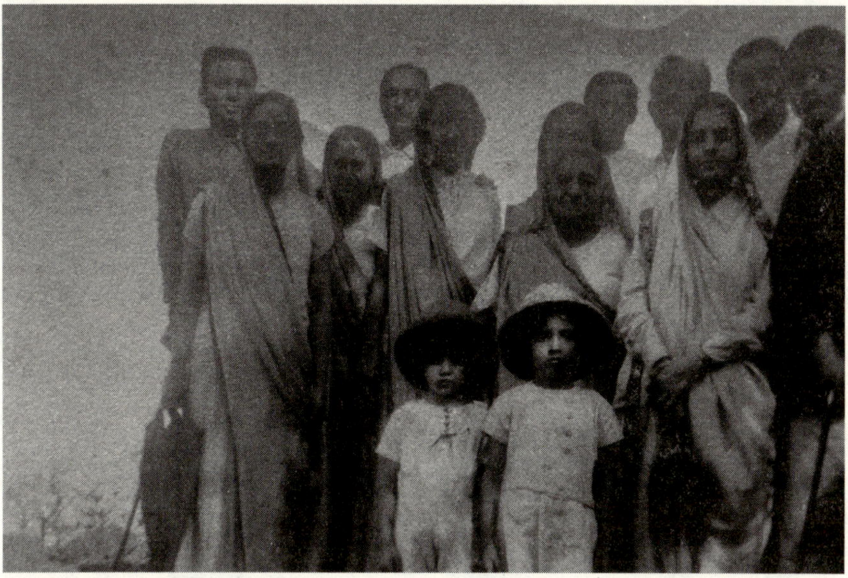

Childhood friends: Young Khorshed Gandhy and Pilloo Pochkhanawala (l to r, front row, standing) with the Adenwalla family members

began through my friendship with Pilloo Pochkhanawala. Pilloo and I met in 1966 at the Bhulabhai Memorial Institute when she wanted to organise the Bombay Arts Festival. She believed the city deserved an arts festival and that it should be an annual event. [That it was not repeated was due to financial constraints.] This grew into a close friendship, and she helped me a lot between 1980 and 1985 trying to find funding for my project of an all-India exhibition of women artists. Unfortunately our combined letters for financial support addressed to different Indian Government institutions of culture were not granted. Luckily a smaller four-woman version of this exhibition was realised in the late 1980s. In this same period Pilloo included me in her project that she was leading with Kekoo Gandhy, to convert the Cowasji Jehangir Hall into the National Gallery of Modern Art. We had several brainstorming sessions and I helped with the paperwork.

'In that same period, again through Pilloo, I came into a closer relationship with Khorshed Gandhy in the early 1980s. At that time, I was showing with

Pundole Art Gallery (Kekoo Gandhy and Kali Pundole seemed to have a wonderful rapport going between the two of them). When Pilloo passed away in 1986, I contacted Khorshed, whom I knew much better by that time, and proposed that we pay homage to Pilloo by organizing another Bombay Arts Festival. Khorshed, being Khorshed, embraced this plan. With the help of several people spread over many disciplines we organised theatre plays, the visual arts show, music evenings and poetry sessions. Chemould became the hub, where we made the plans and held all meetings, and it was Khorshed and her staff that helped make it happen. I for my part took over, what they would call nowadays the curatorial part of the sculpture exhibition called *The Sculpted Image*. This was a huge all-India sculpture exhibition that included eighty-five works, with Pilloo's works as the focal point. *The Sculpted Image* was the first exhibition that took place at the Nehru Centre even before it was completely ready.'

The Bombay Arts Festival brought together pieces of sculpture from Pilloo Pochkhanawala, Adi Davierwala and Meera Mukherjee through N Rimzon, Himmat Shah to Pushpamala N; film (curated by noted film scholar Ashish Rajadhyaksha), poetry (curated by Nissim Ezekiel), theatre (curated by Bhadrakant Zaveri and Toni Patel) and Indian classical music (no curator is listed so Khorshed Gandhy must have been in charge). It must have been a huge undertaking and if you think of doing this without instant communications, without email and WhatsApp and text messaging and mobile phones, it must have required ten times the work that 'Portrait of a Community', a magnificent show of the Parsis in paint, which opened to the public in 2004, almost thirty years later, took.

For this one, the afflatus was Khorshed's. Shireen Gandhy tells the origin story of the show: 'My mother would go to agiaries and sit there and not pay attention to the prayers much. I believe she was a deeply spiritual person but she was also the kind who was impatient with ritual. So one day she was sitting at some prayer service or the other and began to look around and it struck her that there were an immense number of paintings in the agiaries which only the Zoroastrian faithful would ever see. Some of these were genuine art treasures, for instance, one of the agiaries of the city has a portrait by [Manchershaw Fakirjee] Pithawalla.[65] She was also interested in the Parsi painters of the Pithawalla generation and suddenly she thought it would be possible to have a show in which this art could tell the story of the community, a history of the Parsis in India through art.'

Once again, something of this size and of this importance would need a suitably large space. Thanks to Kekoo such a space was now available: the National Gallery of Modern Art. The next step was, of course, a committee. For this Khorshed drew from her friends and from her wide circle of acquaintances but she also knew when she needed expert assistance. The paintings were there, the people were there, the funding would certainly be made available but she also needed an expert curatorial hand. Khorshed found that curator in Priya Maholay as she was then known.

At this point, I should allow Dr Priya Maholay-Jaradi, as she is now known, art historian based at the National University of Singapore, to tell her part of the story:

> 'I had completed my Master's in History of Art and Archaeology at the School of Oriental and African Studies (SOAS), University of London in 2001. I wrote in to Marg Publications for a possible job as research assistant. Radhika Sabavala at *Marg* informed me about an exhibition project titled "Portrait of a Community" which was in the making in Mumbai city and connected me with a committee member, the energetic and elegant Saker Mistri. Immediately upon my return to Mumbai in September 2001, I met with Saker

and founding member of the Committee, Khorshed Gandhy, to see how I could fit into this project. As it turned out, the Committee had been meeting for two years with several ideas for the proposed exhibition. Khorshed and Saker were of the opinion that it was about time they found a project manager and research assistant to tie the various threads related to sourcing artworks, display and research to take the project forward. I was hired to take on these various roles and eventually also became co-curator of this landmark show at the NGMA, Mumbai (2002). This was the beginning of a memorable journey with two remarkable people, Khorshed and Kekoo, whose lives not only contributed to the world of art production, circulation and reception as is widely documented, but whose thoughtful ways and strong ideologies touched many lives outside of the art fraternity.

Stories from the Making of Portrait of a Community

'The "Portrait of a Community" project was not born within a specific institutional context. It was not driven by full-time museum employees nor was there a full-time exhibition team and hence the project worked on ad-hoc appointments of independent specialists from time to time. All of us engaged in the project worked out of a range of spaces which were offered by the committee members: Godrej Bhavan, Gallery Chemould, the Gandhys' residence at Kekee Manzil, Saker's residence at Napeansea Road and the Sir Jamsetjee Jejeebhoy School premises.

'A longlist of desired paintings and photographs from private residences and fire temples in Mumbai and Pune was drawn up. As we pored over these lists to scrutinize the artistic and historical merit of these works, Khorshed surprised me with her impeccable memory as she stored away entire lists and the characteristic feature of every artwork in her personal memory chip. Instead of turning to excel sheets, hardcopies and CDs, one could simply turn to her to retrieve information and minutiae from the big data of this exhibition project. Such was her deep engagement with this show.

'We began working on the content and production of the exhibition catalogue. Khorshed drafted the Foreword and requested Saker and me to edit the piece. That afternoon, I sat in the office space at Gallery Chemould to "clean up" Khorshed's Foreword. Rupal Shah, who has worked at Chemould for over a decade, now sat beside me and said, "You may not need to edit the piece after all. I read Shireen's writing all the time for production-related matters. I can tell you that Shireen and Khorshed have that rare gift of being able to write beautifully and to the point. Their choice of words is perfect and irreplaceable." Rupal was spot on. Neither Saker nor I needed to revise or readjust Khorshed's elegant text. Khorshed displayed remarkable aptitude for colour-proofing, layout and design matters between our trips to Burjor Poonawalla's Comart Lithographers in Dadar and Dhun Cordo's design studio in Mahim. Her long experience and critical engagement with visual cultures was obvious during these discussions.

'Since the NGMA was the exhibition venue, the staff was engaged for the final installation and mounting of the exhibition. Closer to the installation date, Saker suggested how useful it would be to engage Pinakin Patel for display ideas. Pinakin accepted the invitation and graciously stepped in to offer his expertise. Between Saker, Khorshed, Pinakin and myself, i.e., the core installation committee, there were academic, socio-historic and aesthetic considerations. We were often divided on the placement of paintings and each of us came up with a supporting rationale to present our case. In the middle of this, Zarifuddin Khan who served the NGMA as the master installer came up with the same question each day for over a week: "Priyaji, *in sab mein,* curator *kaun hain? Agar aap bataa degi ki hum kiski baat sune, to* easy *ho jayegaa* (!)". [Priyaji, could you please tell me who the curator is of this exhibition? If you tell me whom to listen to it would make work easy!] While Saker and Khorshed tried to placate what could be Khansahib's wrath on some days and plain anxiety at other times, Kekoo displayed his naughty streak as he maintained a single, unwavering response, "Khansahib, you should listen to Priya, *woh thoda* time *ke baad* NGMA *ka* director *banegaa*". [Khansahib, you should listen to Priya; in a little while, she will become the director of the NGMA.] One realised in due course that what appeared to be Kekoo's fanciful world was in reality a route to visualize ideologies and ethics which he thought should drive institutional contexts. Both Khorshed and Kekoo had immense faith in young talent and advocated an inclusive order at the workplace. They treated me as an equal in this complex, multi-layered project. Without their openness to new ideas, I would have never become co-curator of that historic show.

'One evening, our joint curatorial decision was to place a large painting weighing several kilos on the topmost, rotunda level of the gallery. From the time of its opening as a space for modern and contemporary art in 1996 to the POC exhibition in 2002, NGMA had not witnessed an artwork of that weight and volume. As a result, Khan and team were at a complete loss as to how to carry the artwork to the topmost space. The ever-resourceful Pinakin and our man-Friday, Kekoo's cousin, Dara Gandhy, got down to solving this problem. The next morning, Pinakin and Dara were outside the gates of NGMA; they walked up and down the street and across to Regal Cinema and in a while were back with a team of about ten *mathadis* (loaders) who typically wait for the next odd job to come their way for the day. Within an hour the mathadis had secured the work with ropes and other contraptions and lugged the work to the top! As I watched, part happy at the problem being fixed and part embarrassed for not being able to follow the best practices and standards laid out in museum guidelines to handle artworks, Khan directed the mathadis to me for their remuneration. Before I could respond, Khorshed, Kekoo and Dara had organised small covers with their *baksheesh.* The mathadis had never received compensation with as much respect whereby the notes were arranged in little envelopes. As they left the premises, they told us to look out for them should there be more *chitras* (paintings) and *tasveers* (portraits) to be carried up. Kekoo saw them off to the gate and kept offering his salaams reverently.

'The remaining weeks at the NGMA were busy. Visitors of all age groups and diverse registers of the population came to view this exhibition of portraits which had been brought out of private homes and agiaries for the very first time for public viewing. Many of us from the core team contributed to conducting guided tours for members of the public. While Khorshed was unable to offer tours to large visitor groups, she would reserve her energies for walking special guests, friends, film-makers and journalists around. Her tours would begin with facts and figures about the exhibition, its underlying ideas and motivations and then she would gradually navigate the guests through select paintings. It was a delight for Saker and me to watch Khorshed slip into anecdotal/biographical mode with an almost child-like glee each time she paused near the large Adenwalla family portrait, "Jerbai and Cowasji Dinshaw Adenwalla and family". "Can you believe that's me sitting on my grandfather's lap?" she would ask.

'The exhibition was de-installed and Khan and friends swung back into action, as did the mathadis. Every artwork was returned to its lender, often accompanied with personally-written "appreciation and thank you" notes from Khorshed. On the concluding day when we handed over the gallery space to the NGMA formally, once again, Khorshed and Kekoo organised *baksheesh*, this time for Khan and his team. The couple displayed an unmatched alertness and believed in rewarding people from every walk of life.

'A few months after POC, I got married. I shared snippets about my trousseau and shopping experiences with Khorshed. She learnt that I was trying my best to purchase sarees of different regional weaves. She pulled out an antique *gara* lace from her personal collection and went in search of a matching contemporary silk sari. I continue to drape this deep purple saree which holds within its gentle folds the memory of two brilliant, creative and empathetic people who touched my lives just as they touched and blessed several others.'

•

'The show was a huge success and it got grand reviews,' says Sam Maneckshaw, furniture designer and manufacturer, also the youngest member of the committee at the time. 'The opening was so crowded that people had to stand on the street outside.'

He turns over his copy of the eponymous souvenir, looking at the inscription by Khorshed dated 2002: 'To Sam, it was a great adventure and thanks for your wholehearted participation in this project.'

'My friend Kayaan Pundole was on the committee and when she heard what the basic outline of the show was, she said, "You have to have Sam on this committee" and that's how I got to be there.'

In an odd way, his journey was a little like Khorshed's. He had visited these fire temples and seen these paintings all his life. He had begun to experience the world of art but the connection between the two—that the agiary was a treasure trove and that some of these treasures needed to be displayed—came later.

'I knew where the Ravi Varmas were,' Maneckshaw says. 'Some of them were willing to lend; others weren't.' He turns the pages, surveys photographs some of which came from his own collection. 'But I think we got the best into the exhibition.'

•

Museum educator and children's author Saker Mistri was a friend of the family and she had known them for a while. Of course, she and her husband Mehli Mistri, had been invited to Panchgani to the Moral Re-Armament Centre.

'We said we would but we should like to go to our home in Pune and break journey there. We could spend the night and then move on to

Panchgani. This was a good thing because Kekoo was already in his seventies and he enjoyed telling us all about how the whole Chemould thing started but he would also doze off and slump on Mehli and fall fast asleep. Then a honk or a sudden swerve and he would wake up and start talking again without a break.

'That evening we had a good dinner with Kekoo talking us through it and then we went to bed. I thought I had everyone settled in for the night when I was roused by a sound and came out of the bedroom. There was Kekoo with a piece of bread in his hand, dabbing assiduously at a painting. He explained that this was a good way to clean an oil painting.[66] Anyway, we had a good weekend, and we saw a different side to Khorshed and Kekoo there.

'When she invited me to join the committee of the "Portrait of a Community", she must have already been in her eighties but I was amazed at her energy and enthusiasm. We used to have our meetings at the Parsi Panchayat Office and it was all quite a lot of fun. Kekoo would ramble on, Khorshed would cut him short with, "*Ave bas*" but this seemed almost like a pattern between them. There was no rancour, just an old understanding.

'Khorshed's energy was incredible. Once we had a meeting with Ayesha Soonawalla who was doing some graphic design for us and we had gone over to her house; the lift was not working. I knew that Khorshed had had a hip replaced but she was not going to be turned away by a lift! She simply climbed the stairs. She was a joy to work with; the exhibition might have been her idea but she would welcome ideas and suggestions. She could get along with any age group.

'I remember a shoot that was happening which involved Kekoo and Khorshed. Kekoo was supposed to come into the frame at some point and say something. He didn't get it right so he had to do it again and again. He never complained, he never suggested that he was the man who had made Gallery Chemould happen and should not be made to do these "retakes";

he just did as he was told. In some ways, he was a dreamer, a visionary; in other ways he was a loose cannon with a piece of bread in his hand; and in yet others way, he was a well-meaning blunderer with a fund of stories. You knew who Khorshed was immediately; she was gracious, she was generous, she was perfectly dressed. Kekoo? He could be a puzzle because he was often a bit casual about his dressing. He was a gentle maverick and so incredibly low key. If you think of all the people they knew—Mrs Pupul Jayakar, Dr Mulk Raj Anand, Ulli Beier, Rajmohan Gandhi—you would forgive them for name-dropping but they never did. Kekoo was quite happy to come to the NGMA and order an omelette sandwich and chat with whoever came in through the door. I think they were comfortable in themselves and that made them so accommodating of other people. They were incredibly gracious people, both of them so very nice.'

Like many of the members of the community.

('Portrait of a Community' was exhibited at the National Gallery of Modern Art, Mumbai in 2003.)

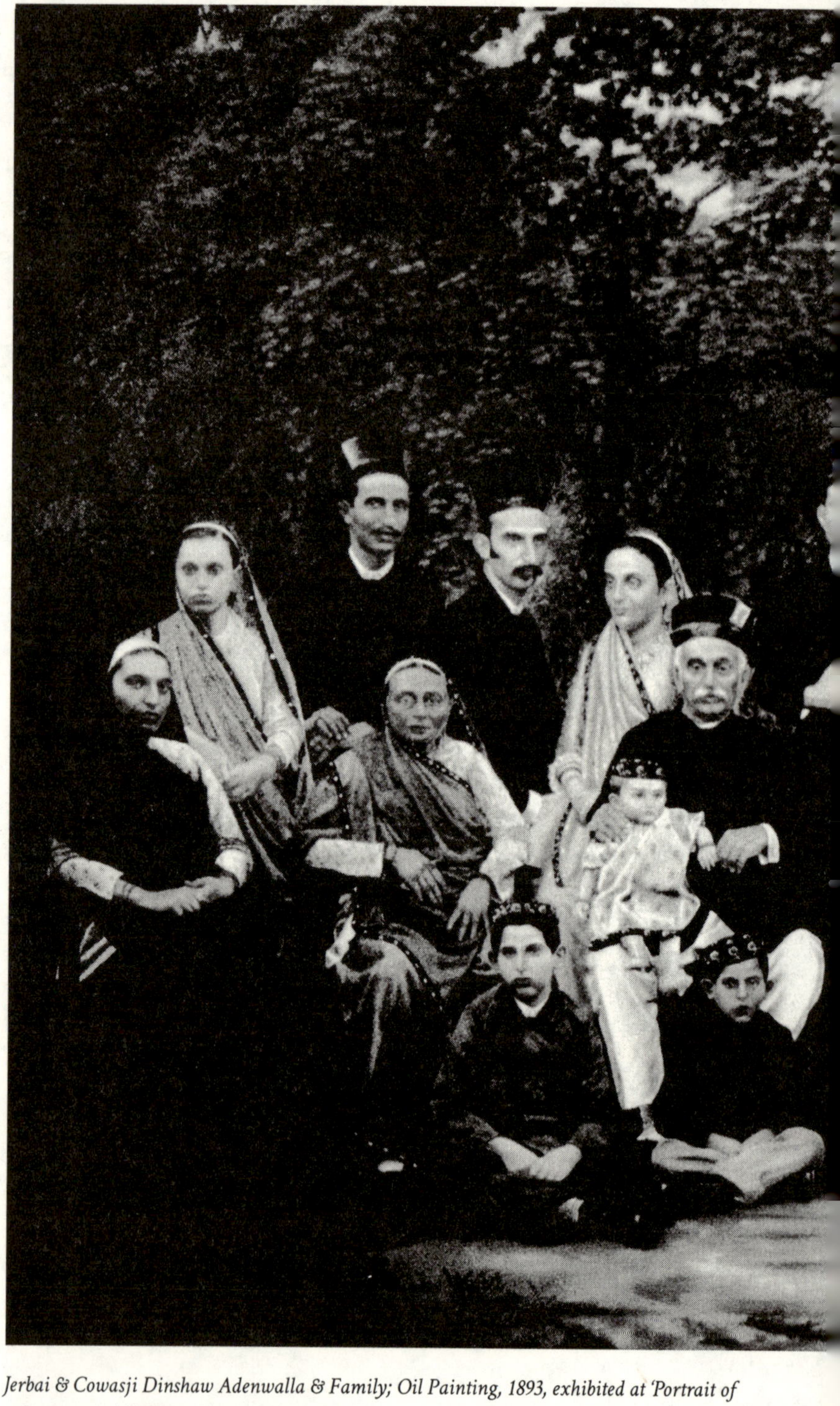

Jerbai & Cowasji Dinshaw Adenwalla & Family; Oil Painting, 1893, exhibited at 'Portrait of a Community', NGMA, Mumbai, 2003

Courtesy: Cowasji N. H. Dinshaw Adenwalla

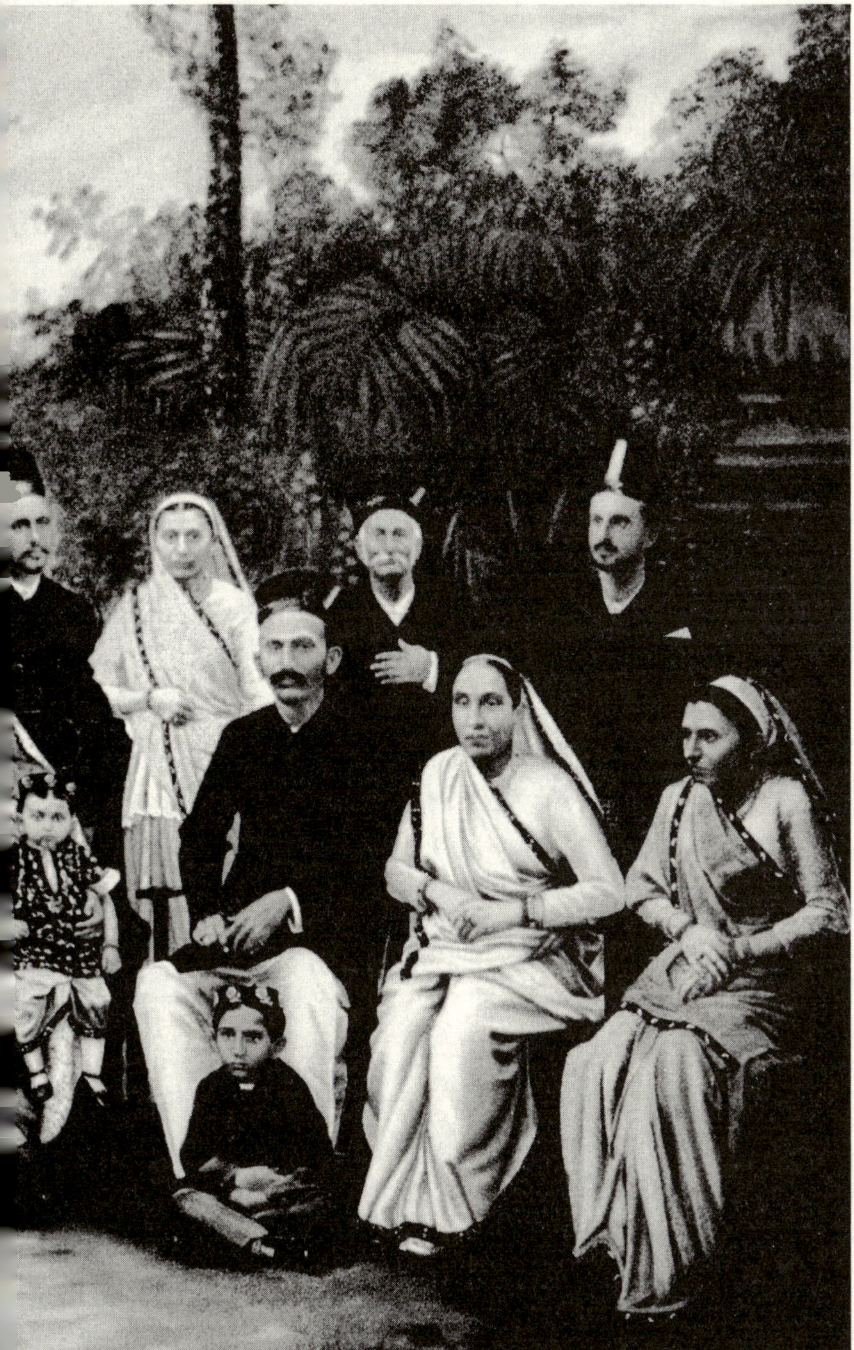

INTERLUDE

crossing generations: diVERGE: Forty Years of Gallery Chemould

It cannot have been very much after 'Portrait of a Community' closed that preparations for the next big show would have begun. For the next year in 2003, the Gandhys would take over the National Gallery of Modern Art for a show that commemorated forty years of the existence of Gallery Chemould.

At this remove, I remember a striking moment of contact, my second, with the Chemould archive. The first was when, as a college student, I climbed the steps of the Jehangir Art Gallery to visit Gallery Chemould. The walls were covered with posters, mostly graphic, generally the names of the painters. In a way, they were one of the many subliminal processes of canon-formation to which we are all subject. The second encounter was in 2003 with Vivan Sundaram's 'piece' in the rotunda of the NGMA. The work was exhibited in twelve large photo albums covered with yellow velvet on a twelve-foot-long table painted in blue. I remember thinking when I walked in: I should sit on one of those chairs and look through the albums. No one else was doing this because one is used to *not* sitting and generally *not* doing in museums and galleries. But then I thought: 'This is Gallery Chemould. This is Vivan Sundaram; they probably want me to sit here.' I sat down and was pleasantly surprised when there were no alarums and excursions. I opened the albums and began to look through the history of the gallery, the history of modern art in this city, as Tasneem Mehta puts it.

The past had been brought into the present in a tactile way. It was magic. When I left, there were two young people looking through the archive. I hoped they would not be the last.

The curators of this show were Chaitanya Sambrani and Geeta Kapur. Kapur had an old association with the gallery, which, she says, began in the 1960s 'with Kunika Chemould in Delhi (my home city). Richard Bartholomew who looked after the gallery in the early 1960s was in a sense a mentor; I later became close to Roshen Alkazi, who ran that gallery until the early 1970s. In the mid-60s, I began going to Bombay quite frequently—to see important exhibitions, to meet artists for my writing work, and for a high share of youthful vagabonding. Like everyone else, I hung out at Chemould and at Samovar in the Jehangir Art Gallery.'

The general modus of association between art critics and galleries in India is that the former write the catalogues for the shows of the latter. Kapur says that many of the artists she admired were showing with Chemould but she was 'a little reticent about gallery catalogues…But because of Chemould's specific history—Kekoo's participation in the Progressives movement, including the critics in the milieu, Mulk Raj Anand and Rudy von Leyden, I felt comfortable associating with this gallery—almost as if it were a supportive "public" art institution. In the same spirit, I also undertook some major projects with Chemould. This was later, in the 1990s, when Shireen, who had been studying in England, came back—a charming young Gandhy on the job. I remember her hanging a show dressed in a white shirt and long casual, stylish shorts!'

When Kapur was asked to be one of the curators of the first Johannesburg Biennale (1995), she chose to show four painters from India: Nalini Malani, Nilima Sheikh, Pushpamala N and Sheela Gowda. 'I

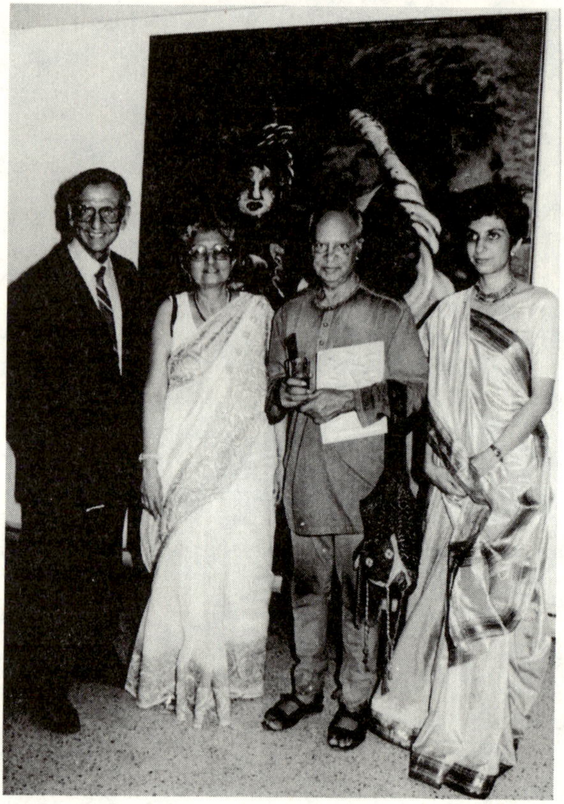

***Silver anniversary:** (l to r) Kekoo and Khorshed, Mulk Raj Anand and Shireen Gandhy at the opening of the exhibition 'Seventeen Indian Painters – Gallery Chemould's 25 Years at the Jehangir', 1988*

suggested that I work with young Shireen (exactly thirty at the time) seeking her/her gallery's collaboration to do the organizational work. This may have been one of Shireen's first international engagements—she could be called the Organizational Curator of the show. All four artists plus Shireen and I went to Johannesburg to mount the show and attend the grand opening and the seminar accompanying the Biennale, where I spoke.

'I worked with Chemould more directly in 2003. Kekoo and Khorshed were still active and engaged with the gallery affairs but Shireen was very much at the helm by this time. She asked me and Chaitanya Sambrani

GALLERY

Chemould

GALLERY CHEMOULD
1ST FLOOR, JEHANGIR ART GALLERY, BOMBAY-400 023 TEL: 244356

PRESS RELEASE

Gallery Chemould's 25 Years at the Jehangir

'Chemould' began as a frame factory over 4 decades ago during which the involvement in promotional activity in the fine arts followed. "Gallery Chemould" as its art division, celebrates 25 years of activity (1963-88) as a professional gallery in the premises of the Jehangir Art Gallery, with the exhibition - "17 Indian Painters". The show opens on 13th Sept. and will be inaugurated by Dr Mulk Raj Anand.

This exhibition offers a spectrum of some of the artists active on the contemporary Indian art scene. It includes senior established artists' like Raza, Tyeb Mehta, Veena Bhargava, Bhupen Khakhar, Paramjit Singh; leading members of the avant garde such as Barwe, Jogen Chowdhury, Laxman Shrestha, K. Laxma Goud, Vivan Sundaram and Prabhakar Kolte; as also the much talked about younger ones with their emerging talents, both from India and abroad - including Saleem Arif, Ranbir Singh Kaleka, Yusuf, Akhilesh, Vijay Shinde and Atul Dodiya.

In keeping with its tradition of fostering varied activities apart from exhibitions, a workshop has been organised in the duration of the current exhibition where school children will have an opportunity to discuss the works on display with some participating artists as well as doing spot paintings in the gallery. Prabhakar Kolte of the J. J. School of art, assisted by Shireen Gandhy of Gallery Chemould will conduct the workshop sessions.

Gallery Chemould hopes that these events will be a fitting celebration of its involvement with the contemporary art scene.

Press release announcing '17 Indian Painters' exhibition

to co-curate a show to celebrate forty years of Chemould's existence. We made a selection from all the generations of artists that Chemould had engaged with, added new and provocative artists and called the huge display at the new NGMA building: "crossing generations: diVERGE: Forty Years of Gallery Chemould". An exhibition spanning four generations of Indian artists curated by Geeta Kapur & Chaitanya Sambrani.'

That a commercial gallery should ask independent curators to conceive their anniversary show was a departure of sorts at the time.

'The curator as both a conceptual and a hands-on entity was familiar in the West from the late 1960s; the waters had been tested, so to speak, and even if they were chilly, everyone had grown used to that exhibitory navigation. Until the middle of the 1990s, the figure of the curator in India was absent, the designation barely existed. We used the more neutral term, "commissioner".'

Kapur remembers the storm that blew up when in 1994, she was asked to re-hang the collection of the NGMA Delhi, '...not to invite new work but just to change the displays of what they already had in the museum. I called myself a curator and conceived a two-part show. Taking up all the galleries of Jaipur House, I reconfigured the works in different ways. When the show opened, I was pilloried. There were caricatures of me in the papers and there were any number of attacks by the artists—on how presumptuous this entity of the curator was. I was rethinking history, the juxtapositions, and thereby unsettling some accepted lineages. That was considered a transgression.'

Kapur puts this down to the ambiguity of the role of the curator which challenges the privilege of the artist and the gallerist, introducing a third party into the relationship.

'When an institution, public or private, enters into a contract with a curator, the curator is supposed to be given the "authority" to select the artists and navigate the route between them and the institution. Artists are

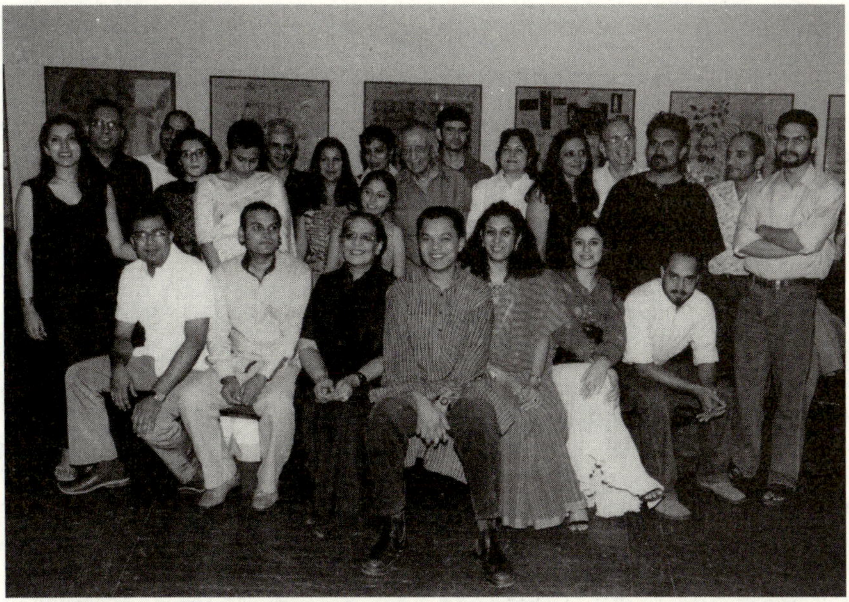

***Preview of crossing generations:** diVERGE, Forty Years of Gallery Chemould, NGMA, Bombay, 2003: (l to r, seated) Jitish Kallat, Subodh Gupta, Geeta Kapur, Chaitanya Sambrani, Shireen Gandhy, Hema Upadhyay, Riyas Komu; (l to r, standing) Reena Saini Kallat, Atul Dodiya, Sudarshan Shetty, Anju Dodiya, Sharmila Samant, Vivan Sundaram, Rupal Shah, Shilpa Gupta, Kekoo Gandhy, Tushar Joag, Shalini Sawhney, Pushpamala N, Sudhir Patwardhan, Gigi Scaria, NS Harsha, T.V. Santhosh*

often very sensitive to this intervening figure—the curator is seen as taking over the autonomy of the artist. It was only when the international art world came calling, when it sought to engage with Indian art, either to have shows or to acquire it for museums, or to set up auction houses here, that the curator became a commonplace of the art world. As it happens, now almost everyone is a curator and there are curators of hotel buffets and curators of fashion shows…But then today artists and curators have, by and large, made their peace. The base line is that artists know the artist/artwork is key to a show and the curator appreciates that the artwork *has* to be shown to its full advantage. There is of course a much more complex set of considerations way above this base line equation.'

Be that as it may Shireen asked and Geeta Kapur and Chaitanya Sambrani took up the challenge. 'The Chemould project took about a year and included fifty-one artists. We had many of the Chemould stars but we also had young artists, unknown ones, and Shireen (with Khorshed and Kekoo in the background but fully in the know) was with us every step of the way. She had not done anything as ambitious and she was happy to scale up her imagination and resources. And I believe that all three of us worked in a manner that was not over-conflictual! Chaitanya and I are very different people and difficult in different ways, expecting, demanding. The process was hard. You can plan something and think you have it down to the last sightline and then in the actual space it doesn't work. At every stage of the way, we had our panics but Shireen and the Chemould team was up to it. They were supportive, efficient and proud of what had been mounted on those semi-circular floors of the Bombay NGMA. When it was over, Shireen wasn't too weary of us; I know because we remained friends and because she asked me to curate the five shows that marked Fifty Years of Chemould (2013-2014).'

• 11 •

Dismounting from a Black Horse

'The variety of Kekoo's commitments, in particular, has lent colour to the gallery—often to the bemusement of the artist showing at the moment. Until the architecture of the gallery was altered, about eight years ago, and the parallel, not strictly art-related activities shifted to an adjoining room, the very first sight that greeted the unwary visitor to Chemould was a desk at which Kekoo convened his meetings with activists, petition-signers and committee-wallahs of every description. You might have come in expecting to spend a quiet half-hour in the company of some melancholy abstractionist works, but the group around the table would conscientise you to everything ranging from high dams through municipal corruption to the demand for a proper museum for contemporary art.

'It's an amusing tableau straight out of Jerome K Jerome: Kekoo encouraging one of his group of oddballs to express himself at length, nodding and generously simulating attention; Khorshed wearing the beatific smile of resignation; Shireen exasperated, but too busy with calls and (other) visitors and the next show, to be able to vent her wrath. And in the background, the artist with his plumb line and spirit level, insisting on just the right degree of light catching the top edge of the canvas, and could they do something about the dripping AC tube please?'

—**Ranjit Hoskote,**[67] poet and art critic

'In their own way, Khorshed and Kekoo were pioneers on many fronts and at many levels. Art openings in those days were not very exciting things: snacks, cutting the ribbon, some desultory conversation and everyone went home. They started this practice of having a contributory dinner somewhere in the area, at Pyrkes or George or one of those biryani places, and those could be boisterous affairs. Perhaps my memory of those times is coloured by nostalgia; perhaps it was that the stakes weren't so high and artists were peripheral; or it could be that we weren't working the system, mainly because there was no system to use. There might have been a few people who could help you and you might want to get to know those people but now you have to embrace the whole system and an artist must ask herself: how far do I want to go to do that?'

—**Meera Devidayal,** artist

Mehlli Gobhai loved to tell this story of the old Chemould, perched on the forehead of the Jehangir Art Gallery.

Shireen Gandhy at her desk.

A Sikh gentleman with some years on him wanders into the gallery. Gandhy pays him no heed; he is not the Gobhai buyer, no savant of the abstract, densely-worked, on-the-point-of-ignition canvases hanging on the walls. He is obviously a tourist, someone who has walked in from the Jehangir Art Gallery's more inclusive space, beneath. She does not notice, perhaps, that he is looking at the paintings, that something in them has him hooked.

He turns up at her desk.

'How much?' he asks gesturing at the work.

'Thirty,' she says, using the euphemism of an age that was unaccustomed to speaking about money, dropping the 'thousands'.

'And if I buy all of them?'

'Still thirty,' she says but she smiles.

'How much will it cost to ship them to Patiala?'

Shireen does a rough back-of-the-envelope calculation and comes up with a figure.

'Fifteen thousand,' she says.

The gentleman is perplexed.

'Thirty rupees for a painting and fifteen thousand rupees to send them?'

It was a guaranteed laugh, one in which we were coopted for as middle-class and bourgeois, we were all still uncomfortable talking about money, and would have been guilty of the same elisions, arising out of the same anxieties.

Many were the joys of the old Chemould. You could drop in unannounced and chat to Kekoo or Khorshed and later Shireen. Across the hall from Chemould, Pinakin Patel remembers, was The Homi Bhabha Library, from which you could borrow art magazines and even artworks. Others remember dropping by at Natesan's or having a bite to eat at Samovar and watching as plans were hatched by the denizens of the art world.

Khorshed would remember, for instance, the RK Laxman show, where the lines stretched down into the street and the doors had to be shut at six in order that the gallery might be closed and the staff might go home.

It was at this show that actor and theatre person Dolly Thakore bought a

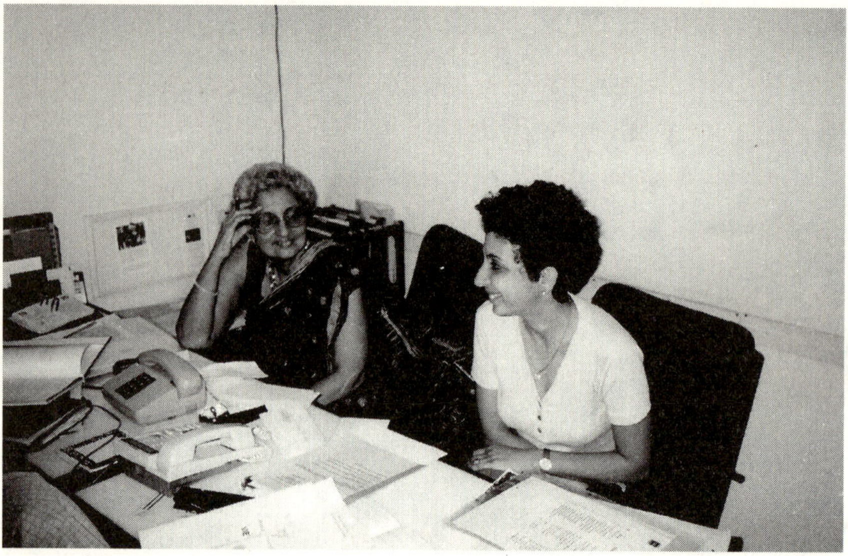

Working in tandem: *Khorshed and Shireen Gandhy sharing a desk at Gallery Chemould*

drawing of one of those iconic paper works of the city's crows by RK Laxman, better known as the cartoonist who invented The Common Man in his uncommon dhoti and checked coat: 'I bought a crow which was swooping down, wings splayed, beautiful in action, but when I brought it home, my son Quasar didn't like it. He must have been about seven or eight and he said: "I want a quiet crow". So I said okay, and I took him to the gallery and he told Mr Laxman what he wanted and Laxman, very sweetly said, "Okay then, I'll do a crow for you" and we got that crow.' The drawing has the corvine standing and looking over his back in a meditative moment. Dolly waves an expansive hand at the art collection that lines her walls: 'The best works on my walls are from Chemould...Vivan Sundaram, Ram Kumar, Shuva Prasanna...and the exquisite framing of canvases given to me by MF Husain and Anjolie Ela Menon...my walls whisper Chemould and Kekoo every day,' she says with a smile and a sigh.

The poet, dramatist and artist Gieve Patel remembers taking on the Jehangir Art Gallery with Kekoo. 'I did show with the Chemould Gallery

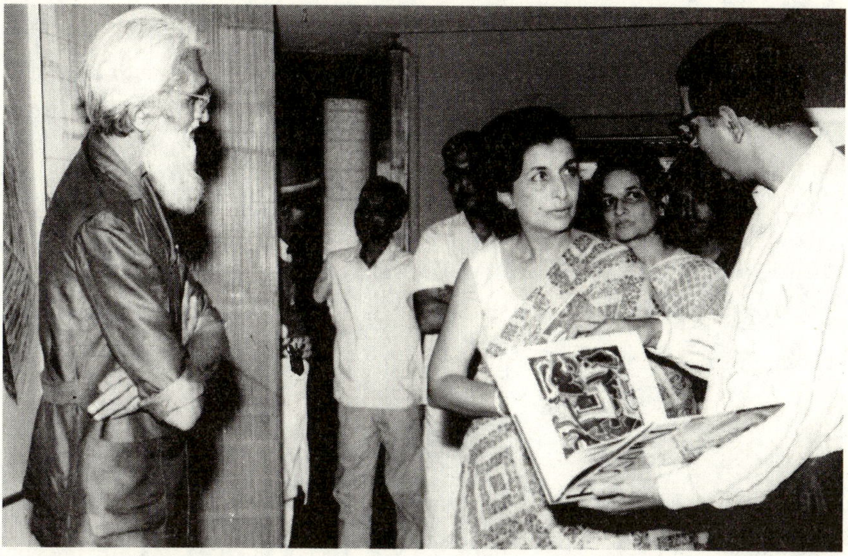

MF Husain, Begum Ali Yavar Jung and Kekoo Gandhy (left to right) at the opening of Swaminathan exhibition

but I have to say I didn't know them intimately. Ours was a professional relationship. I don't think the distance was deliberate on either side. Part of it may have been that I was so busy.'

Patel wore many hats; as a doctor, he spent his mornings and evenings at the clinic and rushed home for lunch and a nap and some work at the typewriter—he is a poet and playwright of note—or at the easel.

'I couldn't just go and sit at the gallery and talk to them as I am told other painters did,' Patel says. 'There were times however when we would come together for a special project. In 1965, the Jehangir Art Gallery began to give out space for weddings. I suppose the idea was that the money so raised would be used to upgrade the gallery but we thought, "No. That's not something you can do." Kekoo and I joined forces to oppose this move. We got together and roused public sentiment against this. We talked to the press; we got in touch with the Jehangir family. We succeeded and the gallery was no longer made available for weddings.'

Archana Hande worked for the gallery as a designer and then went on to making her own art and curating. She has an insider's view of the old Chemould, pointing out that even the support staff had significant art collections too. 'The old Chemould worked like a government office, it is true. But it had a certain vibe. The staff at the old Chemould had their own art collections. Chintamani,[68] for instance? He got every artist who showed there to do a drawing for him. They would do it because they felt he was part of the gallery, the experience, the extended family that Chemould became. The other staff too had their own collections. They never sought to sell them or monetise them, to my knowledge. I learned all of this because in the one year that I worked for them as a designer, I became something of an insider. I was part of the staff and even when I went on to show at Chemould, I was still considered one of them. This would never happen at the new space. Now artists hang out in the office and the staff sits outside. In those days, we all sat around and talked and it became like a friendship, there was something personal. I haven't been with many galleries... but I think that feeling made the old Chemould a special place.'

These memories could be multiplied. Sheetal Gattani remembers having her first solo at Chemould. And almost every young artist came face to face with the grand masters of their own tradition here. Whether it was Atul and Anju Dodiya or Jitish Kallat and Reena Saini Kallat, they all saw their first Tyebs and Barwes and Razas on the curving wall of the gallery.

And it opened itself out to so many more causes.

The painter Atul Dodiya remembers: 'I was part of a Gujarati Writers' Group. My friend Bharat Naik would run a little magazine called *Gadyaparva*. It was devoted to prose and it was difficult to keep afloat. In Gujarat, many painters are also men of literature. There was Bhupen Khakhar and Gulammohammed Sheikh and so we got together and decided that we should raise some money. We got a whole bunch of artists together and asked them for a work. Then when we had got the works, we had to find a venue. That's when Bhupen said he would ask the Gandhys and once again, Chemould threw open its doors for a good cause. For ten days, the show was on and each night was a party. I would bring naashta from Ghatkopar and there were poetry readings, discussions and all the Bombay poets and writers were there too: Adil Jussawalla and Shanta Gokhale; Ranjit Hoskote and Girish Shahane and Abhay Sardesai all took part. The leading Gujarati poet Sitanshu Yashashchandra came down from Baroda, Mani Kaul was there. It was really like a festival. Each and every work was sold and I daresay the people who bought them got bargains because they weren't even priced that high.'

Gallery Chemould had therefore morphed into a city institution. And it reached out in any number of ways.

'There was a time when the Narmada Bachao Andolan was at its height,' says Atul, 'and there was a major protest meeting at Flora Fountain. Kekoo conceived of the idea that one of my paintings would make a good backdrop to this moment, bringing in the idea of the Mahatma into this protest. They were large paintings and I was a bit worried about how they would get there. Don't worry about that, Kekoo said, and so there was a painting as part of that protest.'

•

Gallery Chemould might be seen as part of the landscape but was fast developing into an institution. But the man who had managed two major institutions in the city—the Bhulabhai Desai Institute and the Jehangir Art Gallery—did not seem to think so.

For a while, Soli Batliwalla and Kekoo Gandhy seemed to have had a harmonious relationship, two men who saw eye-to-eye on the city's need for art and culture, for this to be broad-based and available to that chimerical figure of the common man. As late as 1968, they would come together to defend a young artist's right to freedom of speech.

Today Jyotindra Jain is known as an art historian, the author of several books on art history, retired professor of aesthetics at Jawaharlal Nehru University, and former editor of *Marg*. But in 1968, he was in a state of turbulence. In a short essay written for *Aroop*,[69] an issue titled 'Totems and Taboos', guest edited by Nancy Adajania, Dr Jain captures some of the ferment of the self and the city:

'I joined St Xavier's College at Dhobi Talao while attending evening classes in fine arts at Sir JJ School of Arts. The college studies interested me but not enough to erase the lingering childhood fascination for the garish mill labels and my windowsill exhibitions. The local train I took daily from Vile Parle to Marine Lines passed slums comprising clusters of blackened palm-leaf thatched huts. Some of the huts stood out: they were covered with bright, hand-painted cinema hoardings to protect the dwellers from Bombay's torrential rains. My eyes would catch glimpses of a pistol-wielding villain, a kissing couple, or just the blown-up face of a heroine.

'The exciting discussions on Bombay in the context of the rising discipline of Urban Anthropology outside the classrooms of Xavier's on the one hand, and my disillusionment with the JJ School's colonial lessons in Drawing from Memory; Drawing from Life; Perspective Drawing and Sketching on the other, only increased my curiosity for the explosion of the popular visual imagery of the city, which stared at me at every juncture—from billboards, calendars, stickers, magazines, restaurants and shops; on the roadside and from the facades of buildings, in taxis and on the bus. I began to be drawn to the eclecticism of the intervisuality of images from diverse visual sources, often on a single plane—an ambivalent language of collage and citation that facilitated the seizure of aesthetic and cultural meaning.'

Jain quit art school and began work on a series of collages on discarded cinema billboards partially reworking the faces of the filmstars. Encouraged by his artist friends, Prabhakar Barwe, Bhupen Khakhar and Ambadas, he exhibited seven of these works at Bombay's Jehangir Art Gallery.

'The art world of Bombay in 1968 was not ready to accept this as "art". They were shocked. A reviewer in a Bombay newspaper, entitled his write-up "Creations of a Sick Mind". This pleased me immensely. The exhibition opened unceremoniously at eleven am in the presence of a few artist friends and journalists, and was marked by altercations with a couple of hostile viewers. When I returned to the gallery after lunch, I found two police constables waiting at the gallery with a notice to shut down the exhibition with immediate effect. The grounds: obscenity. I complied but not knowing what else to do, sought out Kekoo Gandhy...

'To my astonishment, he not only offered to help, but telephoned Soli Batliwala of the Bhulabhai Memorial Trust and both went to the police commissioner. The exhibition reopened the next day. It was astonishing, because both Kekoo and Solibhai were solid pillars of Bombay's art life yet they, without hesitation, went to the extent of personally visiting the police commissioner to stand up for the freedom of artistic expression of a young, unknown artist who had caused a small public storm with his art.'

•

No one is quite sure how things went sour between Soli Batliwalla and the Gandhys. Soli Batliwalla went from being the man who brought Chemould into the Jehangir to being the man who wanted them out. As Dara Gandhy put it in a classic understatement, 'Somewhere along the way things turned hostile, the Jehangir Art Gallery began to demand a huge rent and wanted us to pay it in retrospect as well. Soon Chemould was fighting a court case.'

The Indian judiciary is not noted for speed and the case dragged on and on. It ran on for twenty-five years and the Gandhys' case was weakened because they had acquired new premises; besides which the emotional costs of a court case were high.

'I would wake up in the morning on the days when I had to be in court and I would feel a dead weight settle on my chest,' Shireen Gandhy says.

'And then I had found the space at Chemould Prescott Road already so our position was weakened a little. I told my lawyer that we had decided to quit and we went to court the next day and announced that we were willing to go. The judge could not believe his ears. A South Bombay tenant who was calling off the battle? Many of my friends thought we had reached a settlement with the gallery and that we had received a payment of some kind. When I told them that we had just walked away, they were aghast too. But I thought of it as coming out of the darkness, as reaching the light at the end of the tunnel. The Jehangir Art Gallery withdrew its demand for arrears of rent and we went our separate ways.'

Khorshed was quite pragmatic about it. 'Quite frankly, we got tired of fighting. Now that we have made our decision to leave, we would like to leave with happy memories. Yes, we will miss this place. But at least we won't have any legal worries. We simply think it is time for us to move out and move on...' she told *Bombay Times.*[70]

But all this would not have been possible, the Gandhy family admits unanimously, were it not for a certain Kurush Jungalwala, Shireen Gandhy's husband.

He was 'the boy next door', living in a flat in a building right across the road from Kekee Manzil. Kurush and Shireen met when she was seventeen and he nineteen and suddenly Shireen began to spend a lot of time in her parents' room. It just so happened that the Jungalwala house was within direct line of sight of the senior Gandhys bedroom.

'She would hang out with them so that she could look into our house and we could keep in "eye contact" at least with each other. We had developed our own sign language from across the street; in those days my family did not even own a telephone!' Kurush says with a grin.

But Noshir Jungalwala, Kurush's father, was also watching. He was the quintessential self-made man, son of an engine driver, who had worked all his life in Hindustan Lever. Of course, like every good Parsi employee, he was loyal to the company, so loyal that he put whatever money he had back into Lever shares, ending up, at retirement with a fair amount of rather valuable equity.

Jungalwala Senior was not very happy about all this window-peeking. Shireen, he felt, might not be the right girl for his son. She was from the 'wealthy' Gandhy family who lived in a bungalow across the road. He thought she might be spoilt rotten. 'His favourite line about me was, "She won't even pick up a plate from the table after eating!"' says Shireen.

Kurush was not to be deterred and eventually the two families became in-laws. Over time, they even became friends. Mr Jungalwala would cross the road to help Khorshed with investment advice. Shireen laughs about it. 'The assumption, based on real estate, was that the Gandhys were the wealthy family and the Jungalwalas were not. The irony was that the Gandhys who lived off an art market that was nascent at the time lived as modestly as their neighbours! And in years to come if Gallery Chemould (now Chemould Prescott Road) owes its success to someone, it would be only possible thanks to the support of the low-key businessman Kurush, now running a successful export operation of footwear.'

Kurush weighs in: 'Kekoo was very keen that I should become a director in Chemould but I refused. He was a smart man. Family wisdom was that he knew nothing about money but he was astute in his own right. He wanted to know what was going on in the business of the gallery and he had a grasp of fundamentals and a strong opinion about them. He might not be able to read a balance sheet or understand a set of projections but he understood what was going on and he was vocal when he felt there was a need. I think his heart got in the way of his head. Some mornings, as he got older, he would be waiting for me to leave the house to take my scooter to the station. He would catch me unawares and ask, "Hey, Kurush, got some dosh?" I'd say, "Yeah" and hand him a five hundred rupee note.'

'But if you gave him money, he would just give it away,' says Shireen.

'Then that was what he wanted to do,' says Kurush. 'And when I gave him that five hundred rupee note, it was his to do whatever he wanted.'

He points to the year 2013. That was the year when some members of the family wanted to sell the family's art collection. It was divided up and some of it was sold at jaw-dropping prices in the first Christie's auction in India.

'How did they come to have an art collection in the first place? Because of Kekoo,' Kurush points out.

Shireen smiles, shrugs.

•

Kurush, as much as Shireen, began to see the need for a larger space for Gallery Chemould.

'In 2006, the artists from the Chemould stable began to get restless. The little space at the Jehangir Art Gallery was beginning to feel too homey, too small. Shireen was also keen on moving out and we began looking out for a space. We looked at several places; some were unavailable, some were asking for too much, and finally we found this space. The gallery moved, the court case was dropped and Kekoo was not pleased. By now he was touching ninety. He did not like the art we were showing, and he began to come to the gallery and write, "Shit, shit" in the gallery visitors' book. It was his protest at what he thought was the side-lining of his artists and his kind of art.'

In his interactions with the Gandhy family, Kurush Jungalwala often seems to have the bemused air of an anthropologist confronting a strange tribe that insists on doing things its own way, regardless of how difficult that way is. He maintains what looks like a detached involvement. Or perhaps it is only the recognition that a family of six independent and strong-minded people is going to develop its own systems which should not be interfered with. However Shireen Gandhy is clear that if Kekee Manzil and Chemould are around today, it is because of Kurush Jungalwala's well-timed and minimalist interventions.

Kurush says, 'If you attend several meetings with the Gandhy family, you'll see a pattern developing. If something is not decided in the first fifteen minutes, the agenda will begin to slip away. Other things will be discussed and eventually, the whole point of the meeting will be forgotten. Then some months later, someone will say: "We didn't really finish that meeting, did we?" and it will start again. I don't function that way.'

He has developed his own way of dealing with this. For instance, Kurush is also a collector, of contemporary art as well as the moderns. However things get a bit blurry. 'I once travelled to Paris and bought three large Vishwadhans. I brought them home and I think a few years later, Shireen sold one or two of them,' he says.

Then he smiles and says, 'I'm democratic that way.'

'Democratic' is Kurush's shorthand for 'I can see that the family won't change so I am going to accept them as they are and work with it.'

Kurush tells me: 'When a friend who was in real estate heard that we had acquired a 5,000-foot property in the Fort area and were going to turn it into an art gallery, he said: "Are you mad? Just rent it out and you can live on the money!"'

But he didn't. He wouldn't. 'Because that was not the reason I acquired it. The gallery is Shireen's passion, she does it brilliantly, the gallery means something, it is history and part of the story of this city in so many ways. That's also important.'

Jungalwala is right when he speaks of an institution rich in history. Nalini Malani draws a beautiful parallel. Her association with the gallery happened on so many different levels and in so many different ways—through Soli Batliwalla who had brought the Gandhys into the Jehangir Art Gallery, through that extraordinary sculptor Pilloo Pochkhanawala who was Khorshed's cousin and Nalini Malani's friend; through their work together in the Bombay Arts Festival...relationships in this city tend to be rhizomatic.

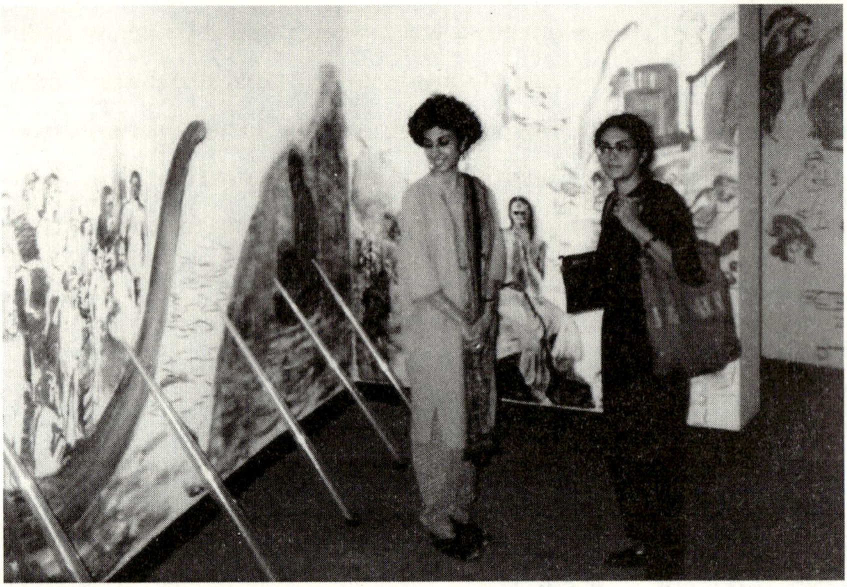

Shireen Gandhy with Nalini Malani during Nalini's exhibition 'City of Desires' at Gallery Chemould, 1992

Malani remembers: 'I had my first group exhibition, which was called *Splash,* with Gallery Chemould, in 1990. That project began when Rajeev Sethi who was a friend of Vivan Sundaram's invited him to do a mural at Shah House in Juhu. Vivan invited me and Bhupen to collaborate on this project. Bhupen had just been to Hungary where he had attended a workshop on reverse glass painting and he said, "Let's do that here; I can teach you this as well." It was such fun working with him. At the time, there wasn't much that came between the Shah House and the sea; nothing had been built there and so Bhupen said, "If they grow bored of the mural, they can look at the reflections in the glass at the coconut palms and the sea". We so enjoyed it that we decided that we would do three works together; in each one, one of us would be the director. So at Kasauli, Vivan planned the work and allocated us spaces for our figures; at Baroda, Bhupen was in charge. And then I had them come over to my tiny studio in Lohar Chawl and we worked on a third in which I directed the work. It was at Chemould that we exhibited our reverse painted glass paintings, and most importantly our combined painted works. We got an avalanche of criticism on these last ones, as people refused to take our combined art making seriously, and accused us of just making a mockery. Interestingly enough, it was much later that their daughter Shireen Gandhy told me that it was the exhibition *Splash* that convinced her to take over the gallery, and to devote her life to art.

'My most important experience with Khorshed and Kekoo Gandhy came with my project *City of Desires*. As a reaction to the upcoming saffronisation I wanted to make an all-encompassing charcoal wall drawing that would cover all the walls of the Gallery Chemould. Of course nothing would be sold, there was nothing to sell, all had to be painted over in the end. But Khorshed loved the idea and so it happened. For the public it was a total shock to see me making the work in situ. Spontaneous dialogues started up about why I was drawing the dispossessed in Lohar Chawl here on the gallery walls. It got a lot of criticism and people did not take me seriously. But it also made a deep impression with the visitors. In fact it was recently in 2014 when on my way to Delhi for my retrospective at the Kiran Nadar Museum of Art, a young man at the airport came up to me and told me how this impressed him when he had visited the gallery as a child. These charcoal wall drawings, and their Erasure Performances, became an essential part of my art practice for over twenty-five years in several museums in India, Australia, Switzerland etc. This could only happen thanks to Khorshed and Kekoo with their spontaneous support for my experimental ideas.

Fascinated by the myth of Medea, Malani and dramaturge Alaknanda Samarth would begin to work on a collaborative project. 'When I was doing the *Medeamaterial* project at the Max Müller Bhavan, Khorshed and Shireen supported it fully, not so much in terms of money, but we, Alaknanda [Samarth] and I had the full support of her staff and everything we needed from the gallery although Shireen was eight months pregnant with her first child at the time.

'When Anuradha Kapur[71] and I worked together on *The Job,* a Bertolt Brecht story that we made into a theatre performance that came out in 1997, Chemould helped as well. Shireen really put her heart and soul into the whole thing. The last all-encompassing public work I did in Bombay was in 1999 at the Coomaraswamy Hall, *Remembering Toba Tek Singh,* a video play; doing theatre had become very expensive and it was difficult to travel [with a show] so I found a mode for working in theatre using performers on video; those [videos] can travel wherever I could find projectors. I had a lot of support from Shireen and the gallery.

'In 2010 I had my last solo exhibition at the new Chemould Prescott gallery space combined with Chatterjee & Lal gallery. This new Chemould space is so much bigger now and that liberates the artist. Their earlier space had a fantastic address in the heart of Kala Ghoda, but it was constricting. I remember going to the new space when Shireen had just bought it. We went upstairs to the floor above the gallery, where there's an entire community which lives and works. Some of them are white-collar workers, some make samosas to sell on the road, and there's even someone who looks after injured birds before releasing them. It was almost as if the people who occupied my wall drawings in *City of Desires,* had moved along with gallery and started a life above them. There's always a sense of the secret life in this city.'

•

Chemould at the Jehangir Art Gallery closed with a show by Jivya Soma Mashe. 'While for my parents this was a completely natural and heartfelt act, I realised that in the context of the larger art world, this was a very important gesture,' Shireen wrote.

Mehlli Gobhai, the painter who had a weekend home in a wadi at Gholvad, took me to meet Jivya Soma Mashe. We spent much of the visit in silence. But when I reminded him of the last show, he raised both his hands in a salute above his head. It was the gesture of a master artist recognising a tribute.

• 12 •

Shireen's Chemould: The Gallery Reloaded

'In the folder of our inaugural exhibition of September 1963, we had said: "Today there is a widening gulf between the painter and the lay public. Conscious of our responsibility in this field, we hope to make our own contribution in narrowing the gap." We would like to think that our endeavour has borne some fruit—it has undoubtedly enriched our lives.

As we cross this landmark of twenty-five years in the Jehangir (and our involvement with contemporary art for about forty-five years) we express our gratitude to all the artists, art-lovers, friends and colleagues from whom we have consistently received support, encouragement and above all, affection.'

—**Kekoo and Khorshed Gandhy**, *'Seventeen Indian Painters'; Gallery Chemould: 25 Years at the Jehangir, 1988*

•

'In a world of crass commercialisation of the art world and commodification of art, it brings to the fore what my parents have stood for; and in turn what lies ahead as the future at Chemould Prescott Road. It will continue to be the gallery which will look out for, tend to and nurture the talent of the best in contemporary Indian art.

Keeping in mind the rapid changes that have happened in the art world, we look ahead to working at international standards, working within international contexts...an inevitability as the world draws closer, where Indian contemporary art does not remain in the ghettos of merely being perceived as Indian art but makes its way into being considered a part of the larger international art arena.'
—From the catalogue of the inaugural show *Shri Khakhar Prasanna* by Atul Dodiya[72] released at the opening of Chemould Prescott Road.

There must have been a time when Khorshed wondered whether there would be anything to hand over to the next generation, even as Kekoo acted on impulse, threw his energy into causes, bought up shows from no-hopers and generally behaved as if tomorrow came with a guarantee. When things began to stabilise a little, she must have begun to wonder who would take over the gallery once they ran out of energy. Adil had done his duty by the factory and the frameshop. Rashna's life was divided between Switzerland and India. Behroze was the high-spirited tearaway who had, early in the game, declared her unsuitability for gallery work.

Today Shireen Gandhy is recognised as a major player, the natural heir, the obvious successor to her parents' inheritance but it wasn't always so. She gave her mother nightmares, she says, with her academic performance. She bounced from school to school, barely making it past examinations despite an obvious and natural intelligence. (Family legend says that she recognised a Ram Kumar painting at the age of four.)

When Shireen finished her board examinations, her mother heaved a sigh of relief at the unexpectedly good grades and thought she was done. But Shireen went off, admitted herself to the Sophia College on Bhulabhai Desai Road, and suddenly came into her own. Soon she was helping out at the gallery and when the twenty-fifth year celebrations came along, she had returned from a degree in arts management from City University, London, and had completed a transformative stint at the Whitechapel Art Gallery.

'That was an amazing space in the way that it reached out to community and was unafraid of the political statement,' Shireen remembers. She would bring all this back with her but no transition is ever easy.

At the time, the artist Archana Hande was working as a designer and curator for the gallery, even as she began her investigation into her signature style. She says:

'It wasn't just a time of transition; it was also a time of transformation for Shireen. It was clear that she had her own ideas and her own vision for the gallery, which had been honed by her time abroad but was also based on who she was. Likewise, the gallery was about who it had been, the back catalogue was tremendous but that history could have dragged it down, slowed its momentum and it could have ended up a cultural backwater, relying on past glories. Shireen had to juggle what she wanted to do with what she had to do because those artists and their work was also part of her history. Kekoo could see all this and his response to it was ambivalent, if you ask me. He would ask pointed questions, he would argue and Shireen would have to try and bring him around to her point of view.'

The problem, Hande feels, is that Kekoo wasn't quite sure how to respond to art that was getting more and more overtly political. 'He was a purist, I think,' she says reflectively. 'He responded very strongly to what had happened in Gujarat in 2002, he was deeply concerned about it but he could not see how the artistic responses mattered. Kekoo would argue with her often. He was very vocal in his displeasure about the new forms that art was taking. He couldn't see what Nalini Malani or I or my generation of artists was doing; for instance, he couldn't relate to video art, installations. He would be extremely happy when a Mehlli Gobhai was showing because he was suddenly back with what he understood. So there had to be a balance between his artists and the experiments Shireen wanted to conduct. I was going through my own set of transitions and transformations, I was experimenting too so I could relate to what she was going through.'

•

Shireen's parents had left her with an enviable roster; almost everyone who was anyone was on it but a gallery that relies on its past is a gallery that is uninterested in its future. A gallery needs to reinvent itself and to do this it needs to keep tabs on the next generation; to showcase them means less time for and perhaps less veneration of the old. Some of the old guard recognised the change and went to other galleries. Some came back, others moved on but the worst loss, everyone agrees, was Raza.

Shireen remembers that rupture with Raza well. 'As a child I was alone a lot because there was such an age gap between me and my elder siblings. We lived in a bungalow so I had no "building friends"; in every school I went to, the other children would talk about "building friends" and I longed for some of those. But it was not to be. At one point in time, Adil was in the United States with his wife. His flat was empty and so when Raza and his French wife Janine Mongillat came, they lived there for nearly six months. I would just go upstairs and hang out with them. It was the beginning of a long friendship. Raza was a member of the family almost, *and* he was also the cash cow. His shows could be relied on to sell out. Even after I took over, we

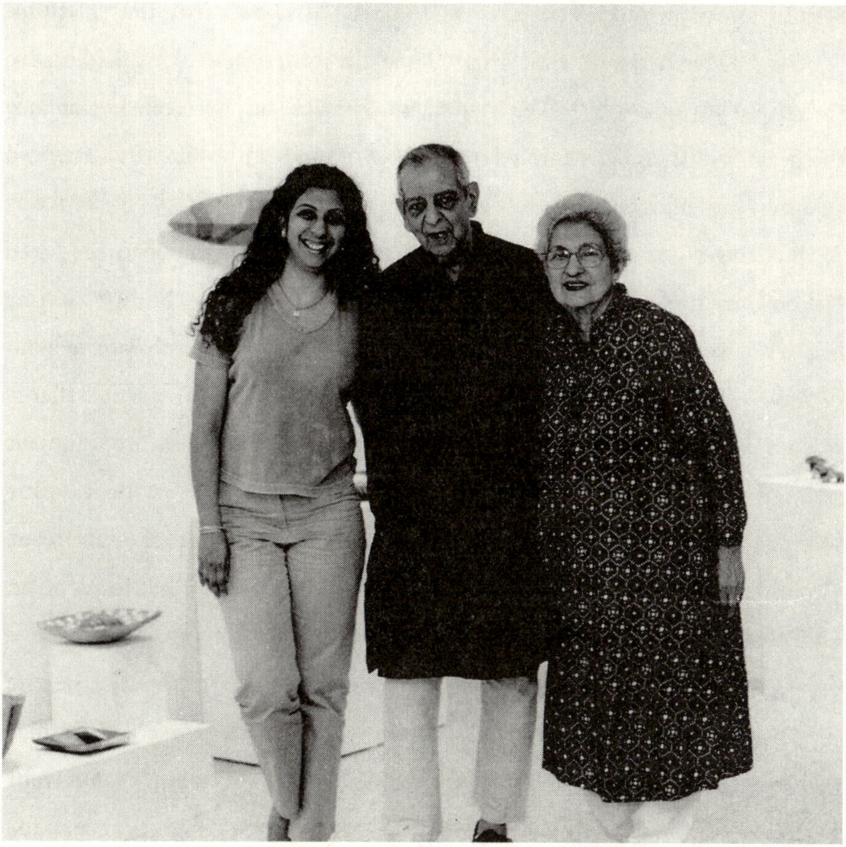

***Family business:** Kekoo, Khorshed, and Shireen Gandhy at Gallery Chemould, 2003*

had many shows with him and he seemed happy enough. Then several years later, he came down and asked to meet me at the Samovar and there, without warning, he told me that he didn't like the way the gallery was shaping. He said he had no time for the artists I was showing. He named names and he was quite savage. I was young too, I suppose, so I didn't back down and the result was that he moved on. That was quite a blow on many different levels.'

As I listened to all this, I could see the other side of being Shireen Gandhy. You walk into Kekee Manzil and you are simply astonished at how the other half lives, surrounded by the best of modern Indian art; by the old retainers and high ceilings and sea views; you don't think of two generations of children without 'building friends'. You think of being Khorshed and Kekoo Gandhy's daughter as an unadulterated positive—you know everyone in the art world; Husain films your sister's wedding, the Gandhys have loads of goodwill among the fraternity. That much is true. But if you are a gallerist in your own right, if you move with the times, work with curators who have strong aesthetic opinions, you might end up hurting some of those people too. You think about a gallery with a tradition that goes back to the time when Tyeb Mehta needed a stipend to keep him going and you don't think about how that very tradition might become burdensome. Shireen explains what happened in that case:

'With Tyeb, I might have made an error of judgement. He told me frankly that now Arun Vadehra of [Vadehra Art Gallery, Delhi] simply came along when his show was ready and put down the money for everything, he bought all the work. Then he looked at me as if to ask, could I do the same? The gallery was making money by then but it was not making that kind of money. I suppose if I had been a hard-headed businesswoman, I would have gone out and got the money from the market or borrowed it from my husband, or whatever. But I didn't want to take that kind of risk and so we lost Tyeb Mehta too.'

•

This is beginning to sound like a litany of loss. It was not an easy time but the Gallery Chemould was also pulsating with a new kind of energy. Some of this had to do with the move to a new space, a huge space, the kind we had not seen in Bombay, in Mumbai, almost anywhere in the country. Here was a barn, a cavern, a hollow, a shell. It could be turned any which way, walls could be deployed, windows opened and the grills outside used so that art might even escape the gallery in an odd way....

But there was also something slightly disconcerting about it. The door was heavy, huge, requiring effort to open it. And every artist who walked in wondered, 'Will what I do get lost in this space?' At the same time, it was such a magnificent space too that they could not help being seduced by it.

Archana Hande says: 'The space in Jehangir was interesting in terms of contact, the contact with the public. We had the usual suspects coming in, the critics, the art world, the writers, the curators, those people. But we also had random members of the public who just dropped in. I remember someone peeking into a Gobhai show and thinking that the gallery was closed and the paintings were all covered up. We had to go and invite him in. That was what I missed, the general interaction. But here it was a different space, spread out, large, inviting. Both spaces made specific demands. I think if Shireen had not moved I would have had to find other spaces for my later work. But I also think, if I want to do a small show, small works, she might think that it would be a waste of her gallery, a waste of her space. I know she also has to think sustainability. This space requires a lot of money to keep going. I don't sell well, I'm an artists' artist so she knows that she might have a show that would not sell. And then to go on giving me a show, year on year, means that she has to consider the cost of that. However, I have to say that she is still open to these experiments, to these shows. Chemould was and still is very much part of many artist movements. For the last two years they have been very much supporting the 2020 artist platform. Again a public event, a multi-disciplinary platform responding to the current state of the country.'

The energy then was as much aesthetic and creative as it was political, overtly political but then art was now overtly political too. A new generation was pushing the envelope, pointing out injustice, calling out the politician, making savage remarks on inequality. Journalist Sidharth Bhatia sees this as a natural process. 'I'm not surprised at the way that Shireen's version of the gallery has turned out,' he says. 'She will find a way to speak her mind, just as her parents did.'

The bridge between the old Chemould and the new one could well be Atul Dodiya, the youngest artist in the 'Seventeen Artists' show that marked the twenty-fifth anniversary (Raza was the seniormost).

At the age of ten, Atul Dodiya knew he wanted to be a painter. But what makes the story truly exceptional was that his father understood his son's ambition. When his son failed the Secondary School Certificate (SSC) examination twice, his father simply bought him 'a year-long first class pass from Ghatkopar to VT[73] [Victoria Terminus] so that I would be able to go to the galleries and see the art there. I went to see plays at the Chhabildas, mostly Marathi, I remember, but also some Hindi. I was also interested in cinema so I would go to the Opera House and see films by Mani Kaul and Kumar Shahani which were on in the morning. I saw *Uski Roti* and *Maya Darpan* there and I was fascinated to learn that Mani Kaul had a show, works on paper, at the Chemould and so I made my way there. This was before the gallery was remodelled; then there was a glass door and behind it was a desk and at the desk was Khorshed Gandhy. The door was closed and the whole thing was so forbidding that I could not make myself open the door and go in. So I didn't see the show; I just went away. I did open that door later but the image of Khorshed persisted. I think, many of us art students, had this impression that she was a strict lady. Later when I got to know the Gandhys, I realised that she was warm and friendly. It was my perception of her.'

For at least three generations of artists and art-lovers, Chemould was the first magical encounter between what you thought art might mean and what art could be. It could be here and now and it could be signed by an Indian name. It could speak to you without the language you were used to in those slick coffee-table books. It could make you so uncertain you wanted to demand, 'Explain yourself' and then you wanted to explain it to anyone else around you. For Dodiya, it was an introduction to history.

'At Chemould, I saw the world: Raza and Tyeb Mehta and Bhupen Khakhar and Barwe. But the most important thing about Chemould was Kekoo and that he was welcoming. As students we would go to the shows at some time but I do remember that Raza was very fond of the Sir JJ School of Arts and when he came to India in the winter, he would often ask Kekoo if he could organise a visit to the school. I was also a very active student and so we would organise a talk by Raza and participate enthusiastically. And Kekoo would come with Raza and sit through the whole talk and he'd turn to us and say, "His show is opening; why don't you come to the opening?" Now that was not something you heard often, a senior gallerist asking art students if they would like to come to the opening of the show of a senior painter. But that was Kekoo. When you did turn up too, he wasn't about to brush by you and attend to more important guests. He recognised you, he put his hand on your shoulder as if you were his friend, he talked to you for a bit. It was wonderful. And at the time, I had no thought, no idea that one day I would be showing at Chemould.'

Was Kekoo choosing his artists or was he being his ebullient self? At this remove, no one can be sure but it is clear that he had the gift of being able to 'walk with kings nor lose the common touch'.

'When I passed out of JJ and started showing, at the Monsoon Show at the Jehangir, for instance, Kekoo would visit and he would come and talk to all of us. He would ask about my family and he would listen with great interest but that was about it. It wasn't that he picked me out; he would talk to everyone. Then there was a show that was being put together for the twenty-fifth year of Chemould's existence. My friends, Bhadrakant Zaveri and Bharati Kapadia, told the Gandhys about this young painter from Ghatkopar. Bhadrakant and Bharati brought the Gandhys to see my work at my studio. (It was then in a chawl; we lived there and when we moved into an apartment in 1987, I began to use it as my studio.)

'They liked my work and asked if they could show me. I was delighted; it was the biggest honour I could imagine. Raza was the seniormost artist; I was the youngest. And in the catalogue there are pictures of the artists; I noticed that only two of us are wearing ties: Raza and me,' says Dodiya.

'I had four paintings in the show. One of them was "Those shoes are mine", a portrait of Bhupen which had him pictured at the door of an office, inside you can see an accountant at work. On the wall next to him, there are words from Gandhiji's favourite bhajan, Narsinh Mehta's *Vaishnav janato tene kahiey je peed paraayi jaane re* (To be a Vaishnav, you must be able to feel the pain of another) and "Boot, *chappal aur aham yahaan utaariey*" (Please leave your footwear and your ego here) on it. The show was in that long gallery of the Jehangir and when you went in, mine was the first painting, urging viewers, I suppose to doff their footwear and their egos at the door. All four of them were sold quickly, almost on the opening day itself. I was delighted; and the Gandhys were happy.

'I enjoyed going to the gallery when the show was on; I still do. I like to watch people experience the work. I like to look at what they are looking at; I like to look at what they are *not* looking at; I like to look at their body language.[74]'

In a way, Atul Dodiya and Shireen Gandhy grew into their space in the gallery at around the same time.

'Shireen had just returned from England; she too would come to the gallery and we began to talk about art. I would tell her the artists I admire, the French artists, the American ones and we would exchange notes. It was in September 1988, I think that they decided to renovate the gallery and that was when they must have been thinking about whom to show in the refurbished gallery and I believe it was Khorshed who said, "What about Atul?" and Shireen says she jumped at the idea. That was how I had my first solo with them. September 1989, my first solo at Chemould; a relationship that has lasted nearly thirty years now.'

In *Shri Khakhar Prasanna*, an invaluable document, Naushil Mehta writes: 'Shireen wanted the first show in the renovated gallery to be a statement—not just about her presence in the management—but also to re-emphasise the gallery's old commitment to spot and nurture new talent.'

You can see how this would be a great way to announce a new version of the gallery. If Shireen had turned to one of the old guard for a first show at the newly renovated gallery, the art world would have shrugged and turned away, thinking, 'Same old, same old' and gone about its business. With Atul's show, there was a completely new vibe.[75] There was in Atul's work much of the modern, much of the contemporary but there was also an unashamed and celebratory cityness, suburbness, Gujaratiness, here-and-now-ness. He could laugh at himself, he could make you laugh, he could also reach into you and connect with your inner baazigar, the one who venerates his seniors but has them in his sights. This was the 'Global Local' with a vengeance.

'My whole family came to the opening of the show,' Dodiya remembers. 'Kekoo got talking to my father and was fascinated by his story; he loved his tales of coming to Bombay from Saurashtra and making a life here for himself and his family. So after that, he would say that he was coming to see the work but he would also ask me to call my father and they would chat.

So it was not just a professional relationship, it wasn't just, "He's an artist—We show him—We call the press in and get him some publicity—We earn money—He earns money—we can all go home now"; it was more than that; I think there was some magic to Khorshed and Kekoo and Shireen now too; you become part of the family.'

Here it is again: that Khorshed-Kekoo streak. You don't just work with an artist or show an artist, he is suddenly incorporated into the larger family.

'For example in 1991-92, I was in Paris and they went out of their way to make sure it would be a good experience for me. They called Raza and told him I would be there and put us in touch. I had done a mural for a private house, for Czaee Shah, and when it was finished, it would go into the house and no one would see it again. That's when Shireen came up with the idea that it should be showed in the gallery, if even for a week or ten days. This was the level of their commitment to art because they were not going to get anything out of this. But they wanted to show it.

'In March 1997, similarly, I was going to show with CIMA in Calcutta. The works were ready and when I told Shireen, she said, "We should have a preview in Bombay." The work was going to Calcutta and it would be sold there but this meant that my friends could see the work here before it left. Again, there was nothing in it for them except for the idea that the work should get the best possible exposure.'

But the family thing works both ways. Atul Dodiya's wife Anju Dodiya is also a painter to reckon with. Like Atul, she too had haunted Chemould as a student of the arts. She says, 'I do remember liking the old Chemould because of its size and its intimacy. It was a quiet space and it had this bamboo matting on the walls when I first began going there. I didn't talk to Kekoo or Khorshed; generally it was Khorshed who would be there, on the phone, discussing something. I would slip quietly past her and go look at the art. I remember seeing some absolutely stunning Razas there; jewels gleaming in the dark. And Tyeb Mehta, it was a Chemould show, I think, but down in the Jehangir. And then there was Prabhakar Barwe too.

'In 1986, I was one of the students they picked for the Monsoon Show at the Jehangir. I remember Kekoo coming down and popping in to see the work. I knew who he was—we all knew—and I was in awe of him. He would throw his arms around the shoulders of the young male artists and chat to them. But for a few days, he didn't speak to me. One day, he did but it was a casual encounter, it was not like he was addressing my art.

'Atul was in the show that marked twenty-five years of Chemould and then they asked him if he was ready for a solo show. That's when Khorshed and Shireen came over to the studio we shared; it was at DK Wadi in Ghatkopar. I was working and showing my work to other artists, to Gieve, to Tyeb, to Sheikhbhai and Nilima, Barwe of course. I didn't show them to gallerists. But when they were planning the show for Atul, Shireen and Khorshed came over and Khorshed said, "You also paint, right?" I said I was guilty. Shireen asked to see the work. I was a bit flustered by this. Not because I wasn't ready to show my work, maybe it was just unexpected. And as luck would have it, they were sitting on my paintings. They were on the studio bed and my paintings were under the mattress.'

Shireen Gandhy told Naushil Mehta about that moment in *Shri Khakhar Prasanna,* 'This was risky business. If Anju's work was good or bad, there was no worry. But if her work was mediocre, this could be a diplomatic minefield. I mean, look. Here was Atul, our artist, who was becoming my friend. How could I ever explain to him? I'd probably end up losing him...not just as an artist...but also a friend. Reluctantly she took out four watercolours from under a mattress and showed them to us. Four self-conscious self-portraits. Here was something special. At once, we invited her to participate in a group show at Gallery Chemould.'

This was followed by a solo show and another Dodiya joined the

Chemould cohort. For Anju Dodiya, the old Chemould was where she saw herself, it was the frame of the right size for her work.

'When Shireen was giving up Chemould, I said I would miss the gallery deeply, I could see myself in that space, I could see how my work would fit there. I liked the intimacy it created, the feeling that you could never be too far away from the work you were seeing. But when I saw the new gallery, I found it exciting too. My scale grew; I began to get ambitious, although at the beginning it was also intimidating. Scale is exciting but there's also that feeling: "Can I do this?"'

But here's the thing.

It wasn't just the artists who were changed by the dynamics of the new gallery. There was a change in the way the viewers, the gallery-hoppers, the flaneurs, experienced art as well. Anju had a show at the Chemould Prescott in which she invited viewers to erase a work.

I don't think Anju would have thought of doing this in Gallery Chemould at the Jehangir. I don't think I would have thought to help erase a work there. But here you could expand and be anyone. And so I climbed a ladder and got hold of an eraser and went to work. In so doing, I had a strange, intense experience. I was doing this *cum permissu*; the artist herself had asked us to participate in the erasure but now I was aligning myself with the iconoclast. What am I doing? I asked, as I worked industriously with a lovely slab of eraser, the kind I had always wanted as a boy, half blue and half red. Why am I doing this? Because I can? That is stupid and no reason. There are hundreds of things I can do and I do not. I am on the side of beauty, I am on the side of self-expression, why am I participating in an erasure? Why am I almost enjoying this? But there was something that was driving me on and I worked for a bit before coming down and gathering myself. As I walked away, I remember thinking: She's made me act, she's made me confront something inside, something a little darker than I thought. It was exhilarating and disturbing. I felt as if I had made an odd new connection with art.

Perhaps the source of that invitation came from a dark place too. 'I was going through a serious crisis. I was wondering what exactly I was doing,' says Anju. 'My work was variations on a theme, a fictional retelling of a life. I could also see that my work followed a linear trajectory. And I was beginning to think: what is it I am doing here? I tried to do other things but they were not working. I changed media but whatever I did, I felt as if I were doing the same thing. And so I conceived of the idea of doing these three drawings, I would give them exactly what I would give every other drawing I had done. I would plan them and make them precious, investing them with attention and love, I would execute them with formal care. I would make sure they were "finished". And then I would ask the viewers to erase them. This was my way of testing whether I could let go, whether I could let it go. I wanted to see if the process of watching them go would revive me, take me somewhere else. I had a ladder so that people could climb up and erase the top part. I had the erasers on a stand like the one where votive candles are lit in a church. I wanted to sacramentalise it. I remember seeing some young people get totally into the process of erasing my work; they were working hard at it, as if on a mission. And that was when it struck me: this can go anywhere, there is no limit, I've told them to do it and they're doing it. It was a very unsettled space. I found links to a history of erasures: to the attacks on Husain's work, the destruction of the Bamiyan Buddhas, even the work of time in slowly bringing art to dust. But it was interesting, I grew detached. I love the fact that the viewers came into the work and finished it, in more ways than one. In my work, I have often fetishized the pencil and other instruments, the sewing machine too. And now the eraser came in, it became a weapon, a violent thing, iconoclastic. I believe it was the last exhibition Khorshed saw. She was frail then but she made it to the opening.

She had a glass of wine and she looked at the work and she whispered to me, "Lovely watercolours."'

Of course when you throw a piece to the iconoclasts, when you invite its end, it is not going to sell. No gallerist is going to be delighted with that. 'But Shireen was excited. She welcomes new experiences. If it's different from what you always do, it's better for her.

'The erased work came back with me. They're in the store. I love the quality of a slow fadeout.'

Here then is another point of departure. In the old dispensation, the art was central, the viewer came to the art as a finished product that would provide enlightenment at best or some kind of emotive experience at least. In this new world, and Chemould Prescott located itself there, art was an experience, an immersive experience. You could be part of its making as well.

•

There's another high-powered art couple represented by Chemould. This is Jitish Kallat and his wife Reena Saini-Kallat. Jitish Kallat and I go back a long way to the time when I was writing for the *Sunday Review* and he and Justin Ponmany would do our illustrations under the name Jitish and Justin. You can see why the Monsoon shows were not quite the backwater the rest of the world (and I) imagined them to be. For it was there that Kallat also got started.

'I was basically an art school student when I first met Shireen. Chemould was one of the few leading galleries at the time and Shireen would be exceedingly kind. She would hand out catalogues and more importantly, she was always friendly and welcoming with students. Our first interaction was at the college Monsoon Show at the Jehangir Art Gallery that takes place after the final year and I was showing a painting I had done during the vacation. It was called "Flower Child Operates the Funeral of a Schedule", a self-portrait with a watch dangling in my mouth and ants coming to get it, a

Daliesque image. Shireen came and saw the painting, and when I was sitting there, she came to the glass panels near Samovar, took off her watch, dangled it from her mouth and tapped on the glass; then she came in to say hello. But she still had this watch clutched between her teeth as if it were a cigarette while she was speaking! She asked when she could visit the studio. I was very prolific at the time and so I said, "Any time" and after she came to see me, we fixed my first solo show in 1997; it was titled *PTO*, and it was held across Chemould and Prithvi Gallery.

'This was the Chemould at Jehangir Art Gallery and two of my early shows in Delhi were also hosted by Chemould.[76] I suppose I was something of an oddity; I was barely twenty-two or twenty-three when I had the show. I was this really young person in the gallery and everyone was, I think, supportive and indulgent. At the time, no one would have given an artist that young a solo show; I remember Shireen had come to see my studio in Borivali and she asked if I would like to do an exhibition at the gallery. Afterwards we went to lunch and somehow the discussion drifted towards my age. She denies it now but I remember clearly her face fell when I mentioned how old I was. I got the impression that if she could travel back in time she would have gone back and erased the offer.'

Reena Saini, as she was then known, had the same qualms as Anju Dodiya. 'Since Shireen launched Jitish's first solo exhibition in 1997, I felt that it would not be professionally appropriate for me to sign up with the same gallery as Jitish, even though we were not married then. I approached Dadiba Pundole of Pundole Art Gallery to share my work and he offered to give me a solo. When Shireen found out, she said, "I've waited for you to be ready" as she had been following my work for a while and I was most excited to have the two premier galleries of the time, come together to launch my first solo exhibition in 1998 called "Orchard of Home-grown Secrets" with a large body of work shown across both venues.'

Jitish Kallat is one of the few artists to tell it like it was. 'The old gallery was charming and pleasant but it had its limitations. You could not work with sight lines. You could not place one object in relation to another and develop a meaningful dialogue between the works because of the narrow and curved nature of the space. The move made it possible for me to show the larger works that I was doing.'

And there were also works that the old Chemould could not show. The conceptual artist Shilpa Gupta remembers: 'I was very young, just out of college really, when Shireen offered me my first solo. But the work I was doing then, required a large square space, so when Arshiya Lokhandwalla invited me to participate in a three-person group show, I chose that, as the work could fit into the front part of Lakeeren. It did not occur to me at the time that one was supposed to associate with a gallery, or how today, the gallery is seen as such a close partner of an artist. I was honoured that she had offered me a solo, honoured and surprised, but to me the space was a part of the work and the narrow arc of the old Chemould was not where I could have spread the circular hair strands of the piece I was working on.'

This is where you see the interaction between artist and gallery space. A gallery should not circumscribe the vision of an artist but once s/he has settled into a gallery's embrace, its physical limitations will play some role in defining the ambitions of each show. Consider Vivan Sundaram's trajectory as an artist who was in on the birth of the gallery.

'There was a great deal of excitement when Kekoo Gandhy came to visit the Fine Arts Faculty, MS University in Baroda in 1963, as he had announced that he and his wife were going to start a gallery of contemporary art in Bombay,' Sundaram wrote in an email to me. 'My teachers introduced me as a talented student. After I graduated from Baroda in 1965, I did not go back to Delhi but came to Bombay where I lived for a while in Readymoney Mansions at Worli Naka. It was on the sixth floor and I had a lovely studio. At

Gallery Chemould, Kekoo introduced me to Khorshed, who was very open and friendly. She always greeted me with her gentle smile, asking me to sit with her at her small desk at the entrance. Through them I met many senior artists, such as Jehangir Sabavala, Pilloo Pochkhanawala, Adi Davierwalla, Ara and Mohan Samant. I became friendly with Mohan and visited him at his studio that faced the sea at Walkeshwar. I was very impressed by his paintings and listened to him playing the sarangi. And then there was the lovely Samovar Cafe beneath it, where often the Gandhys also had lunch and a great place to meet a range of people.'

His first show should have been at Chemould you would have thought. After all, the gallery would not have objected at all to his political leanings. Sundaram remembers: 'Whenever Kekoo saw me, he would say, "Hey comrade, come sit down, let's talk politics!"' But the works were just too big. Thus, Sundaram's first show 'was at the Taj Art Gallery. Kekoo and Khorshed helped in promoting it. Subsequently, I went to England on the Commonwealth Scholarship to study at the Slade School of Art in London, where I did a post-graduate course in painting and in the history of cinema, and became active in the student movement of May 1968. I returned to Delhi and in 1972 when Pablo Neruda got his Nobel Prize, I did a series on his *The Heights of Machhu Pichhu.* I showed them at the Jehangir Art Gallery with Bhupen Khakhar, Gulammohammed Sheikh and Nagji Patel. Once again Kekoo and Khorshed helped to mount the exhibition. In 1974, I showed paintings at Chemould. Some of the works had political references, such as *The Famous Mrs G,* an authoritarian portrait. Kekoo was not disturbed by any of this. On the contrary, he enjoyed it. Many of my shows were at Jehangir Art Gallery but were put up by Chemould, because of the size of the works.The show titled *The Discreet Charm of the Bourgeoisie* was one of these. 1976 was a politically significant year for the nation. The Emergency was declared on which I did a series of drawings and took the risk to show them in the Jehangir Art Gallery, as they were complex works, allusive in nature. Kekoo in particular supported this show as he was very opposed to the Emergency.

'*Signs of Fire* which was exhibited at Chemould in 1985 were watercolours and boxes that referred to a forest fire at my residence in Kasauli,where I had set up the Kasauli Art Centre. My 1986 *Paintings* show, which included my largest painting *The Sher-Gil Family*, which was at Jehangir Art Gallery, was also supported by Chemould Gallery.'

'There would be many shows including *Paintings* in 1990. 'That was my "last" painting show, signalled by the title of the largest work 'Easel Painting'. Shireen bought the painting which adorned the living room of the Gandhys' house in Bandra. Kekoo would remark with a mischievous smile "What a loving portrait you have painted of Geeta in a rocking chair".

'In 1992 *Collaboration/Combine* was my first multimedia exhibition, which combined photographs, large stone columns, engine oil and paintings on wood with objects. This was again in the Jehangir art gallery. Shireen was now proactive in her parents' gallery and took the installation of this demanding show. There were two stone columns, each weighing 2000 kgs. In Delhi, I had mounted them using a system of chains and pulleys. When I suggested we use the same in Bombay, I was told the strong Marathi workers would lift the stone blocks with their own muscle power. Shireen and I watched with bated breath as they hoisted the columns. Shireen wrote a text saying this was a novel experience. Krishnamachari Bose was at the JJ school of Art at that time and he said he would help and he brought other students.'

All well and good but if you read between the lines you can see that for someone like Sundaram, Gallery Chemould at the Jehangir was a space that was constricting his work. At the new version of the gallery, *Trash*, Sundaram's largest body of photographs based on an 60 x 20 x 10 foot 'installation made of found objects and garbage of a cityscape' fit perfectly. 'Also included were videos and a large room-size installation, titled *12 Bed Ward,* (which included a theatre performance conducted by Rehan Engineer). Even this space was not large enough, so Shireen agreed to collaborate with Sree Goswami of Project 88 and hold the show in two galleries. *Objet Trouve,* the readymade with trash, had become my privileged medium. So when I thought of sculptural draped figures in 2011, it logically followed that the title *Gagawaka* should come from the existing names, icons in a manner of speaking. Thus came the idea that garments made out of second-hand items, even rubbish, could be draped on mannequins and that became *Making Strange.* When worn by models they came alive on the ramp, as they did in Delhi's Rabindra Bhavan galleries. Shireen loved the event. We couldn't replicate the ramp but we did have about half-a-dozen people walking informally around the gallery when *Making Strange* was shown at Chemould Prescott Road. I was very moved when I got a two-page hand-written letter from Khorshed saying how she loved the ironic humour of the exhibition.'

The new gallery made things much easier for Sundaram. Not everyone had the same response.

I remember Mehlli Gobhai's response to the new space.

'I will miss the old Chemould,' Gobhai said.

'I find that door means exercise,' I said. 'It seems forbidding, as if asking people to stay away.'

'I can't say I mind that much,' he replied and as always I found it difficult to tell whether he was being polemical or practical. 'But it's going to be a challenge to conquer the space when I show there.'

Here it should be noted that Gobhai spoke of his canvases in the same way as arenas, as victims, but his work did expand to fit the new space in a series of constructed canvases.

But it isn't only the size and the scale of the gallery that has changed. (I cannot imagine Vivan Sundaram's *Trash* show in the old Chemould; and this may be taken as a synecdoche.) It is the size and scale of the artist's ambitions and the size and scale of their world.

Jitish Kallat points out another significant change in the way Chemould operates vis-a-vis its artists. 'If I look at most of my early international exhibitions, these happened without any links with the gallery. In the late nineties and early 2000s, a few Indian artists were possibly more internationally active than the galleries were because these were the days before the art fairs. Artists were represented in biennales, museums; and there was also the burgeoning international artist networks like the Triangle Artists Networks. At present the situation is very different and most of our key galleries participate in international art fairs but all this has happened in the last twelve years or so.'

This has made all the difference. Anju Dodiya puts it well. 'Our generation grew up with minimal needs. We only wanted to make art. [Prabhakar] Barwe's famous dictum was: if you can afford paint and canvas, good; if you can't afford paint and canvas, use paper and watercolours; if you can't afford watercolours, draw; if you can't afford paper and pencil, use rice paste and make collages. But *make art.* I began by drawing on the dining table; then when the work got bigger I moved to the bedroom. When we finally got our studio, I had one side of it and worked on the floor but when I got up from drawing, my hips would bump into the wall behind because there was just no space. We made do because all we wanted to do was make art. And recently I met a young woman who said she couldn't make art because she didn't have a studio.'

The conceptual artist Shilpa Gupta, who belongs to the same generation as the Kallats, says, 'We may be the first generation who can make a living out of art, even though that came much later to me than most of my peers. I could stop working as a graphic designer and become a full-time artist only around 2005-'06, almost a decade after leaving art school, I feel our generation has, in a short span seen and experienced a lot of extremes.'

This means the role of the gallery has changed too. Reena Saini-Kallat believes, 'The gallery plays a vital role as a mediator in helping communicate the artist's ideas to a wider audience just as views/opinions expressed by visitors are relayed back to the artist. Hence it is crucial for the artist and gallery to share affinities in the way they think and their approach with how the work should get represented. Since Shireen grew up in an environment with frequent interactions with artists, she understands the artistic and intellectual needs of artists. The gallery has had a long-term commitment to the work of many of their artists. After all, it is often the gallery that stands by the artist holding faith in the work even before it gains recognition from the outside world.'

All these artists are what might be described as 'hot tickets'. They would be welcomed almost anywhere in the art world. They stay with Chemould partly because it has worked for them but also because of Shireen.

Reena Kallat says, 'There are many similarities between Shireen and me in how emotionally sensitive she is as a person. She has always extended herself well beyond the professional boundaries of a gallery/artist relationship to make us a part of her extended family. Our working together over two decades has been a great learning curve for both of us from where we started. We can freely share our minds, exchange ideas and opinions, express differences if any, trusting the other will understand.'

Proximity brought the families closer. Jitish Kallat says, 'Since we moved to Bandra in 2005, we got closer to Shireen's family because we would often meet Kekoo while going for a walk at Bandstand and we would walk with him for a while before parting ways because there was always a mini assembly of people around him and people who would want to talk to him. He remained active with local civic issues even when he was of advanced age and not in great health. The relationship has lasted for a long time because I think we have both valued this collaboration and friendship. When Chemould and Bodhi Art Gallery came together to present a solo exhibition titled *Sweatopia* in 2007, twenty years after *PTO*, it was because there were some works that I could not show at Chemould. For instance, one of the sculptures was fifteen feet high and would not enter Chemould. I had also spoken to Amit Judge [of Bodhi] about my long-standing relationship with Chemould and that I saw this show as a celebration of a twenty-year old association. I would say that he was very graceful in the manner in which he phrased it, saying that he would jointly present the show and bring an added value to it.'

Shilpa Gupta adds, 'What I admire about Shireen is that she is concerned about the art, first and foremost. She looks straight at it, instead of at the possibilities of the transactions behind it. Even if she is confronted by something that no one can "possess", she is driven in a quiet and beautiful way, by what she sees rather than anything else. I have worked with galleries across the world and I think Shireen is a rare human being, like her father. The way they love and embrace art is truly heartwarming. It is from a moment, from a place, or a city, which once had another name, which one does not know exists. New gallerists from other cities will come and stay with her when they are in Bombay. When we were in Kassel recently for the Documenta, Priyanka Raja of Experimenter in Kolkata, and Shireen shared a room. I can't imagine two gallerists from France or Italy doing that.'

Reena Saini adds: 'Chemould has consistently taken risks with providing a platform for showing art that might be disruptive and provocative while challenging conventional norms. In the 1990s while I was still at art school, I recall encountering some of the most interesting artists from India showing new and exciting cutting-edge, experimental work at the gallery. A few years ago, when I completed a sculptural work that was to be shown at the Chemould booth in Art Basel, Miami Beach, I used salt to create the fairly large textual component on the floor. While this would be considered troublesome to exhibit at the art fair since the text would have to be recreated every time visitors walked around and disturbed it, Shireen never once questioned my decision; interestingly she also managed to place this complicated work in a good collection. She is someone who not only recognises how integral the medium is to the meaning of the artwork but is both respectful and appreciative of the artist's decision. She has always placed the evolution of the artist's work over any commercial interests.'

•

Geeta Kapur describes the new expansive space as 'one of the most beautiful exhibition spaces in the country and has been rendered so by an open plan that you can expand or turn into a maze.' And even before a decade had elapsed, a new milestone loomed on the horizon. Fifty years of an art gallery. Shireen decided to go with Geeta Kapur to curate a series of shows.

Kapur says, 'The five exhibitions I curated for the Fiftieth Anniversary were together titled "Aesthetic Bind". The shows took place from September 2013 to March 2014; each show was thematic and had a separate title.[77] Each show sought to unfold a different aesthetic and all the different meanings of the word, "bind". There were fifty-plus artists in the five shows—long-standing artists from the gallery shared space with young and unknown artists, and with artists who had never showed with Chemould. We made a beautiful catalogue for "Aesthetic Bind" with the dedicated designer, Anusha Yadav. It was several years in the making and becomes, I believe, a good exhibition book that includes, aside from the curator's text and a rich representation of the artworks exhibited, sheafs of artist-gallerist-curator correspondence: personal, anxious, descriptive and often purely technical—we were talking about inches, gaps, adjoining walls, and the way sound would carry or not carry through the gallery. It is an archive of the making of five exhibitions by fifty plus artists, one curator, Shireen and the Chemould team.

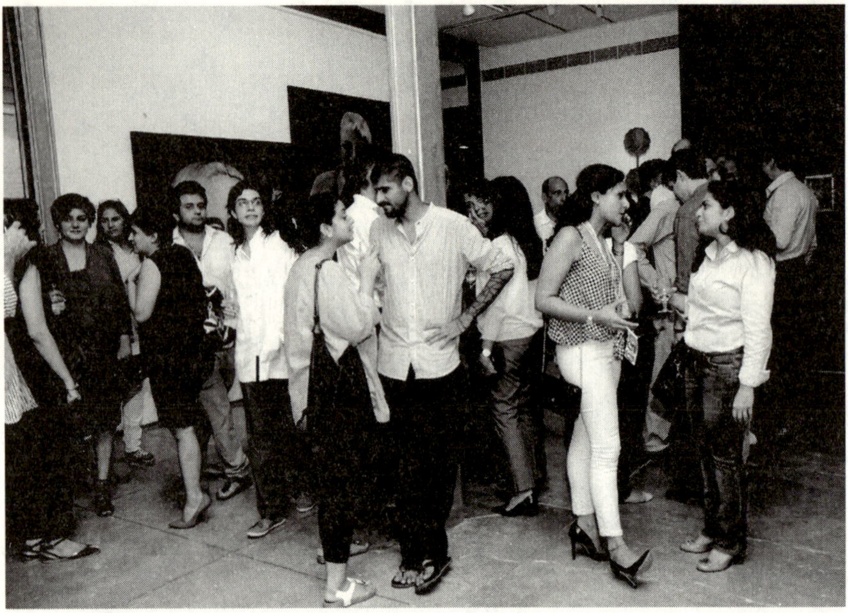

Visitors at the preview of 'Aesthetic Bind: Subject of Death': Chemould Prescott Road celebrates 50 Years of Contemporary Art, September 2013

'In those two years, only on one instance Shireen said to me "Do you know how many times you've been frenetic and behaved crazy and unreasonable with me!" I was going through a phase of bad health and much stress. I was not as mobile as I used to be; the two crutches had just come into play. Despite that the entire team worked perfectly; from Sandra and Rupal and Priti to Firdaus, Vithal and Naina. I haven't worked with many gallerists, I am sure they too have a good environment for work but here I have known twice over that the willingness to work, to change, to change again and again if necessary and to make it seem as if it is effortless—and that they trust you still—that comes from the way the Gandhys have functioned. It comes from their belief in art but also from their social commitments, and their generosity of spirit in a world shrinking with fear and retrograde ideologies.'

•

One of the last interviews I conducted for this book was with Atyaan Jungalwala, Gen 3.0. At the time, she was part of a campaign working against Mumbai's Coastal Road, three generations of social activism showing up, except that in this case, the war is being played out on social media. She says, 'I think activism has always been a part of our way of life; I think my grandparents were always involved in some cause or the other and so was my Mom.'

Galleries also run in the family. I asked her whether she saw herself running Gallery Chemould.

'Not in the way it is now but in some form or sort, yes, perhaps.'[78]

AFTERWORD

The Origin of This Book

> 'I remember the last time I went to see Khorshed; Kekoo had flown away by then. We were sitting at the dining table in Kekee Manzil, Rashna, Behroze, Khorshed and I. She was quiet and appeared self-contained. She was drinking her tea and suddenly, said, "Jerry Pinto". Surprised, we turned towards her. I asked, "What about Jerry Pinto?"
> Rashna asked if there was something she wanted to say, but she shook her head.
> Then she punctuated the long silence twice more...with just those two words... "Jerry Pinto".'
> —**Bina Sarkar Ellias,** founder editor of *International Gallerie*

Since the time I enrolled at the Elphinstone College in 1981, the Jehangir Art Gallery had always played some kind of role in my intellectual life. I am not sure why I went there although I did so regularly. I suppose I had the feeling that art was one of the elements of a sentimental education, part of a process by which you grew up and found your place in the world. I had the hazy notion that art improved you in some way, though I would have been hard pressed to define how and to my good luck, no one ever asked. Or it could have been much less high-minded: going to an art gallery was a signifier of a sort; it suggested that you were invested in the life of the mind and that you knew something more than the other poor swots who were just trying to get their degrees and get jobs.

Besides the Jehangir Art Gallery was across the road.

There were two other reasons. The toilets of Elphinstone College were malodorous beyond belief so many people went across the road to spend a rupee. And there was Samovar, the Bohemian café where, legend had it, you might just meet MF Husain and he might just sketch something on a napkin for you and make you rich beyond your wildest imaginings.[79]

I discovered Chemould only by accident. I was at yet another bad show at the Jehangir when a Parsi woman said to her friend, 'I don't know why we bother. Let's just go upstairs to Chemould; at least we'll get some real art there.'

I followed after a few seconds and discovered the hermetic quiet of Chemould. Khorshed Gandhy was at the desk; in my earliest memories of it, you had to get past a desk as if you were entering a tiny private club. It was an odd shape but that also seemed right. After all the brightly-lit and somewhat-too-large halls of the ground floor, there was something distinctive, almost personal about Chemould's space. I do not remember what the first show I saw there was; but eventually, I stopped going to the Jehangir Art Gallery; I walked straight upstairs, willing to take my chances with what the Gandhys had up on their walls.

I often felt there that I did not know how to be in the presence of art. I had problems of the usual adolescent kind; was it decadent? Was it bourgeoise? Was it a con job? When my friends found out, they wanted to know why I was going to galleries. I would sometimes say that it was the air-conditioning and the quiet; I would sometimes say it was the art. I think by then I had begun to understand that being in the presence of the disquieting and the discomfiting and the sometimes incomprehensible can rewrite your boundaries but so slowly you don't even notice when you stop wanting to understand, to parse and dissect and you begin to respond.

So when I began to climb those stairs as a professional journalist, I was a little better equipped than I thought I would be. (Not as well equipped as Ranjit Hoskote and Girish Shahane, or Nancy Adajania and Anupa Mehta, the other Elphinstonians who would become formidable art critics but I could manage.) I did go to review the art and interview the artist but as often as not, it was just because there was a place where your presence was not questioned. Without quite understanding how it became that way, I think Chemould grew into a space where you had the right to be. You didn't even have to look at the art. I would often go there to do precisely that and get dragged into discussions about the city and politics by Kekoo Gandhy, its mercurial founder. He would tell me what I should write about, he would tell me who to talk to, he would insist on feeding me at the Samovar, where Mrs Khanna would smile kindly upon him and keep young artists from disturbing us, promising them that Kekoo would meet them later. Back upstairs, several hours later, Khorshed Gandhy would remind me, 'Do you want to talk to the artist too?'

Khorshed was the backbone of the gallery; Kekoo its wings. Their life together was the stuff of which legends are made; only they were the legends themselves. She loved him and hated him and anchored him. He loved her and probably would have hated her too if he had taken time to think about it, but he grabbed her hand and whisked her into the blue yonder, taking risks no one else would dare at the time.

•

They left the building as they did everything else, with grace. When an artist wrote saying a show was ready, Khorshed would reply with a polite letter. The burden of these letters was: Shireen runs the gallery now; she will decide.

I asked Khorshed once whether she thought the gallery had changed much under her daughter. 'The city has changed. Art has changed. How can the gallery remain the same?' she asked.

Through those tumultuous decades, Khorshed and Kekoo began to see the fruits of their labour come into being. They had grandchildren across the globe. The gallery had moved out of the Jehangir Art Gallery and had morphed into Chemould Prescott Road. Indian art was selling well, with almost every other auction bringing news of a fresh price peak scaled; and many of these were paintings they probably knew, by artists they probably had nurtured in one way or another. The National Gallery for Modern Art was finally settled into the beautiful and eccentric building across the road from the Chhatrapati Shivaji Maharaj Vastu Sangrahalaya, once known as the Prince of Wales Museum.

I would love to leave them in this *dakshinayana* but I also remember a darker time. Kekoo had been in a decline for a while before he died in November 2012. He vanished from public view, choosing to spend more and more time at home and then withdrawing even further, to his bedroom. Perhaps he felt increasingly out of place in all the worlds through which he had moved so effortlessly. Perhaps the city had belied its early promise of an easy and accommodating cosmopolitanism. Perhaps the demons that had haunted him could no longer be held at bay by relentless movement, by constant reinvention, by a steady stream of people to see and issues to confront.

'I could not enter that room,' said Shireen. 'I knew I should but I could not. I did not know what to say to him. I did not know what he wanted. When I did go, I would sometimes catch a look of hope on his face, as if he were expecting something. But I didn't know what it could be.'

I had always enjoyed Kekoo too but in a way that was part response to spectacle and part bemusement. I could not make him out. I knew he seemed friendly, even fond of me, but this net was so wide, and it reached so far and took in so many people there was nothing in this fondness to make me feel that it was aimed at me. It was something in the nature of *agape*, disinterested love for all humanity and that made him seem at once approachable and distant. That meant I was not likely to seek him out though I was always happy to see him.

When Kekoo died, I thought about the man who appeared in a cameo in Salman Rushdie's great novel about my city, *The Moor's Last Sigh*.[80] I wrote a Facebook post about Kekoo's departure. I was invited to a Gathering of the Gandhys where tea was served and it was suggested that I might write a biography of Kekoo, Khorshed and the art gallery that they had created. I could have access to the files, I was told, I could write what I wanted and I would have access to the family as well.

And so it began. The Gandhy siblings kept tabs on the work but without undue interference. Khorshed however was always present in Kekee Manzil and since I visited often, I got to know her well. Like so many deeply intertwined couples, Kekoo's departure after sixty-eight years of marriage had left her deeply shaken but she was still interested in my work.

'What are you doing?' she asked once.

'Writing a book on Chemould.'

She looked doubtful but then that might have been her response, a Pavlovian reflex, no, perhaps it might be called the Sancho Panza reflex that develops when you have the scars of dealing with a Don Quixote.

'It's about how you and Kekoo built Chemould...'

'What Kekoo? I did all the work,' she snapped.

She was not exaggerating. Everyone in the art world at the time remembers the presence of Khorshed and Kekoo's engaging persona. Geeta

Kapur puts it well: 'I remember Khorshed at her desk at Chemould in Jehangir Art Gallery. Gracious but stoic, holding the ground with artists and visitors as her gregarious husband hung out at Samovar with artists, went about the city dialoguing, provoking, supporting forms of activism in the art world and in the social and cultural centres of the city. Kekoo. He was a remarkable man, not just for his commitment to the art world, but also for his wide range of commitments to democratic, secular and what one might broadly call Gandhian and socialist values. Something of a maverick himself, Kekoo was comfortable in the company of even the more anarchic artists. Khorshed, in contrast, was the one with contemporary art as a project firmed up by her own style of commitment.'

Once again, it seemed history would repeat itself. Kekoo had gone away and Khorshed was here doing the work. She and I would talk about this and that, about artists and archives. But the moment I turned back to my files, to the piles of paper and letters and catalogues, she would roll her wheelchair out of the room. She was no needy old lady who wanted to talk. She had spent her life being an independent tough-minded woman, an institution builder and a feminist; age was not going to wither that.

But even after she left the room, her spirit would linger in the letters I would be reading. Here she was organising a visit for an artist to Switzerland; there Kekoo and she would be toiling up the stairs of the Governor's Bungalow to set up an impromptu exhibition of contemporary Indian art for the Shahbanu of Iran (she bought two paintings; and more about this is in Part Two), here she is again writing to another artist about how the general public responds to his work.

And her cheque books reveal a giving heart. Almost all of them are made out to people she was supporting in one way or the other. Some of these were artists who needed help in their early days. Others were people she had met and befriended after the riots of 1992-'93, when Kekoo and she worked tirelessly in Behrampada, one of the Muslim settlements worst affected by the conflagrations that followed the demolition of the Babri Masjid.

•

Pinakin Patel, long-time friend and collaborator, told me the story of Khorshed's going: 'One night, we were attending a talk at Jnanapravaha and Shireen got up very suddenly and left. I didn't know what was going on but I got up too and followed her. When I got to their home, there were Behroze and Rashna and they told me that she had been calling my name in her semi-comatose state. I said: "Here I am". The family was deep in a discussion about what should be done now. Shireen, the hard-core radical, wanted to take her back to hospital. I looked at all of them, at the faces of Adil and Behroze and Rashna and after a while I asked if I could have some time with her alone. They said sure and I went into her bedroom and I leaned down close to her and I said, "Look darling, how wonderful your complexion is, there are roses in your cheeks. Here's your chance to die with grace. Why do you want to go to hospital where they'll just poke you and prod you everywhere and give you some more months of assisted living? *Ab jaa tu, dikri, jaa* (Go my darling, go). You've led a wonderful life and you've had some wonderful times. It's the best time for you to go."

'I came out and told the children I thought she should be allowed to remain in her own home, with her children and grandchildren around her, to live out the rest of her time in peace. I said it protectively, I said it out of love, I wanted her to go with grace. Then I went home to Alibaug and the next morning, they called to say she had passed away.'

At her funeral, her son Adil Gandhy read out her last requests. She wanted no memorial service and no solemn faces. She wanted laughter and stories. She wanted a celebration of her life, in life.

'"Don't cry for me, Argentina", may be sung,' she wrote.

•

I spent many happy mornings in Kekee Manzil, trying not to be distracted by the view of that old pretender, the Arabian Sea; trying not to be distracted by the art on the walls around me and the many beautiful items of furniture; trying to be the good biographer of an enterprise built around a shell of space that must be animated and reanimated by what happens inside it.

And one day, as I walked out of my wonderful workspace and was crossing the little patch of park before you hit the Bandstand, a Muslim couple stopped me. They were middle-aged, care-worn in the way that poverty can grind you down.

'*Suna hai ek aadmi rehta yahaan,*' said the man tentatively. (I've heard a man lives here.)

I thought I knew what he meant but I waited.

'*Ek bada aadmi.*' (A big man.)

'Shah Rukh Khan?' I said and pointed to Mannat, the star's bungalow that is next door to Kekee Manzil.

'*Nahin, wo nahin. Ek aadmi jo garibon ka madat karta hai,*' he said. (Not him. A man who helps the poor.)

The sun is hot as I walk down the Bandstand, where a piece of sculpture stands, donated by the Gandhys to the city they loved.

And I think: When all else fades, it is kindness that remains.

Envoi

How the earth turned green; a Warli legend

Mahadev and Gauri looked down from the heavens and found the earth bare of trees. They descended, armed with bags of seeds. Mahadev set off in one direction and Gauri in the other, planting seeds along the way. They walked for many years, covering the parched brown earth with lush green trees.

Gauri grew old and grey, Mahadev lean and weary. Thus they met, their bags empty, their good deed done.

'Who are you?' asked Mahadev, as he met an old woman hobbling along.

'I am Gauri,' replied the woman.

'And I am your husband, Mahadev. Our work is done, let us go home.'[81]

(Taken from Lakshmi Lal's *The Warlis: Tribal Paintings and Legends*)

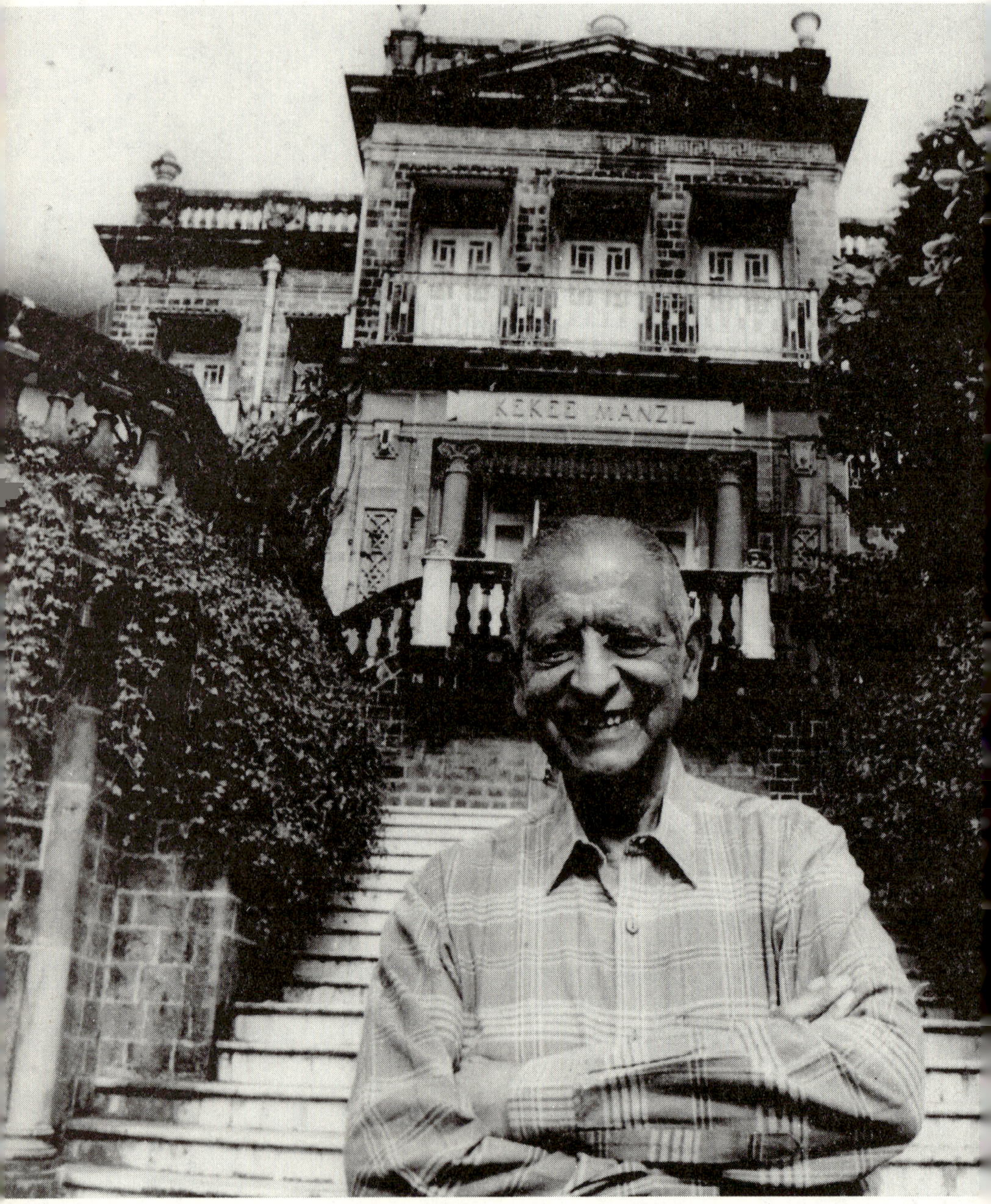
KEKEE MANZIL

PART TWO

Kekoo and Khorshed in Their Own Words

The Beginnings of the Art Movement

Kekoo Gandhy

Among the European painters who came to India during the War was Walter Langhammer, an Austrian. He was a contemporary of the famous painter Oskar Kokoschka, who was professor of the Academy in Vienna in the 1930s. There was this Parsi girl called Silloo Vakil from Bombay who was studying with him and she used to say to him, 'Walter, you must come to India one day,' and he would say '*Ja, ja.*' So when Hitler came along and he had to leave Austria, he wrote to Vakil, saying that he would like to come to India. And she walked into the office of Sir Francis Low, editor of *The Times of India,* and said, 'I am the daughter of Rotarian Vakil and I would like you to promise me something.' She was cheeky enough to do that. The result was that Langhammer was appointed as the first art director of the TOI. The year must have been 1936. And at the time it had the only colour annual number.

Langhammer fell in love with the light and colour of India and all the young artists. Here, he would often say, he saw a future in the modern art movement—he felt it was all over in Europe. So people like Ara, Raza, Husain, Souza and Raiba, the great names of the Indian Progressive Art Movement, became his students. Every Sunday, it was open house at his studio on Nepean Sea Road.[82]

He would tell them what makes a good painting. He would share his experiences of Europe and tell them about events in the art world, seen at first hand. They found a windfall in this readymade teacher. And he had so much love and affection for them. It was not just the artists alone—the people around them too were responsible, in a way, for the birth of the Progressives. There were factors like the excitement over the prospect of impending Independence, the feeling that now Indian artists would not have to go through Westminster, that India would have its own embassies in different parts of the world, and that we would be able to make our own connections.

Remember that in those days, Indian artists had no means of going abroad or of following trends in Europe. Of course, there were magazines, but the unexpected arrival of all these Europeans—most of them Jews fleeing from Austria—really started the Progressive movement off. Apart from Langhammer, there was Dr E Schlesinger and Rudy von Leyden, both German. Rudy was the chief PRO of Volkart Brothers, a Swiss trading company based in India, and he had a younger brother, AR Leyden, a sculptor who styled himself as a painter after Langhammer and was called 'little Langhammer'. They had arrived before Langhammer because their father foresaw the arrival of Hitler by two or three years. They were all warm and outgoing people, generous too. The founder chairman of Larsen & Toubro, a Danish gentleman called Holck Larsen, was one of the earliest art patrons. They were also the 'in people' of the time. They were written about in the papers very often.

With Langhammer came a lot of professionals, doctors…a sort of mini-influx of Jews. They valued art and provided patronage. Schlesinger was so attached to Mohan Samant, one of the Progressive artists, that he would travel by local train to Goregaon to see what he was up to. They had a great enthusiasm for Indian artists—who else was interested?—and they pioneered buying. They were not the only foreigners to influence the new art movement.

Towards the end of the War, with operations ongoing in North Africa, Italian POWs were brought in by the British and domiciled in camps all over India. Captain Dust, an Englishman, decided that these able-bodied men should be put to some work. Among them were car mechanics, painters and waiters. He selected those who could use a brush and formed a separate unit in the army called MURART. The idea was to get them to paint and use their work across all army establishments in South Asia. Dust went to [Lord Louis] Mountbatten with a proposal and, imaginative as he was, Mountbatten accepted the idea and put him in charge. He was given a building at Chakala near Sahar airport. The POWs were equipped with soft boards and were asked to paint. That is how these Italian men started creating paintings here in Bombay.

Meanwhile, back on vacation from Cambridge (I never went back) during the War, I met a Belgian gentleman who had landed up in India called Van Damme. His father had been a framer and restorer of the great Flemish masters. He had heard a news story back home about the many gods and goddesses that Indians kept in their homes. He knew that India would be a captive market to sell frames. Our acquaintance led to the establishment of the Chemould Framing Factory in 1940. He gave me know-how, we got the finance together and my brother Russy and I set up the factory.

Around the time Dust was putting together his idea, the Chemould factory was in a plot behind our bungalow called Shapur Baug in Chakala. The Leela Hotel stands there today. It was a very pretty place with mango and chikoo wadis. The British requisitioned the ground floor of this bungalow for MURART. Wood was scarce because it was requisitioned for the war effort. We did not know how to continue with our business. Luckily, MURART said they needed frames for all these paintings they were churning out and they started supplying us with wood. We worked exclusively for them.

For soldiers, the Italians were really good artists. They would come home on Sundays. We handed the kitchen over to them and they would prepare all these risottos. They were lonely people, far from home, so we tried to help them by selling the private work they did, not the ones they made for MURART. Food was rationed at the time, but they were soldiers and had everything. They used to bake lovely cookies. We began to invite over our friends and other Indian artists. Everyone had a good time and after dinner a hat was passed around. For Rs 100 or 200, you could pick up one of the finest paintings of the time and everyone was happy.

Collecting art was really started by a few individuals. Though there was no art movement or recognised artists around, Bombay's first generation of collectors were quite generous. Ratan Tata's father, Naval Tata, was a very kind man. We had a party at his house in Juhu and in one night sold ten or twelve paintings, some of the private work of the Italians and some by our own Indian painters. Bombay then had the right mix of socialites and patrons. We were, of course, trying to make it a fashion statement, so that people would feel that it was the in thing to buy art. Since there were no galleries then, all this was done at our homes.

Much later, in the early seventies, when Holck Larsen was still chairman of Larsen & Toubro, I remember telling him that Jamshedji Tata believed that by picking out talented people from across the country and nurturing them, he was doing the greatest service to the country. Immediately, he told me to name an artist and he would look after him. So a Bangladeshi refugee called Bhushan was installed at the factory, supplied with materials and told that all he had to do was create art. He stayed for three years.

But coming back to the early forties, one Christmas I was at Porcupine Point in Matheran and I met Schimmel, another Austrian. When he learned that I ran Chemould, he asked me to meet his good friend Langhammer as soon as I got back to Bombay. In those days, we were making mouldings for paintings, but Langhammer asked us to make frames. And he explained to me his vision for Indian art. He really believed that contemporary Indian art would make a mark and have an impact on the art scene in the world. He even compared it in terms of impact to the French Impressionist movement. When he said 'Indian art', he was referring to the various schools—the Bengal school, miniature paintings, the influence of Indian sculpture. India had a great store of inspiration to draw from and the colours and light of India would make the difference, he felt.

Meanwhile, the Progressive artists were working hard to establish their own identity. They were working on a very deliberate policy of establishing their own personalities and not using past traditions to express themselves. At that time, the JJ School of Art had two sections—Indian and western—with different principals. Jagannath Ahivasi looked after the Indian section and at the Western section was Charles Gerrard, a Jew from England. But the question on everyone's mind was: where do we go from here?

People like Souza and Ara were not sticking to the academic conventions of painting and nor were they students of the Indian section, which concentrated on miniatures. All the encouragement from Langhammer and his circle of art collectors at the Bombay Art Society, a most vibrant and prestigious body, gave them a place of their own. They said: We are what we are. We don't want to copy the West. We are products of our immediate environments and want to establish our identity by being contemporary.

The Bombay Art Society was set up in the latter part of the last century by the masters of academic painting, most of whom were traditional artists from the academies of the West. There, artists were taught to take a canvas, prime it, grind colour and be responsible for the painting right up to the varnishing stage. For the Indian artists who were learning from them, all this was very new. Oil paint was not part of the Indian tradition. The Indians were experts at watercolours on cloth, or murals and frescoes.

This was one of the earliest exchanges between the West and India in art. The society had an annual event, a gold medal for the artist of the year, and without doubt it was the most prestigious art award. Artists before the Progressives like Dhurandhar, Haldankar and Pithawalla had won this award. Later, artists like Husain and Amrita Sher-Gil were also honoured.

Leyden introduced me very enthusiastically to Ara. Ara came from a humble background and I remember Gallery Chemould sponsored his first exhibition at Chetana in the late forties. Rajeswar Rao, the writer, came down from Paris and Mulk Raj Anand was back from London, and we were keen that it should be a big success. I remember inviting people down the road from my home—doctors, dentists, people we knew personally, we told them to go and they bought paintings for Rs 200 or so.

Leyden supported Ara for a long time. When Ara made some money from the exhibition, he wanted to give it to Leyden. But Leyden opened a bank account for him with that money and told him that he was on his own.

I shared a close personal relationship with KK Hebbar. I first met him at Langhammer's studio and we shared a lot of enthusiasm for the independence of the country. We hero-worshipped Nehru. But after the Chinese conflict we could not possibly go on like that. We remained great friends, despite the fact that our ideologies had changed. He was the one who introduced me to Gerrard, who was then Dean of the School of Art.

Husain was a favourite of Wayne Hartwell, who was the librarian at the USIS, opposite Khadi Bhandar. You could walk straight into his office off the pavement. This was in 1946 and he was one of the most consummate buyers of our set, as well as a very good friend. He and his wife loved the work of Husain and Chavda. Don't forget that Husain was a nobody then. He was to rise to great heights later, but at the time it was Chavda who was sought after. He had a powerful personality. Unlike most of the others, he was an educated, sophisticated and quiet person. One of Husain's paintings, 'Doll's Wedding', was part of a Chemould exhibition and was picked up by Hartwell. He took it home with him and we heard that it had changed hands. It was finally sold for 35,000 dollars in the mid-eighties and I know Wayne had bought it for Rs 300 in the 1940s right here in Bombay.

I can't say honestly that I was interested in art to begin with, or that I had any great knowledge of it. I got interested through my friends Langhammer and Leyden, after seeing their great enthusiasm for contemporary Indian art. I was moved by their belief in the future of Indian contemporary art. And once I began interacting with the artists—they were such beautiful, trusting people, Ara and Raza and Hebbar—I felt I could be a go-between. As a Rotarian, I was meeting a certain class of people, and I felt I had a distinctive role to play and, in particular, a vested interest in the framing of their art.

I had a vested interest in seeing a picture transformed by a frame, when it would stand a better chance of finding a buyer. Indian art then had no market, and it gave me a lot of satisfaction to be part of a process that sold paintings. There was no commission in those days. Then came a time when artists would leave their paintings—Raza, Palshikar, Ara, Gade, Raiba. Raiba was so badly off that we had to give him a job at the framing factory. But the great thing was that they trusted us.

They would all leave their paintings with us. We had a place called Haroon House next to a stationery mart behind the Reserve Bank. There, we displayed some of the paintings that came to us for framing. The Metro Cinema opened with a lot of fanfare and we took a portion of the wall on the first floor and called it the Metro Art Corner. When people came out after the show, they would see the paintings. And we had a window on the first floor of the Taj from 1944 to 1948. Then we realised that we needed a bigger place, since we were selling a fair number of paintings there. My father had a godown on Princess Street, which we turned into a framing shop. Roshan Kalapesi showed initiative in displaying art and framing all the paintings. The Progressives made their first sales through this shop and the Artists Centre at Rampart Row.

So that became the first regular place for display, where we showed all these paintings that the artists had left behind. Then Homi Bhabha, who was setting up the Tata Institute of Fundamental Research(TIFR), came over after lunch and started examining our frames with a great deal of interest. He was very meticulous about framing.

We soon recognised discerning and interested art patrons and started holding private exhibitions. We had previews for Homi Bhabha, which is why the TIFR has the best private collection of 1940s art. The contagion spread among our set from Langhammer and Leyden to Homi Bhabha and Farrok Mulla,[83] PRO of the Tatas. They were all patrons of the Chemould shop.

At our first Husain exhibition, I looked out of the window and saw my wife's uncle, the founder-owner of *Parsiana* magazine, passing by. I just pulled him in and said we needed a crowd. The poor man had no idea what was going on. But Husain sold so well that we were flooded with work from artists all over India. After that exhibition, our sales of frames and art shot up from Rs 5,000 per year to Rs 20,000 per year. That is when Mulla, Langhammer, Leyden and I got together—Sir Cowasji Jehangir was there too—to discuss how we could handle this sudden growth of interest. The implication was that artists in Bombay needed a gallery. So we put this to Sir Cowasji Jehangir, who was already a patron, and though a political person (he was a crucial mediator between Gandhi and Jinnah and was active in the Legislative Assembly), he also bought art.

He hailed from a long line of visionary benefactors. Two hundred years ago, his great-great grandfather had founded the Bombay University

Convocation Hall, the next generation gave the city the building where the National Gallery of Modern Art is housed, and the next sponsored Elphinstone College. He granted the funds for setting up the Jehangir Art Gallery in 1951-52. The museum gave the land and they had a tripartite agreement. He had the foresight to put nominees of the Bombay Art Society on the management committee of the Jehangir Art Gallery; the idea was to differentiate the promotion of art from the sale of art.

We were invited by the committee to set up a gallery on the first floor. We started the Gallery Chemould. I was persuaded by artists like [FN] Souza and [Shiavax] Chavda not to do this. They said, 'You will never recover your investments.' Somehow, we did not make losses but our profits from the framing company certainly fell. Since I was already with the Bombay Art Society set, I was really in the thick of things and with the help and support of my wife Khorshed, we continued to promote art independently as the proprietors of Gallery Chemould.

It has given us great joy to support the art movement and see it grow from strength to strength. Today we continue to support exhibitions like the one my wife put together called 'The Portrait of a Community', which opened at the National Gallery of Modern Art in October 2002. We have both retired from the running of the Gallery Chemould, which our youngest daughter Shireen continues to run, and the framing factory has been taken over by our son Adil.

—As told to grand-daughter, Anisha Imhasly.

A Compassionate Master

Perhaps because of the relevant affluence of my home background, I was at an early age awakened to my social conscience and felt a desire to help people. Later I was to experience many conflicts between this desire and my own personal ambitions for success and popularity. I became aware that fulfilment could not be achieved by pursuing one goal. More deeply I began to realise that there was no one ideology, social, political or moral, which could give me what I wanted; that the question was not of adherence to a group or an idea but was more personal; and in this way all the more pervasive in my life.

I recall theorising a great deal about the need for detachment, about peace of mind, about not living on reactions of others, but in fact when I was in a crisis, my behaviour was far removed from my theories. When this continued, it became frustrating and made me restless.

It was at this stage that I first encountered Baba through a friend who talked about the Kundalini Shakti—the dormant soul force in every human being, which association with a 'Siddha' could help awaken. I enjoyed staying with Baba in the L-shaped ashram, for that was its shape in 1962, as much as I enjoyed the hot springs at Kothawalla's half a mile away! I would return to Bombay with a feeling of well-being, of the 'battery having been recharged!' Reading the experiences of the 'awakened Shakti' in the *Guruvani* and witnessing some of these phenomena with my own eyes, I longed for these experiences in my own life. With the many, many problems that my ambition was landing me into, I began to believe that there was no recourse other than the 'awakened Shakti', which could deal with the mess and confusion I was constantly creating around me! When I asked Amma,[84] all she would say was, 'Keep coming more often.' This used to irritate me, as I thought I had gone often enough! Baba's words were 'Spend a little time morning and night on *japa*.' I did so as regularly as was practicable, but nothing spectacular has happened so far—no visions, no blue lights!

Years have rolled on and my friendship and respect for Baba has turned into an inexplicable devotion and a faith—a faith not without reason. I have been the recipient of his help on many occasions. In times when I have not known what to do—he has shown the way. For example I faced a great dilemma at the time when my daughter wanted to get married to a Swiss, at very short notice. She was determined to leave India and get married if we did not agree. We loved her dearly and we felt a little time was called for before she hastily plunged into this important decision. However, Baba's guidance, which was not based on caste, religion or social custom, at this juncture helped to find a solution which has led her to be happily married, and she is, at the same time, on the closest terms with the family. The young couple felt doubly blessed to have had the privilege of being married by Baba; the marriage ceremony was arranged by Baba at the ashram itself.

Yet another example was when we had a prolonged strike in our factory, due to a professional racketeer who had a hold over our workers. Although they realised they were being misled, the workers had gone along with him too far to retract. My faith in Baba had grown tremendously, and his interest and advice helped in no small measure to consolidate my decision to stand firm and have patience. The strike lasted for three months, and although the process was long and painful, the results were not only rewarding, but it created an atmosphere between labour and management free from any acrimony and bitterness.

My respect for Baba which has turned into a growing affection for him is slowly turning into love for people in general and a compassion for those with whom I differ. Now and then I feel a sense of bliss and joy which provides a peace of the heart to enjoy my work without an undue hankering for results.

If I am not a recipient of '*Shakti*' in the manner of the experience of many other devotees of Baba whom I have got to know at the Ashram, I can hardly deny being a recipient of Baba's grace. I find myself being constantly an instrument to lead other people to Baba, who are perhaps more 'ready' spiritually and have flowered fast in his presence. I cannot be grateful enough for a faith that is growing slowly but surely. While old forms and ideas are crumbling, I feel it is a privilege to be a participant with Baba, and other great souls of his stature in the building of a new world order, based on personal change of man and his motives with fresh values and goals. Who knows, this may enable man to contribute more effectively to human happiness than he has done so far?

—From a collection of articles about Bhagawan Nityananda (Baba), p. 54

The Art of Thinking Bigger

This is a story about how thinking big can lead to something even bigger. It is a true story. It happened right here, in the Rotary Club of Bombay, and it can happen again. So listen up!

The year was 1969. I was a member of the International Service committee, and Rotarian Chinubhai Kilachand was its chairman. Shantilal Mehta, then the District Governor (DG), gave a call to clubs to create truly grand projects to build Rotary's image. In response to this call, we, in collaboration with Jehangir Art Gallery and Max Müller Bhavan, organised an exhibition of paintings by young emerging artists of the Society of Contemporary Artists, Calcutta, from 23rd to 29th January, 1970.

While the gallery contributed the exhibition space, former District Governor Naval Ardeshir sponsored the production of a handsome catalogue. Individual Rotarians played host to the artists, which included names like Bikash Bhattacharjee and Ganesh Pyne. Everything was free for them.

In his inaugural address, DG Shantilal vindicated the worthiness of our cause. 'To help or to give service to the most talented in the land is the need of the hour, and the greatest service that we can render to the nation,' he said, quoting Sir Jamshedji Tata.

Our Rotarians worked hard, individually and collectively, to ensure brisk sales of paintings. The exhibition was a resounding success.

But more was to come...

They say God helps those who help themselves. The subtle hand of fate was working, unbeknownst to us, beneath the surface. Present at this exhibition, by a stroke of pure luck, were some visiting Rotarians from major European cities such as Zurich, Dusseldorf, Essen, Hamburg and Brussels. So enthused were they by the work of the artists and the Rotarians, and by DG Shantilal's rousing speech, that they proposed an international exhibition in Europe.

I will never forget this moment at Naval Ardeshir's home in Bandra, when, after dinner, the Rotarians from Europe went into a huddle, and emerged with an offer to do for us what we had done for the Calcutta artists. 'Put together an exhibition of paintings from all over India, and we will organise everything at our end,' they said.

Overriding opposition from those who felt that we were sailing into unknown waters, or that it was an elitist cause, unworthy of Rotary involvement, Chinubhai and I accepted the proposal. In this grand endeavour, the Rotary Clubs of Bombay, Delhi and Calcutta came together to collect the best of Indian art.

Now we had one big worry: who would foot the astronomical bill of flying these paintings to Europe? Providentially, help arrived from unexpected quarters.

The Shah and Shahbanu of Iran happened to be visiting Bombay at the time of our exhibition, and staying at the Raj Bhavan. We approached them through the good offices of Lady Jehangir (wife of Sir Cowasji Jehangir, after whom Jehangir Art Gallery is named), and at their request, took some paintings to the Raj Bhavan for a special viewing. They not only bought some of these, but asked for the exhibition to be taken to Teheran as well, offering the services of their national carrier, Iran Air, free of charge.

The costs of flying the paintings out were taken care of. And in the bargain, my wife Khorshed and I were royally hosted as guests of the State in Teheran. (Incidentally, the royal couple had quite a soft corner for Zoroastrians!)

The showing in Teheran was a grand success, making the front pages of the local dailies. I was invited to give a talk on contemporary Indian art at the Rotary Club of Teheran.

My wife and I escorted the paintings—steering the exhibition through its winding route. The exhibition ran for several months in Europe, including a full month in Dusseldorf. So it helped that we had our own bases there. My daughter Rashna was living in Zurich; her husband, a Swiss national, was then serving in the diplomatic corps. And Chinubhai was running a government-aided art centre called 'Sona' in Dusseldorf, and also had residential premises there. But for this, the hotel and organisational expenses would have been killing!

At Dusseldorf, I had the privilege of interacting with Rotarian Werner Schmallenbach, who was, so to speak, the Pope of the art world. Sitting here at Sona through many an afternoon, amidst our small staff, he warmly helped us network with other art centres in Europe.

The cost of travelling to each exhibition centre was taken care of by the cultural council of that nation. Air India helped generously in various ways. Also, we had the unflinching support of Bombay's stalwarts—some of them Rotarians—like Sir Cowasji Jehangir, PP Ambalal Kilachand, Neville Wadia, Lalchand Hirachand, PP Pratap Bhogilal, JRD Tata, and the Mafatlals—both Rashesh and Arvind. The exhibition moved forward without financial hitches.

But nonetheless, approaching the end of this travelling exhibition, the last big hurdle loomed large: who would bill the big bill of flying back home?

Again, this worry was taken care of quite providentially. Rolf and Utte Rettberg, a German couple residing in Frensheim, near Heidelberg, offered to take over the entire exhibition and use it to establish an Indian art gallery abroad. Gallery Surya, as it came to be known, continued for many years to be India's show window in Germany.

In 1970-71, this project got us our first Significant Achievement Award from Rotary International. Our club was the toast of the District!

I daresay, that was our first lesson in the art of thinking big. Some big projects have followed after that, but none that seriously challenges it in scale or spread or grandeur of vision. (Am I wrong, fellow Rotarians? I would love to stand corrected on this point!)

I think it is high time we all got together and did something like this again. Something that shows Rotary as being a truly global organisation, that towers above petty considerations in the service of all that is noble and grand in human nature. What do you say?

—*The Gateway*, 23 April 1992

•

'Mirroring the Past': an interview in the catalogue of 'Seventeen Indian Painters'[85]

Among the second generation of contemporary painters, Bhupen Khakhar has always been interested about the times in the late 1940s when a new art climate was emerging in Bombay. Here he interviews Kekoo Gandhy to get a flavour of those days and Kekoo's own involvement in it.

BK: ***It is said that Bombay provided the first impetus to the modern art movement. How did this come about?***

KKG: There was a series of events which brought this about. Different people in key positions through their personal involvement were contributing towards the whole. Bombay has always been a cosmopolitan society and it was essentially this fundamental factor which contributed to the intermingling of different cultures so vital to any growth. We are now talking about the 1940s, let me see how many people involved I can recall and the roles they played.

George Keyt, the Sinhalese artist, was living for a prolonged period in Bombay and he was certainly amongst the moderns. Mulk Raj Anand had returned from England and being a close friend of Keyt, Mulk was one of the earliest art enthusiasts. Amrita Sher-Gil had shone and disappeared like a meteor. Karl Khandalawala, an ardent admirer of Sher-Gil, had authored a book on her work which was published by New Book Company. (To digress a little, this fifteen-inch book with twenty full-page colour reproductions was priced at only Rs 40 in those days! I bought several of these and gave them as presents to my Italian artist friends.)

Then of course there was the famous European trio of Rudy von Leyden, Langhammer and Schlesinger. They had settled in Bombay in the mid 1930s because of Hitler's anti-Semitic activities.

BK: ***Would you say that theirs was the major contribution during that period?***

KKG: I have no hesitation in declaring that this is correct. Each one had his own distinct role to play. Rudy was an art critic, writing in those days for the *Times of India.* With his discerning eye, he would pick out the wheat from the chaff when he reviewed the annual exhibitions of the Bombay Art Society. Raza tells the story of how overwhelmed he felt when Rudy in his art review mentioned his watercolour as the most refreshing painting in that year's exhibition![86]

Langhammer was the art director in the *Times of India.* His annual numbers of the *Times* with their full-colour reproductions of the moderns was bringing them to the notice of the public. Besides, every Sunday morning his home became the rendezvous where the young artists like Ara, Raza, Samant, Gaitonde received critical comments about their latest works.

Schlesinger was an important art collector in Vienna. He had to leave everything behind. In Bombay, he picked up the young painters' works with real enthusiasm and helped several of his European friends to do the same. Kathe Langhammer,[87] Walter's wife, told me while she was reminiscing last year that Schlesinger not only found a room which became the Bombay Art Society's salon on Rampart Row but he continually got his friends to buy the paintings. Only when pictures sold, did the young artists get launched, was Kathe's comment.

BK: ***Can you give an idea at what prices the paintings were sold in this Salon you just mentioned?***

KKG: Ram Chatterjee had organised an exhibition in aid of the Artists' Aid Fund. He has a copy of this catalogue in his possession where artists contributed their paintings. Husain sold at Rs 50, Bendre sold at Rs 40, Hebbar at Rs 60, and Langhammer who was the most expensive sold at Rs 190! You only have to add a couple of zeroes behind that number today to get a comparatively young artist's painting. We have moved on, have we not?

BK: ***Kekoo, now let us talk about your background a little. You started with the frame factory so how did you get involved in art?***

KKG: Two distinctly different factors got me involved. It was war-time when we set up our factory with a Belgian partner who had the know-how of manufacturing frames. The factory was located in Marol, almost a jungle area and I used to drive out in 'Victorias' (horse carriages) from Andheri Station to the factory every morning. On the way to Marol was the Italian Prisoners of War camp. They were turning out pictures, panels and murals for various army camps in South-east Asia. It was called MURART. They heard about our framing factory and approached us for their supply. Just as well, because being war-time wood was difficult to obtain and their quota of wood kept us going for some time.

BK: ***Were you interested in their work?***

KKG: I was interested in how my frames looked! It increased my vanity to see a good frame making a painting look better.

BK: ***Is this how you came in contact with the artists?***

KKG: I had an idea. The MURART artists did some private paintings. These paintings could be sold. I invited many friends and some prominent personalities to MURART for a function. We all got together. They met the Italian artists. Their works were sold.

BK: ***Who was the leading artist among the MURART ones?***

KKG: Giovanni Pinto.[88] I have a painting by him. The Cricket Club of India had also bought his painting. It is still hanging in their Dining Room.

BK: ***What is the second factor that you mentioned earlier?***

KKG: Prof Langhammer also came to know about our framing. He insisted that I should make mouldings of his design for his paintings. At first, I resisted, thinking I could not make special frames for one individual artist. However he convinced me that there was a whole group of young painters in whom he had a lot of faith. They would one day create a big demand for my mouldings, he said.

BK: ***Is that how you first established touch with the early painters like Ara, Husain, Souza, Hebbar and others?***

KKG: Yes, these painters introduced by Langhammer started coming to my office to get their paintings framed. That made it necessary for me to open a retail framing shop at Princess Street. Ara was soon to have his first one-man exhibition at Chetana Restaurant which was inaugurated by the well-known writer Raja Rao. He could not afford to pay for his frames so we took interest in seeing that the paintings got sold amongst our family and friends. This was my next opportunity to sell paintings. I was by now continually putting framed paintings on display at my shop and several of the customers like Dr Homi Bhabha and others were buying paintings of these young artists.

BK: ***With your growing interest in art by then, was your activity confined to Princess Street?***

KKG: No, I was participating in some committees to sponsor exhibitions of artists in different parts of the city, eg. [Shiavax] Chavda's exhibition was held at the Taj, Raza's was at the Institute of Foreign Languages, Jamini Roy's first exhibition in Bombay was at the Salon and of course several others. Bakre, Souza, Gade were at the Salon from where the main thrust of art activity was continuing.

I had planned an exhibition in Delhi in 1948. I knew that many businessmen who came to Delhi for FICCI's annual conference and stayed at the Imperial Hotel used to be at a loose end in the evenings. I organised an exhibition in All-India Fine Arts & Crafts Society (AIFACS). On one wall were displayed fifteen paintings of Amrita Sher-Gil borrowed from Helen Chamanlal and on the opposite wall were works of Raza, Ara, Husain, Palshikar, Hebbar, Chavda, Gade, DG Kulkarni. The show was a great success and paintings sold. Many people came to see Amrita Sher-Gil's work including Pandit Jawaharlal Nehru who was brought by Pan Narielwala to the exhibition.

We opened our Framing Centre in Calcutta by having an inaugural exhibition by Bombay artists. These artists were Palshikar, Gaitonde, Raza, Husain, Hebbar, amongst others.

BK: ***Was Bombay Art Society the main centre of art activities in those days?***

KKG: The annual exhibition of the Bombay Art Society had established the tradition of giving a show window of the best art of the year. Its Gold Medal was a much-coveted honour. Sir Cowasji Jehangir was a patron in the real sense of the word. Though his personal collection was miniatures and ancient sculptures, the present-day artists were encouraged and promoted through the important status he gave to the society as its active president.

The annual exhibition was an important social event. The Governor always inaugurated it and the ladies came dressed in gloves, hats and elaborate sarees. To be seen at that function every year made you a part of the 'art-elite' of Bombay.

The opening was followed by a party which the Langhammers always hosted in their home. Kathe was a fabulous cook. On one such occasion Chavda made an on-the-spot sketch of the guests, including the artist Topolski.

BK: ***Can you tell me any significant incidents in the art field in Bombay between 1950 and 1960, just prior to the time you started your Chemould Gallery at the Jehangir?***

KKG: Late Allen Currimbhoy and his wife Priti had started the Roopa Art Gallery at the Taj Mahal. Then of course there was the popular Bhulabhai Institute. Many prominent artists from Bombay had their studios there and the place was humming with actitvty including theatre workshops of [Ebrahim] Alkazi.

Soon after Bal Chhabda started 'Gallery 59' also at the Bhulabhai. It is interesting how he entered the art field. Bal had recently returned from Hollywood and wanted to make a film on an Indian artist. I introduced him to Husain and Gaitonde; they became good friends, soon afterwards Bal launched his art gallery. He started exhibiting the works of Ram Kumar, Akbar Padamsee, Gaitonde, Tyeb Mehta, Krishen Khanna, Husain and Raza.

BK: ***Tell me about the prices at the time.***

KKG: The prices were around Rs 300-500 but during one of Bal's group exhibitions, Raza fixed his price at Rs 1200. He created a stir especially among the artists. They felt it was much too high. However the painting sold! As far as I remember, that was the first time paintings of a contemporary artist were sold in Bombay for four figures.

BK: ***Tell me about how Chemould entered the field as a professional gallery.***

KKG: I was beginning to see the trend that paintings were gaining in importance and with my own interest in contemporary art, it was the most obvious diversification for our Chemould Organisation. Luckily for me, some people connected with the Jehangir Art Gallery also felt the same way, especially because Bombay did not have a sponsoring gallery whereas there were already two established by then.

Besides, the sales at the annual exhibition of the Bombay Art Society had touched an all-time low and artists needed other outlets for selling their paintings. Unutilised space on the first floor of Jehangir Art Gallery was offered me to equip into a gallery. Thus it was that on 16th September, 1963, Lady Hirabai Jehangir inaugurated our gallery.

BK: ***Since you have worked as a promoter of contemporary Indian art for more than forty years, how do you see the place of art in our society today and outside of India?***

KKG: I would say a sea-change has taken place. When one talked of Indian art in those days—even twenty-five years ago—we had to be specific that it was not the traditional art one was speaking about but of the living art of the day.

It was the period when the long ignored miniature paintings had come into high fashion and people discussed the people of Kangra, Rajasthan and Moghul paintings. Looking askance at the contemporary painters, their questioning was: 'Why are you abandoning your great cultural heritage?'

However to quote J Swaminathan, 'The fact that the art of former times moves us today does not mean that their ideologies still serve as tools for establishing rapport with nature and eternity.'

It was the intelligence, the questioning, the creative urge of those few pioneering artists which placed our modern art on a firm threshold. We have moved beyond our own expectations to a full circle where culture today has become, both politically and socially, a powerful weapon and art a significant investment.

Khorshed Gandhy

Diary fragment from 2010

We are both at a stage in our lives where we hate one another intensely. We have often fought and shouted at one another but there was no hate. Somehow all this has changed and the chasm between us is so wide that only by shouting and screaming and even by throwing things at one another, are we able to communicate. What a "picle [sic]" to be in. A pickle is both sweet and sour—it has all the ingredients thrown in to make a pickle. It can give it a flavour as well as burn the tongue. Your lives at the moment is [sic] burning your very souls—making your lives into a façade where the reality is so different from the outside appearance. The reality is rage and hatred for one another—intolerance of any slight hurt or criticism. It is a false life that you lead where on one hand you meditate supposedly trying to reach the GOD within you and yet realizing that you are so so far away from that reality. That MRA through daily guidance can cleanse out the untruth, the falseness and yet there is total dryness within which does not allow for the fountain of sweetness, the freshness and purity of sparkling spring water to cleanse your heart and mind.

To put down in words how you perceive Kekoo and then how he conceives (of) you and how he has to contend with a strong dominating personality. My perception of Kekoo:

A split personality which changes every few months. The lows of depressions and then the highs in which Kekoo goes, gets me intolerant. At best of times, find so little care (love which I experience from Dara in so much measure—even from Rashna and Behroze). At best of times, the care is totally absent. The latest example being Sunday morning where he kept me waiting in the hot sun for so long that walking back was more tolerable than just waiting. There can be umpteen such examples.

I could enumerate instances where it is the Ego pushing him and yet the selfishness in his actions is also so entwined.

Sunday 29 August 2010

Kekoo, in his hey-day has achieved many things in his life and has been quite successful. He has taken risks such as taking an exhibition to England with very little money and yet managed to live for six months there, taking exhibitions to Antwerp, Germany etc. He has the courage and the vision to achieve what he set out to do.

Today at the age of ninety, his ambitious nature, as it were, is not tamed or is not in control. He still wishes to be noticed, to be counted so he indulges in acts which don't make sense but only brings scorn and bad name to himself and his family. What then is the answer? I can't say I have the answer but I can only suggest that Kekoo should spend five or ten minutes every morning (before rushing off for his morning walk at 6:30 am) just sitting still and going within. To ask God or his inner self what Kekoo should be doing for the day—or whatever thought that comes to his mind. To practice this five-minute meditation (or prayer) can bring a new stability in his life and a new direction can be at least experimented.

From The Archives

Kekoo's Birthday Bash: Or how to turn a party into a crusade

This was a letter written by Bernard and sent to me by Rashna Imhasly-Gandhy who thought it summed up Kekoo Gandhy and his family's relationship with him. I thought to condense it and slip it into the chapter on who Kekoo was as a person but on second thoughts, I believe it has its place as an insight into the Kekaesque transformation of an event into an idea and from then on into a movement of sorts.

Matheran is one of Maharashtra's loveliest hill stations. It is one of the places to which the Parsis have always retreated for the summer. Many own bungalows there; others simply rented bungalows. My friend, the painter Mehlli Gobhai would often talk about how he spent the sultry months of April and May there with his mother and grandmother. In the background hovered the redoubtable Bapsey Sabavala who had a collection of dolls. No ordinary dolls these; they were porcelain dolls, made in France and dressed in Mechlin lace and real silk. She loved these dolls and would often send them out with a chauffeur.

'I remember there would be a knock on the door in the middle of the morning,'

Mehlli told me, 'and outside a driver would be standing, looking slightly sheepish. In his arms, he would be cradling one of Bapsey's dolls. He would ask for my mother and when she came to the door, he would say, "Veronica madam day-spend[89] ke liye aayi hai". My mother would receive the doll and set it down carefully in the living room on one of the arm chairs and lock the room, lest we boys should do her some harm. From time to time, I would peep in at this forlorn little figure, slumped in a chair. In the evening, my mother would tell her bridge-playing friends at the club of the visitation and they would giggle at the mad heiress. But Bapsey would have the last laugh. She would traipse past my mother and yodel, "Naughty, naughty, Perin, you mustn't spoil dear Veronica. She came home with a bad tummy from all that rich food you fed her." It was an object lesson in taking your passions seriously.

Perin Gobhai laughed and confirmed the story but she took pains to remind me gently: 'She wasn't only an eccentric. She started Swabal Stores so that unemployed Parsi youth could find jobs. She raised money for charity and worked for animal rights. And it was Bapsey who saw Mehli Mehta playing at some restaurant in Matheran and recognised his talent. She insisted that he come to Bombay. She made it possible for him to come and she supported him in a number of ways and that may be how we got a Zubin Mehta too.'[90]

Rashna remembers her Uncle Mehli Lalkaka telling a similar story where they carried the joke further when Bapsey's doll was sent by the rikshawalas to spend the day at Woodlands, the family home in Matheran. They used to ride with their riding companions Themi, Nanny and Siloo Umrigar who lived at the Umrigar Lodge. The doll named Rosie was sent on by the Woodland's mali with a note by the Lalkaka brothers, Ratan and Mehli, to the Umrigar sisters to say that Rosie needed to be looked after, fed and entertained as Bapsey was busy all day. They added in their note that Rosie loved to hear stories. When the doll was supposed to be fetched and sent back to Bapsey in the evening, they visited the sisters and found Rosie tucked into bed and one of them reading her a story. They burst out laughing as the sisters had taken their joke very seriously!

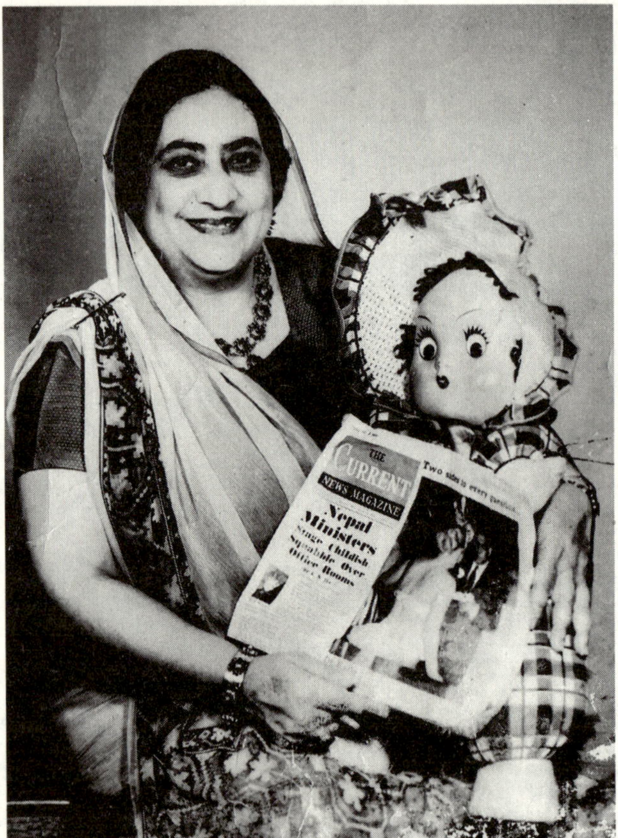

Bapsey Sabavala with her doll

Matheran was dear to many Parsi hearts and then came the news that the government was considering a motorable road that would go straight up to the hill-station from the plains. This would make the hill station more accessible to tourists but the costs in terms of ecology, quaintness and quiet made many old Matheran residents angry.

Kekoo joined the battle with a birthday party. Now read on.

Monday

16 January 1995

Matheran Woodlands

Dearest Nishi,

Two metal benches face each other below the white lions. Together with the potted plants next to them, they are the last remaining signs of yesterday's birthday bash for Keka. For a whole week Keka had planned this event, not out of vanity, but because in his paradoxical and Kekaesque way, he has found that that best ego massage lies in contributing to something bigger than himself.

It started with him walking in the garden, sprucing up the plants, watering the rocky red clay. It soon became too much for him. He summoned Surkri and her drunkard husband Peddu and made them dig flower beds around the trees and carry stones about for little rock-garden corners. Soon they couldn't cope either and so Keka contracted half a dozen labourers from the bazaar, and they flattened the driveway, replastered the entrance columns and adorned them with the "Woodland" marbles.

Keka's trips to the neighbouring malis (gardeners) became more and more frequent. He would disappear in the morning and by early afternoon (if we were lucky) he would come back with his arms and plastic bags full of plants and cuttings. By Saturday, the neighbours' gifts had become too heavy; the malis themselves had to carry the stuff for him.

He wouldn't neglect the other details either. Last week, at 11 pm, I was reading, Rashna had gone to sleep when Mamaijee woke up suddenly. She got up and glanced into the dining room. 'You know,' she said with a voice of brave resignation, 'I think Kekoo has gone mad.'

I was about to laugh, but then I thought I had better make sure. I went over and saw him leaning over the dining table, which was covered with the stalks of dry plants. He was trying to string these together. For a brief moment, I thought Mamaijee was right: Keka was really going potty.

Then he looked up from his 'work' , saw me, and smiled.

'I want to make a "toran",' he said. 'For the entrance gate. Don't you think it would look nice?'

I nodded more out of concern than conviction.

The next morning as he came back from Dasturi, where he had dropped our visitors...he allegedly stopped at the gates of various forlorn bungalows and set about cleaning their nameplates.

One day he sat pensively on the garden wall, looking at the Woodlands staircase. He called me over and began to describe how he envisaged the seating arrangements for the PARTY—'Two benches here, the chairs there maybe a few rugs here and there? And don't you think it would look nice if we repainted the staircase with red matti?'

But if there was madness (there wasn't, or just a benign variety) there was also a method to it. However much he seemed lost to his plants and plans—and blissfully deaf to the growing vociferousness of Mummy's and Mamaijee's railing—he never lost track of the greater political design of his endeavour which was 'HOW TO SAVE MATHERAN'. And the fact that we had two heavy downpours on the seventh and eighth of January (you should have seen Matheran; we were huddling indoors as the rain hammered on the roof and thick mist was racing through the garden) was for him like a sign that mad or not mad, Ooperwallah was on his side. And so he would take to the bazaar like a proselytizing darvesh. As soon as his garden duties allowed him leave, he would visit hoteliers, the ghodawallahs, the bazaaris, the cobblers and talk to them about HOW TO SAVE MATHERAN.

And, devious as he is, he went about it with true bazaar diplomacy. Once I accompanied him to the market, and as usual he fell back because he accosted a lingering ghodawallah and began talking to him. When he caught up with me he explained: 'I was doing a bit of canvassing against Pappu Divarkar (president of the Municipality and a known supporter of the road). But I had to do it cunningly, and so I asked the ghorawallah, "Why is PD so unpopular in Matheran?" and then I went on and said that he certainly was very unpopular in Bombay!'

Soon rumours started trickling in—mostly from Ashok after his morning shopping that Keka was on an invitation spree—not only the hoteliers (both those from the pro- and contra-road factions) were invited but also ghorawallahs, malis (of course!) and bungla-owners. And one good morning Dina told us that he had overheard Kekoo sahib invite the mehtar for the Sunday afternoon function; which led the latter to protest and say 'No, no, I am coming in the morning. Why should I came in the afternoon as well?' so that Keka was forced to explain that it wasn't to empty his chamber pot but to attend his birthday party!

So you can imagine the assemblage of characters trickling into the Woodlands Compound yesterday afternoon. 'Trickling' is the word: while a German photographer (Nirmala Devi,[91] chela and worse, Kekoo chela) came already at 3 pm for the four o'clock function, Jimmy Lord and 'Mr. Dhansakia' (another Parsi hotelier) came at five, the ghorawallahs trundled in at 5:30 and as the meeting was well underway, the owner of the 'Sakvill' hotel made his grand entrée. A rickshaw drew up along the tiles specially laid down in the garden by Keki Seth, and stopped at the venue only to unload an old crotchety man in flapping trousers. He had hardly time to sit down and swallow the sweets when Kekoo called him up to speak—and according to Rashna his was the most poetic speech, talking with affection about the 'Rani', the little old Matheran train which is now almost gasping its last, and the beautiful winds in the trees, which invigorate the travellers (but not him, because he looked miserable).

Believe it or not: but what could have turned into a tedious and embarrassing *khichdi* of Papa's all-embracing mix of class and caste became a success: it was a birthday party full of grace and affection for Old-is-Gold Keka; and at the same time we witnessed the birthday of a small movement of people who went away with the conviction that something needed to be done about Matheran but (even more important): that something COULD be done about the place they all love. It was quite remarkable and a proof of your grandfather's great humanity and his gift to bring people together, to acknowledge and empower them. The way he handled the meeting was vintage KMG and great politics: he started the meeting on a humorous tone—he had beaten up the little rascal Narya and wanted to atone publicly for this 'sin'—then he withdrew and let others speak—Rahul Dev, the Contractor, the Corporator, the ghorawallah, Jimmy Lord, and yes, even his son—and every now and then he would interject with a personal anecdote or suddenly raise a point when it threatened to become gossipy. In the space of two hours he transformed, in front of his mischievous family, a higgledy-piggledy assortment of Matheran characters into a group where everyone was respectful of the other and each got connected to a worthwhile cause... —Enter your mother.

(Rashna Imhasly takes over here and the letter becomes more conventional. This letter has been lightly edited to bring the spellings of Hindi words into consonance with common use.)

APPENDIX 1

But What Is a Gallery?

(or A FINE TIME TO BE ASKING)

'The perfect relation between an artist and a gallery would be that when the artist comes up with an idea, even one that might be contrary to the impulses and pressures of commerce, works that cannot be sold for instance, the gallery should be supportive. When I was doing 'City of Desires', it was the first time that a gallery was turned into a public studio but Khorshed supported it. And of course, artists know that galleries have overheads, they have to pay the rent and their staff so they do want a mix of works that can be sold and works that simply need to be done. The other requirements are so simple: a space, an openness, the right lighting, a good catalogue.'
—**Nalini Malani** in conversation with this author

'That there were all three of them, Kekoo and Khorshed and Shireen, was important to both the old gallery and the new one. There was a lot of discussion, a lot of conversation, and I think sometimes, these conversations are at the heart of the gallery. That's where the idea of the gallery is shaped, in those political discussions, in those heated arguments about what art is and where it is going.'

—**Archana Hande** in conversation with the author

Just for a moment, consider the art gallery. Not Chemould but any art gallery. Not an art gallery when it is alive with work on the walls and floors and hanging from the ceilings; not when people are experiencing the art, not when an aesthetic is being hammered out in some way, your aesthetic, mine, the city's, the world's. Not when hushed voices are discussing prices and futures and investments.

When is an art gallery not an art gallery? When it is waiting?

For the gallery lives the dichotomy of that big/small word 'art'. We have been told that true art is priceless and that only a Philistine would ask about the price tag.

We have been told that a work only needs a viewer to make it art.

We have been told that we make something art by the simple fact of our attentive viewing, our opening up to it, the conversation it begins with who we are.

We don't believe any of it.

Most of the time, we think it is art if it cost someone a lot of money.

And so, it is in an art gallery that we seek out art. All over the world, the educated middle class and the leisured will 'confess' to enjoying time spent wandering in art galleries and museums. (This is not a confession, it is a boast. Or perhaps even a claim, a claim to being civilised.) The art gallery then is a stepping stone to the museum. The difference is hierarchical. Many pieces will appear in the art galleries and many names will come through but only some will be what is called 'museum quality'.

The art gallery asks for no payment to enter its portals although some open their doors now only by appointment and all of them have ways of ensuring that it isn't just anyone who wanders in off the street. The museum asks you to pay to come in and see what it has.

The art gallery wants you to buy; the museum is not for sale but the gift shop allows you to indulge in the retail therapy that is thwarted by the museum's policies and the art gallery's prices.

The museum is large, the art gallery is small and both want you to believe that they are there for you and that they are exclusive; that some kind of filter has been at work so that you have got the best of art and culture within these cool, neutral walls.

But turn now simply to the art gallery. It is a strange thing, located at the intersection of art and commerce. The project is large—it will define how mankind sees itself; the project is dramatic—there will be a constant coming and going—the artist, the viewer, the buyer, the critic, the dilettante, the student—and each one will have her role to play and some will gasp in recognition, some will be silenced, some will be repulsed, some will be moved to buy, some will sneer, whatever. But all this only because the art gallery is hollow. It is a shell and it must be brought back to life each time a show opens. Without the art to animate it, it is a staging space—and in this it most resembles a hotel. Here is the pretence of habitation but all is hushed and silent until an occupant, a PAX to use the language of the hospitality industry, enters the room. In the case of the artist who takes over the gallery, the desire must be to personalise, to reinvent everything to create the best possible staging. This may explain the peculiar and specific charge site-specific work carries with it. Instead of the work coming to the space and finding its way in, it must begin with where it otherwise would end. What artist trained in paradox—and how many artists can resist the siren call of the paradox—could resist?

But, at the same time, it is possible to talk about the nature of a gallery, of Gallery Chemould in the time of Kekoo and Khorshed and Chemould Prescott in the time of Shireen Gandhy. This is true all over the world. 'The only gallery that showed Indian artists in all of Germany,' one often hears or 'They're not really into video art'. This predilection is determined by the gallery people, it would seem, but it can also be a host of other factors at play. One of these is size. The old Chemould was small, it was enclosed, it was tucked away, not on the street. You had to know about it to get there, and if you were not part of the cognoscenti, you might not even notice it.

For some artists, the very things that were negatives became plus points. Mehlli Gobhai often said it was the womby feeling that he loved, that he liked being away from the rush and noise of the streets.

'I like that aspect of the gallery: that people have to pass the Jehangir, pass the lavatory, and climb up the stairs. What I personally value in the gallery is that it's off the street. I prefer galleries like that because I like the fact that someone who wants to see my work is making the effort to go in. I'm all for democracy in art, but my work may not reach out to everyone.

'The same people who come to the Jehangir sometimes come up to Chemould. If they've just come with the idea—*Chalo, upar shu chhe? Joy-nay avye* (What's upstairs? Let's go and see. This is in Parsi Gujarati if it does not sound like standard Gujarati to you)—then they beat a quick retreat. One of them got angry—"Are these paintings? You call this art? You're fooling the public!" I rather liked that. For an artist to be controversial in 2003 is quite rare.'

For other artists though, these were precisely the failings of the gallery. Jehangir Sabavala did not like being tucked away. His shows with Chemould were at the Jehangir Art Gallery, the Museum Gallery and always had a Delhi component (via Kunika) or a foreign excursion (to England, for instance, and Scotland). Kekoo remembered him stationing a man at the Jehangir Art Gallery with a clicker, a people counter, to check how many people had visited. I remember him being in the gallery for most of the day, ready to talk to people, to anyone who came in. With his elegant Victorian manners, he managed to charm the local yokel while never suggesting to the art buyer that he was stooping to conquer.

Sabavala was far too much of an art-world animal to be impressed by the very things that made Kekoo such a treasure for the rest of us. He wanted a gallery owner who was committed to the success of Sabavala, and this does not sound like such a bad thing, surely; the Gandhys, after all, also recorded that he was their first sell-out show. Sabavala was too much of a senior statesman to ever say anything politically incorrect/undiplomatic; and when it came to paying tribute, the painter dusted off some old clichés.

'My association with the Gandhys has been extremely long, both professionally and as a family. There is no question that they are the pioneers. We have also had the mutual luck to have had sell-out shows even in the 1960s and the 1970s. It really has been an extremely fruitful relationship,' Sabavala said to writer Anupa Mehta.[92] You can smell the carefulness in his words. This was a tribute piece and his contribution to it was pablum, the standard clichés you trot out when other feelings lie hidden.

Shirin Sabavala, his wife, had no such qualms. When I asked her about Chemould, she arched her eyebrows, 'Once at a show, a collector came along and Kekoo grabbed hold of him and began to tell him about another artist whose show was coming up next. He kept insisting that the collector see this fellow's work. Now how is one supposed to respond to something like that?'

The painter Ram Kumar also had a similar experience. 'I remember there was a time when I was having a show at Chemould Gallery and I had invited Neville Wadia[93] to come and see the show. I was waiting for him on the steps of the Jehangir Art Gallery when Kekoo joined me there. Neville Wadia showed up and immediately Kekoo started a conversation about the problems of the Bombay Art Society or some other body in which they were both involved. They talked for a while and then Neville Wadia looked at his watch and said he had to go somewhere else and left. He didn't see the show. I remonstrated with Kekoo who apologised sincerely. When I had a show with them in Calcutta, I invited Satyajit Ray to see it. And I told Kekoo, if he should come, please don't waylay him. Let him see the paintings and then you can talk to him as much as you want. He took it well.'

•

The artist who is in the gallery at that moment is the animating principle of the gallery. At that point in time, the bigger picture does not matter. (It does, but the artist cannot be made to feel that nor should s/he be expected to.) Kekoo's eye was firmly on the bigger picture and it cost him some relationships and some friends.

But now let us consider the gallery in its specific situation in India. Nalini Malani said to me, 'The history of contemporary art in this country is the history of the galleries.' And if that is so, how are artists shaped by this impulse or how are they deformed by it?

Again, Chemould becomes something of an outlier. Tyeb Mehta told M Rahman of *India Today*, 'By ensuring a fixed income for me in the early years without pressuring me, Chemould helped me to remain independent and work my own way.'[94] Satish Gujral said to Gaurav Jain, on another occasion: 'Kekoo Gandhy helped artists the most in Bombay.'

It wasn't only money; there were other roles for galleries to play. There was a time when artists seemed to be the go-to guys for charitable causes. There were frequent auctions of paintings and artists were expected to donate pictures. In a single letter, Raza talks about requests from Rippan Kapur of CRY and the HelpAge people. 'The HelpAge wants me to contribute a canvas for an auction sale at the Taj. It seems a prestigious project and humanly worthwhile. I intend to participate. The forty per cent that will come to me will have to be collected by you. The CRY people also want a canvas—a smaller one. Howsoever laudable the effort, the choice of painters is not going to be as good but we cannot neglect "children" so here too I have to participate, Rippan Kapur is a very agreeable person and most helpful.' In a letter dated 28 June 1984, Paritosh Sen wrote: 'Pritish Nandy and Maneka Gandhi are organising an art show at the Jehangir Gallery next month to raise funds for animal protection in the country.

'I remember that of the four charcoal drawings I gave you a few years ago, you sold three. You should have one remaining with you. I shall feel deeply obliged if you would please hand it over to Pritish for their show. I am sending two drawings from here through Gallery 88. Since I am not participating with any of my paintings, I thought it would be a good idea to make up for it by contributing more than one drawing so that money earned from the sale of the three drawings would be substantial...Please price the drawing for Rs 15000.'

Sounding board? Storage space? Postal service? There were other letters expecting hotel bookings, help with selections, any number of requests. All this came into sharp focus when I happened to read a conversation that cultural theorists Ranjit Hoskote and Nancy Adajania had with artist Anju Dodiya in the Dialogues Series from Popular Prakashan in 2011 where they talked about the 'gallery reflex'. The conversation began with Ranjit Hoskote addressing Dodiya with a question:

'Anju, we'd like to open this conversation by asking you about that vital subsystem of the ecology of contemporary art that you inhabit as a practising artist, the gallery. We have often thought and talked about the fact that the Indian art world is premised so strongly on the gallery system, and that many of the other institutional forms of the art world are absent or weak in India—such as the museum, the foundation, the cycle of public commissions, the artist residency system and the biennial. We have had a heroic period of gallery practice, if you will, in the 1960s and 1970s when pioneering gallerists worked closely with their artists to promote their work and find ways of supporting and extending it, even within the considerable limitations of a struggling, semi-socialist Third World economy.'[95]

Anju's response was simple: she wanted to make art; the gallery was tasked with something else.

But this conversation alerted me to my own myopia, specially since I had accepted the primacy and centrality of the gallery to the art world without too much question.

Because if art galleries are central to the art world then they become central to art practice and that opens up another can of worms. However benevolent they may be—or may seem to be—to create a focal point around a single set of institutions is to risk a certain homogeneity. You're going to paint for the gallery and into the gallery. Its limitations will become your boundaries. Its shape will determine your practice. Its aesthetic will begin, I suspect, to invade yours.

For instance, it was a debate over what exactly a gallery should do for an artist that caused the rift between MF Husain and Chemould. The Gandhys had worked on his hugely successful retrospective in 1969, which featured furniture for Bal Chhabda in a suite called Salle de Bal and an Ambassador car which was painted over with gopis with the understanding that he would do his next one-man show with Gallery Chemould. He did indeed have a one-man show the next year, but he wanted Chemould to buy his entire show. 'It was time the galleries started buying art, not just keeping them on consignment,' he told Ila Pal.[96]

Kekoo said no, Kali Pundole said yes and so Husain moved to Pundole. It cannot have been an easy time or a good break because MF Husain was already selling well in those days. Kekoo told Pal that his turnover at the framing shop went from five thousand to twenty-five thousand because of Husain.

Shireen remembered this incident in a speech she made at a show at the Jehangir Nicholson Art Foundation which showcased Nicholson's relationship with these two premier galleries. 'My parents were to go on holiday, but due to the death of a family member remained in India. In that period when they were to be away, Husain went ahead and had his exhibition with Pundole, marking a severe end to his relationship with Chemould and starting a life-long one with Pundole. My furious mother felt jilted and let down and went on to write a letter that became famously quoted as the years went by, where she says: "Promises are like pie-crusts, meant to be broken.."'

To understand some of these conflicting notions, I thought I should turn to Ranjit Hoskote and Nancy Adajania. And since this chapter relies heavily on the insights they provided, I thought it best to keep the interview intact.

The city's premier art critics remember visiting Chemould regularly in the late 1980s, walking across from the Elphinstone College, where they were both studying.

Nancy Adajania recalls, 'Kekoo and Khorshed were always warm and welcoming to everyone. It didn't matter who you were—a student, a collector, an activist, a filmmaker. Kekoo and Khorshed were both equally active in getting people to focus on civic issues as well as questions of cultural infrastructure. Kekoo would be preoccupied with his pet project, that of lobbying the Union Government to establish a branch of the National Gallery of Modern Art at the Sir CJ Hall. That was a dream that he shared with the sculptor Pilloo Pochkhanawala. Khorshed remained strongly concerned about the forces of illiberalism that were threatening what she saw as the bedrock of postcolonial India—a liberal, secular order that embraced diversity. She was indefatigable in writing letters to politicians, bureaucrats, and editors. Both Kekoo and Khorshed worked hard to mobilise the art world as well as civil society.'

Hoskote remembers Kekoo as a man energised by the organisation, the size and the spectacle of the Bombay Arts Festival in 1987. 'This festival was held in memory of the artist and cultural activist Pilloo Pochkhanawala, who had organised its first edition. The sculpture section featured artists like N Pushpamala, and was accompanied by an illuminating text by Ashish Rajadhyaksha. Nissim Ezekiel organised the poetry readings on the terrace. [Hoskote was one of the readers. He was only eighteen then but was already reckoned as one of the new voices.] But Kekoo was all over the show, and many of his interests, especially his commitment to non-metropolitan artists of rural background, were reflected in it. Bulu Imam from Mithila and Jivya Soma Mashe, the Warli artist, for instance, were represented. The festival was powered by the same inclusive, democratic instinct that had always characterised Kekoo, and he was voluble as ever as he navigated viewers around.

'Kekoo was the man with the cultural and political vision, and these twin interests had been rivals for his complete attention since the Emergency. Khorshed, who also had strong political convictions and was a staunch believer in a liberal and participatory democracy premised on social justice, held the gallery together as a functioning economic entity with a consistent cycle of programming. By the early 1990s, it was clear that Kekoo's political interests—in communal harmony, neighbourhood activism, saving trees even—had taken over. For him, the gallery was as much a meeting place and forum for people associated with all these activities and interests, as it was a strictly artistic or business enterprise.'

Excerpts from the interview

JP: What is a gallery?

Nancy Adajania: The gallery is not merely a venue for exhibiting art objects, although that is how it is usually perceived. Ideally, it should braid together the expressive and the discursive, affording both aesthetic edification and political provocation. When I am in a gallery, my eye often travels to the empty spaces between objects, which act as poetic pauses. They offer us the potential for contemplation, highlighting the interrelationships between works but also revealing the dissonances between them and pulling them apart.

When you walked into the old Gallery Chemould, on the first floor of the Jehangir Art Gallery, the first thing that you saw was the table where conversations took place, a flourishing *adda.* A lawyer would be talking to Kekoo about regulations pertaining to civic issues. An activist would be discussing censorship with Khorshed. An artist would be waiting to discuss her next exhibition. You actually saw the art only a little later, as the gallery's curved main wall segued away from these conversations and established its own arc, only to return to the world of ideas and propositions. In this way, Chemould became a site for a lively public sphere—a sphere of active exchanges, where manifestos were born, statements issued, gatherings convened, festivals planned and presented.

In the late 1980s, as students at the emphatically left-wing Elphinstone College, we were very interested in the politics of resistance in Dahanu, and thus also in Warli art. When we spoke to Kekoo and Khorshed about this, Khorshed showed us the book they had published, *The Warlis: Tribal Paintings and Legends*, edited by Lakshmi Lal. I remember the earth-coloured dust jacket of the book. Khorshed also introduced us to Yashodhara Dalmia's *The Painted World of the Warlis*, published by the Lalit Kala Akademi but available mainly through Chemould's efforts. At a time when subaltern art was still being described patronisingly as 'folk' or 'tribal' art, and accorded little respect, the Gandhys had included Jivya Soma Mashe in their gallery programme, and had presented a special display of his work at the 1976 Biennale de Menton.

For the Gandhys, the notion of the gallery as a space in which they would nurture and display artistic talent was intimately linked to the larger Nehruvian narrative in which aesthetics and social justice went together.

Ranjit Hoskote: The gallery, as we see it today, is only the most recent version of what the gallery has been and the role it has served, historically, as an institution. Even its stereotypical *mise en scène,* the objects arranged as singular artefacts in a white cube, does not date back further than the early years of the Museum of Modern Art (MoMA) in New York. Before Alfred Barr's re-visioning of the museum space along the lines of Bauhaus exhibition practice, as he had experienced it in Europe, museum and gallery spaces conveyed a hushed, neo-classical opulence, with their walls dressed in rich red, green or powder-blue silk. In such interiors, the bourgeoisie enjoyed the feast of culture. It was in critical, revolutionary response to this model that the Bauhaus artists adopted either hessian lining on their display walls, or else painted these walls in very pale shades of off-white, cream, or white. Bourgeois culture was opposed in artisanal or clinical vein.

Even the metric that most of us, as contemporary curators, take as axiomatic while hanging an exhibition comes from the specificities of Barr's personality, choices, and career. The height at which paintings are customarily hung, five feet from the floor to the centre of the work, was defined by the fact that Barr was illness-prone and often wheelchair-bound. That was the height from which he could enjoy the impact of the paintings.

In looking at the gallery of today, too, one cannot avoid considering how it was shaped by market forces. Perhaps Le Salon des Refusés, in its various editions, can be used as an important point of departure, gesturing towards other moments in the development of the gallery. In 1863, there were so many paintings that were rejected by the Academicians who controlled participation in the annual Paris Salon, that they were accommodated in Le Salon des Refusés, literally 'The Room of the Rejects'. Soon enough, the Impressionists, who had led the 'rejects' triumphantly, couldn't be bothered to wait for the annual salon. Their friends became their greatest supporters, and soon there developed showing rooms or the viewing rooms, where the early dealers presented new work to viewers and potential collectors who came from all walks of life, although the most influential among them were members of the haut bourgeoisie and the more adventurous aristocrats. Side by side, you have the dealer, the journalistic hack, the pamphleteer, and the art critic, all beginning to take the positions we see in today's art world, around a venue that we recognise as the 'gallery'.

A pivotal moment in Bombay's art world was the opening, in 1952, of the Jehangir Art Gallery, a public gallery that was open to a diverse viewership, irrespective of class, caste, level of education, or degree of entitlement and opportunity. Later, during the early 1960s, nearly two decades after Independence, individual entrepreneurs like Kekoo Gandhy and Kali Pundole founded their galleries in Bombay. The template of the white cube could not be imported here because there were various constraints, some infrastructural, some financial, and so they began to indigenise the template. To today's eye, the hanging formats and systems might seem quaint, for the gallery has transformed itself along international lines now. But these were the necessary first steps.

We've come a long way now to the gallery that is off the street—behind a heavy door on an upper floor, with a doorbell to be rung for admission, and thus diminished in its democratic potential—where you have a white cube or a black box in order to show video art, where wall text is set onto the walls via vinyl transfer, where the space can be reordered within the limits of the architectural constraints of the building, through the deft use of dry walls.

That is what has changed. Between the 1960s and the 1990s, things were rudimentary but there was a great energy, animated discussion. Gallery openings were simple affairs and the people who came were the ones who wanted to see the art, not the ones who wanted to be seen.

There's another dimension to this. Indian galleries have had to play a much more central role in the making of art history, due to institutional deficits that have hobbled our museum scene. Private galleries have been building collections, holding retrospectives, commissioning substantial documentation and analysis of artists and periods, publishing books on artists and films on them. This is the kind of work that other art institutions, such as museums or academies, should have been doing—providing a platform, a laboratory, a research centre, for art criticism and art history. There have been some changes, of course, as evinced by the generous curatorial vision of Rajeev Lochan at the National Gallery of Modern Art, by R Siva Kumar in Santiniketan, the curatorial commitments of the Kiran Nadar Museum of Art, and a few other institutions.

But for both of us, so much of the dialogue that distinguished this period happened at the kidney-shaped Gallery Chemould, which mounted some very memorable exhibitions, allowing Nalini Malani to paint on the walls, for instance, to create ephemeral artworks that had no monetary value because they could not be taken away and framed on a wall, and would, in fact, be erased. At Chemould and at Pundole, there were day-long conversations with Badri Narayan, Akbar Padamsee, Jehangir Nicholson.

JP: You speak of 'the dangers of the gallery reflex'.

NA: By the 'gallery reflex', I mean the kneejerk response of many Indian artists to seek the security of the gallery system—not only in a financial sense but in the sense of offering a sacred *temenos* in which art can be securely presented. As time passes and artists make art that lays claim to public space or political urgency, the gallery reflex becomes more and more troubling, even untenable. Can the artist intervene in the larger public sphere, and, upon being shaken by sometimes violent reactions, rush back into the safety zone of the gallery, claiming artistic immunity?

Like all institutions, the gallery, productive as it is, suffers from certain flaws. I think back to an earlier generation of artists who were very important to us—Akbar Padamsee, Tyeb Mehta, VS Gaitonde, all of whom spoke of their artistic 'autonomy'. But they never addressed the fact that this autonomy was guaranteed by their participation in the gallery system. A system that, in the final analysis, was premised on commerce and the relationships between collectors and artists. Whether overtly or subliminally, that generation of artists—and artists to this day!—internalised the demands of the gallery system. What were the collectors' preferences? A particular medium. A certain signature style. A vocabulary of images. These came to define many artists, who then either ceased to explore anything beyond these demarcations—or downplayed the value of any experiments that did not fit within these limits. Krishen Khanna once said to us that, much as he admired his contemporaries, they remained trapped within the 'four edges of the canvas'.

In the 1950s and 1960s, artists in West Europe, North America, and in Japan were rushing *out of* the gallery system, to work with refuse, in derelict spaces, producing work that was barely recognisable as art from a conventional perspective. In the 1950s and 1960s, in India, artists were rushing *into* the gallery, both to secure their careers in a precarious postcolonial economy, and also to give themselves a degree of legitimacy as artists, which the gallery gave them, as did their allegiance to institutions like the Lalit Kala Akademi.

Unlike the Gutai group in 1950s Japan, with artists jumping through paper screens, costuming themselves in electric robes, emphasising the performative aspect of art, Indian artists of that period were fixated on galleries, and on producing work that would be acceptable to the gallery space. There was a strong dependency syndrome. There were, of course, exceptions to the rule—such as Akbar Padamsee's transdisciplinary Vision Exchange workshop of the late 1960s, where he and Nalini Malani and also Gieve Patel made experimental films. Another exception, created outside the gallery system, were the films that some Indian artists made under the aegis of the Films Division, including MF Husain's *Through the Eyes of a Painter* and Tyeb Mehta's film, *Koodal.* Through such endeavours, some artists sidestepped the gallery system—but these remained eclipsed or treated as aberrations until very recently.

Acknowledgements

First to Khorshed Gandhy, guiding spirit of this book, and to Kekoo Gandhy, the elf in residence, the anima, the will 'o' the wisp, sorely missed by the city that produced him.

Then to the Gandhy family and the Gandhy family's families for their complete openness, their patience and their accessibility.

And to the Chemouldates, all those who worked with and at the Gallery for helping at every step of the way.

Also to all those who gave of their time and their knowledge, sharing their city and their memories with me.

And to Ravi Singh but *cela va sans dire.*

And Renuka Chatterjee who bore the brunt of my irascibility. Herewith a public and heartfelt apology.

And Maithili Doshi who gave us such a great design.

It takes a village to make a book. I have been lucky in my village.

Endnotes

1. Jayati Vora, *Man's World,* issue dated December 2003
2. Princess Street was named after Mary, Princess of Wales who inaugurated the street in 1905. After Independence it was renamed Samaldas Gandhi (no relation to the Gandhys) Marg.
3. Page XIII, The Bombay Art Society (1888-2016), History and Voyage, Volume 1 by Suhas Bahulkar, translated by Anil Rao, published by The Bombay Art Society, Mumbai, 2016.
4. For more on the Progressives, see Yashodhara Dalmia's *The Making of Modern Indian Art: The Progressives,* (OUP, 2001)
5. John Clark, *Modern Indian Art; Some Literature and Problematics*; School of Asian Studies, University of Sydney, 1994, p 13.
6. For this part of the account, I am indebted to Victor Rangel-Ribeiro's *Souza: The Man, The Artist, His Loves & His Times,* p 60.
7. My generation of writers from Elphinstone College—across the road from the Jehangir Art Gallery and Gallery Chemould—produced Girish Shahane, Anupa Mehta and Nancy Adajania, three of the four editors of the Art India Magazine. On the same benches sat the young man who would reinvent art criticism in the city, wrenching it from the hands of an old guard, Ranjit Hoskote. Just having an art gallery around doesn't make art critics or artists; but having access to the best work in the country as Chemould offered, is always a good thing.
8. (A colonial phrase, WC stands here for water closet. Now commonly referred to as the toilet or restroom.)
9. Ibid, p68
10. Rudolf von Leyden (1908-1983)
11. Walter Langhammer (1905-1977) came because his wife Kathe was Jewish.
12. Emanuel Schlesinger (1896-1968)
13. *The Time of My Life: Memories, Anecdotes, Tall Talk* by Krishen Khanna (Viking, Penguin India, New Delhi, 2002) pp 99-100
14. *Do Raha,* 1952, starred Nalini Jaywant, Shekhar, KN Singh, Murad, Agha. It had music by Anil Biswas and some songs can still be found on YouTube.
15. This was a Chemould show and marked the end of the relationship between Husain and Chemould.

16. For more on Samovar, read Usha R Khanna: *The Making of Samovar; How a Mumbai Café Became a Metaphor for a Generation* (Spenta Multimedia, 2007).
17. For more on the Bhulabhai Desai Institute, read Shanta Gokhale (ed): *The Scenes We Made: An Oral History of Experimental Theatre in Bombay* (Speaking Tiger, 2015). The book deals with two other sites and focuses on theatre but will give you a feeling of the excitement of exchange in a city of intellectual porosity.
18. Karin Zitzewitz lists the firm of Desai and Aris, a fledgling firm, she calls it.
19. R Raj Rao: *Nissim Ezekiel: The Authorized Biography* (Penguin, New Delhi, 2000); p128
20. *Mumbai; A City of Dreams* edited by Malvika Singh (Academic Foundation, New Delhi, 2011) from Jehangir Sabavala's essay, 'A Rebel with Many Causes'; p136
21. Jayati Vora's story from *Man's World*
22. Fugga means 'balloon' in English but the implication here is that these are hot-air balloons; the double 'guh' produces an effect of a snort of contempt which the word 'balloon' will never give you.
23. Pupul Jayakar (1915–1997) was one of those cultural tsarinas who earned her claim to the title. She was best known for her work in the revival of the arts and crafts of India.
24. The Zitzewitz interview in the 'crossing generations: diVERGE: Forty Years of Gallery Chemould' catalogue.
25. Dnyaneshwar Nadkarni 'Triumph of the Camel's Hump',*The Independent,* September 13, 1993
26. Lady Temple was the art teacher of the poet Adil Jussawalla, the writer Saker Mistri and the painter Anjolie Ela Menon when she was Anjolie De. Lady Temple was a colourful character who taught at school and gave private lessons at her home near the Colaba Post Office. None of her students seem to remember her first name; she was the wife of Sir Richard Temple, she said, and this could have been a little in-joke, so perhaps it is best to remember her as the colourful Lady Temple. She gets short shrift from Souza too. He includes her in the company of English memsahibs like Mrs Newsom, Mrs Blundell, "who instead of doing needlework painted to pass the time between playing with teacups and chaprasis..."
27. I have not been able to find any reference to why Calcutta was chosen but it could be that Rudy von Leyden had something to do with the choice. In 1946, Satish Gujral says, in *A Brush With Life: An Autobiography* which he wrote with Khushwant Singh (Penguin Books, 1987), von Leyden "had organised an exhibition of the works of the Calcutta Progressives in Bombay. He tried to get artists of the two metropolises together."
28. For more on Roshen Alkazi see Feisal Alkazi: *Enter Stage Right: The Alkazi/ Padamsee Family Memoir* (Speaking Tiger Books, 2021)
29. Ila Pal: *Beyond the Canvas: An Unfinished Portrait of MF Husain* (Indus/Harper Collins, 1994, New Delhi); p75
30. Part of this was even made public in the catalogue for the fiftieth year show, DiVERGE: There was a wonderful set of emails from the magisterial Geeta

Kapur, including one which read: 'I have got the seventeen minute video of KM Madhusudan, History is Silent Film that I was looking for from him. I want to show it in this exhibition but with one request. The video had throughout a grating, whirring sound (of an old 16-mm projector running) which I would prefer not to put on headphones—it's a great nostalgic sound—but I don't want to disturb the more or less silent works in the show. Will you agree to turn over your little library behind the counter into a dark showing room for the video? Let the books etc remain intact and show up in the light and shadow of the video—it will be all the more like an archival work. We will mark the presence of the work adequately and let the sound spill be a low murmur which I would like to hear. Madhusudan (he is by the way a key figure from the Kerala Radicals Group of the 1980s and colleague and antagonist of Krishna Kumar) may then be written to by you, giving an outline of the five exhibitions and invitation for this guest appearance in Citizen-Artist. I AM SURE THIS IS POSSIBLE.' (Love those capital letters. JP)

31. Homi Bhabha was a nuclear physicist, the founder of India's atomic power programme and the founding director of the Tata Institute of Fundamental Research. He was also an aesthete who built up a magnificent collection of paintings for the Institute and a painter himself. He died in an air crash in 1966.
32. Pipsy Wadia was an art lover. Homi Bhabha's sketch of her is in the TIFR archive. She is described as Bhabha's long-time companion by Coomi Kapoor in her book, *The Emergency: A Personal History.*
33. Stella Snead was a surrealist painter best known for works like 'Ecstatic Cow' and 'Tiger in the Sky'; her show at Chemould, Mehlli Gobhai remembers, was photographs of the patterns left on the sand by crabs digging their lairs.
34. Ila Pal: *Beyond the Canvas: An Unfinished Portrait of MF Husain* (Indus/Harper Collins Publishers, New Delhi, 1994); p 130
35. To calculate what that means, you should consider that between 1975 and 2019, the inflation rate has been close to 2000 per cent.
36. 'Undoubtedly the pioneers' by Anupa Mehta, *The Independent,* Mumbai, 13 September 1993
37. 'A picture of success' by M Rahman, *India Today,* 31 October 1998.
38. For more on PROYOM, please read Nancy Adajania's masterly *The Thirteenth Place; Positionality as Critique in the Art of Navjot Altaf* (Publisher, 2016). The first chapters of this book present an intelligent critique of the Left's engagement with the arts.
39. It is difficult to say exactly what Ebrahim Alkazi meant to Bombay and then to India. He started the Theatre Unit, which staged some of the most important plays, still remembered for their dramaturgy and their experimentalism. At 36 years, he headed the National School of Drama for which he had written the curriculum. He staged Dharam Vir Bharati's *Andha Yug* in the ruins of Firoz Shah Kotla. He was also a notable collector, connoisseur and gallerist.
40. Nandini Bhaskaran: *The Hindu Magazine,* 7 March 2004, p1

41. When political activist, actor, playwright and poet Safdar Hashmi was brutally murdered in broad daylight while performing a street play in a working class area just outside Delhi, the spontaneous revulsion and outrage grew into SAHMAT. For more, see sahmat.org or read Sudhanva Deshpande's fascinating book, *Halla Bol*.
42. *Sushobha Barve: Healing Streams: Bringing Back Hope in the Aftermath of Violence.* (Penguin India, 2003)
43. At the time, I nodded sagely but later, I discovered I had no idea what a Hermes archetype meant. Rashna explained: 'CG Jung introduced the concept of archetypes into psychology. They are preexistent patterns of being and behaving, perceiving and responding—they are patterns that are part of the collective unconscious. As archetypal figures, the Greek gods describe the basic structure of a personality that is recognizable. The Hermes archetype plays the role of the communicator, trickster, guide of roads and boundaries. A man who embodies this archetype will find it difficult settling down to do just one thing as he responds to the lure of an open road or the next opportunity, he shifts levels with ease. He is like quicksilver or Mercury, his Roman name. Hermes has the best of communication skills and always has innovative ideas. He was known as the friendliest of the gods to men and was said to bring luck.'
44. From www.ngmaindia.gov.in/ngma_mumbai.asp Visited on 06/08/2019 at 15:34pm.
45. *Yeh Un Dinon Ki Baat Hai; Urdu Memoirs of Cinema Legends* selected and translated by Yasir Abbasi, (Bloomsbury, 2018), p 35, where Kaifi Azmi writes with reference to Sahir Ludhianvi: "I was in Lucknow at the time when Sahir first arrived at India's Temple of Arts (Bombay)."
46. See www.caravanmagazine.in/reviews-essays/being-here. Site visited on 06/08/2019 at 15:56pm. This was so delightful to read and to consider as a possibility. Nissim Ezekiel reading out Adil Jussawalla's poetry while Arvind Krishna Mehrotra is listening. As someone interested in the story of Clearing House, a poets' cooperative, it is as if I were in at the start, the poems over which the Jussawalla-Mehrotra friendship may be said to have begun.
47. Ila Pal: *Beyond the Canvas: An Unfinished Portrait of MF Husain* (Indus/Harper Collins Publishers, 1994)
48. Karin Zitzewitz: *The Perfect Frame; Presenting Modern Indian Art; Stories and Photographs from the Collection of Kekoo Gandhy* (Chemould Publications, 1987)
49. Viewed on NDTV, https://www.ndtv.com/video/news/news/gond-the-enchanted-forest-470933, viewed on 17/08/2019 at 21:48
50. This story is from Jyotindra Jain: *Jangarh Singh Shyam: A Conjuror's Archive* (Museum of Art and Photography/Mapin, 2018)
51. For more on this read *A Fine Disregard: What Makes Modern Art Modern* (Harry N Abrams, 1994) by Kirk Varnedoe, one of the most readable books on modern art I have come across; or even *The Anxiety of Influence* (Oxford University Press, 1973) by Harold Bloom.

52. For more on the Rotring pen and Jangarh Kalam see *Jangarh Singh Shyam: A Conjuror's Archive*.

53. The Weavers' Service Centre was initiated by Pupul Jayakar in 1955, and invited leading contemporary artists to work with weavers and craftsmen, an idea of cross-pollination, of siloless work, that was part of the Nehruvian ideal.

54. Nissim Ezekiel in 'Art Notes of the Week', *Mid-day*, December 2, 1983

55. Yes, I know. This is a variant of Khorshed's version. Don't let it worry you.

56. *Celebrity* magazine, August 1984

57. 'Mining threatens Bihar's old tribal and rock art', Gunvanthi Balaram, *Sunday Times of India*, 28 July 1996. p7

58. 'Preserving Heritage', Vrunda Rahatekar, *Mid-day*, 10 July 1996, no page number on the cutting.

59. Clipping of a piece by Meher Pestonji: 'Tribal Art: The Endangered Heritage'; paper not stated, 17 July 1996,

60. Gunvanthi Balaram piece

61. Georgina Maddox: 'Putting needle to paper', *Mumbai Mirror*, 23 July 2005

62. 'Life begins at seventy-two [sic]' by Meher Pestonji, undated clipping from a newspaper, courtesy the author.

63. In an email to me, Jyotindra Jain, that remarkable art historian wrote, "Whenever folk or tribal artists encountered new surfaces for painting such as paper, canvas, board, etc., they invariably moved from static iconographic imagery to narrative story telling—this is true of Warli, Pardhan Gond, Madhubani, and several others." This may well be what happened here.

64. Horst Ulrich Beier, known as Ulli Beier (1922-2011) was a writer and scholar who helped develop literature, drama and poetry in Nigeria and Papua New Guinea. He founded the influential magazine, *Black Orpheus*. He spent his last years in Australia.

65. One of the great masters of his time, Pithawalla was called The Rembrandt of the East.

66. Do not try this at home; you will leave food particles behind which may attract fungus and other insects which might eat at the canvas of the painting. If you have a painting that needs cleaning, take it to a restorer.

67. *Man's World*, to Jayati Vora

68. "Chintamani," says Shireen Gandhy, "was one of the old guard, the classic 'faithful Nepali retainer'. He was a fixture, an institution at Chemould and everyone loved him as they love Vitthal now. He had a book and at some point during a show, he would ask the artist if she or he could draw something for him. And they all did. When we moved out of the Jehangir Art Gallery, he quit. It was something to do with the change in scale but I lost many of the old faithfuls. It was sad but it was also a relief in some ways because we could not keep on working in the old way."

69. *Aroop*: A series of arts, poetry and ideas; Volume 3, Number 1, January—June 2018: Totems and Taboos: What can and cannot be done; Editor: Ashok Vajpayee. Pp 46-48

70. *Bombay Times*, July 19, 2007
71. Anuradha Kapur is a theatre director, professor of theatre and formerhead of the National School of Drama, Delhi. In 2004, she won the Sangeet Natak Akademi Award for her contribution to theatre.
72. *Shri Khakhar Prasanna* by Naushil Mehta and Atul Dodiya, catalogue celebrating a show of the life and works of Bhupen Khakhar. Chemould Prescott Road was born in February, 2007, on the eighty-seventh birthday of its founder Kekoo Gandhy with this exhibition of Atul Dodiya, *Shri Khakhar Prasanna.*
73. Victoria Terminus, as the station was once called, represents the southernmost tip of the Central Railway Line, from which trains first began their conquest of the subcontinent. It was then renamed Chhatrapati Shivaji Terminus and then re-renamed Chhatrapati Shivaji Maharaj Terminus. In the minds of earlier generations, it is still VT and that was how Atul Dodiya said it to me and how I transcribed it.
74. In *Shri Khakhar Prasanna,* Naushil Mehta tells us of one of the specific observations Atul Dodiya made at the show: "How did people respond to dark watercolours? As soon as they saw their reflections in the glass, they whipped out their pocket combs!"
75. But since it was about Bhupen Khakhar, there was a connect to the history of the gallery too.
76. Kallat is now represented in Delhi by Nature Morte
77. *'Subject of Death'; 'Citizen Artist: Forms of Address'; 'Phantomata'; 'Cabinet Closet Wunderkammer'; 'Floating World'.*
78. This has already begun with Chemould/SHIFT a gallery space in Colaba, co-authored by Atyaan Jungalwala and Sunaina Rajan. It will focus on discovering and nurturing new talent.
79. My own introduction to Samovar was much less exalted, though, quite the reverse in fact. I did not go to Samovar while in college because I could not afford it. It was not expensive but such money as I had, I needed for books. The first time I did go, I ate nothing and I drank nothing. I was doing a story on the art market for the *Illustrated Weekly of India* and I had to interview a reputed and somewhat weather-beaten art critic. He told me that he should be writing the piece and that I would have to buy him lunch since I was not going to pay him and he ate his way through much of my fee for the piece. Then he pocketed the tip I had left for the waiter and I had to replace it. It was a fine introduction to the obverse of the art world.
80. He plays Kekoo Mody, the owner of an art gallery in Cuffe Parade. Aurora Zogoiby shows her work there. I thought this a rather *pheeka* portrait, a non-speaking part for a talkative man, and asked Salman if he had indeed modelled his character on Kekoo. 'Yes, I did meet Kekoo G and knew him just a little and stole his first name for my book.'
81. Lakshmi Lal: *The Warlis: Tribal Paintings and Legends,* Bombay, Chemould Publications and Arts, nd.

82. If it matters, the exact address was 20, Nepean Sea Road, now Laxmi Jagmohandas Marg. This I got out of Lakshmi Lal's book, *My Brush with Art* (Rupa & Co, 2004).
83. Other than his illustrious career with the Tata Group, Farrok Mulla (1911-1990) was an amateur photographer and painter. He was a patron of the arts who supported the painter Rasik Raval (1928-1980) for many years.
84. Amma refers to Swami Prajnananda.
85. These were: SH Raza, Akhilesh, Paramjit Singh, Vivan Sundaram, K Laxma Goud, Prabhakar Kolte, Saleem Arif, Tyeb Mehta, Veena Bhargava, Yusuf, Bhupen Khakhar, Prabhakar Barwe, Ranbir Singh Kaleka, Laxman Shrestha, Jogen Chowdhury, Vijay Shinde, Atul Dodiya; 13 to 21 September, 1988
86. Rashna remembers: 'Rudy was invited as the chief guest to Raza's exhibition in 1982 at Gallery Loeb in Bern, Switzerland, which I organised. In his speech, at the opening Rudy remembered Raza as a rising star when he first exhibited his work at the Bombay Art Society as a young student and said he was honoured to be present as the chief guest to an artist who had now risen to be one of India's leading stars. Many of the ex-retired Swiss employees of Volkart and SLM who had been employed in India, and who had bought early Raza watercolors when he was unknown were present. Hennig Holck Larsen has also flown in for the opening. Many of those old India hands bought his vibrant oil paintings and the show was a sell-out, much to the amazement of the Swiss gallery owner.'
87. The Langhammers lived in India until 1957 when they had to return to Europe because, as she told Lakshmi Lal, her husband's chronic amoebic dysentery had reached a near fatal stage.
88. In the Adil Jussawalla archive, I found notes towards a profile of Kekoo, one that unfortunately, Jussawalla never completed. There he notes that Pinto was captured in Africa and brought to India.
89. One of those delightful formulations which is no longer in use. In my childhood, children often went to 'day-spend'; I think they now have 'play dates'.
90. This story of Mehli Mehta's discovery is borne out by a little book on Matheran written by Dinoo Bastawalla, *The Hill of Beauty.* Bastawalla deserves a book of her own; she was an amateur political cartoonist and holder of séances which were conducted in a cupola of a building in the Fort on full-moon nights. Mehlli Gobhai told me that she once asked his mother, Perin Gobhai if she would like to speak to Mr Gobhai when he had passed on. 'We didn't have much to say to each other when he was alive,' said Perin. 'What would we say now?'
91. Nirmala Devi (1923-2011) was the founder of Sahaja Yoga. For more information shrimataji.org.
92. 'Undoubtedly the pioneers', *The Independent,* September 13, 1993.
93. Neville Wadia (1911-1996) was the head of Bombay Dyeing and father of the current chairman, Nusli Wadia.
94. M.Rahman 'A Picture of Success', *India Today,* October 31, 1988, Tehelka, 16 April 2011, page 56

95. This conversation is one in a series and at some point, I felt I would be cannibalising the entire piece here and so I would suggest that this chapter be read in conjunction with Ranjit Hoskote and Nancy Adajania: *Anju Dodiya (The Dialogue Series),* Mumbai, Popular Prakashan, 2011, p 66.

96. Ila Pal: *Beyond the Canvas; An Unfinished Portrait of MF Husain* (Indus/Harper Collins Publishing, New Delhi, 1994) pp 121.

Index